Thinking
in Pictures

Thinking in Pictures

**Dramatic Structure
in D. W. Griffith's
Biograph Films**

Joyce E. Jesionowski

University of California Press
Berkeley / Los Angeles / London

Photographs courtesy of Killiam Shows, commercial
proprietor of the Biograph Collection, and the Museum
of Modern Art, New York City.

University of California Press
Berkeley and Los Angeles
University of California Press, Ltd.
London, England
© 1987 by
The Regents of the University of California

Library of Congress Cataloging-in-Publication Data

Jesionowski, Joyce E.
   Thinking in pictures.

   Bibliography: p.
   Includes index.
   1. Griffith, D. W. (David Wark), 1875–1948—
Criticism and interpretation.   I. Title.
PN1998.A3G755   1987
791.43′0233′0924   86-30793
ISBN 0-520-05776-7 (alk. paper)

Printed in the United States of America

1   2   3   4   5   6   7   8   9

To Stefan who started it;
To my parents who supported it;
To Hal who lived with it.

Contents

List of Illustrations

Some sequences have been condensed for purposes of illustration. Usually the entire sequence is covered in the text in shot order, but for reasons of space it would not be possible, and it is not essential, to illustrate every shot in an *ab* sequence of intercutting. In some cases shots have been extracted from larger sequences to illustrate a comprehensive structure built over the course of the film.

Acknowledgments

No book is ever the work of one person. Thanks are due to the many generous people who helped make this one possible: the librarians at the Library of Congress who arranged access to the paper print collection in Washington, D.C.; Charles Silver and Ron Magliozzi, who provided access to prints from the Museum of Modern Art's Collection; Kristin Thompson, who shared her method for frame reproduction; Anne Morra, who arranged access, space, and time to reproduce stills from Museum of Modern Art prints of the Biograph films; John Fell; Bruce Kawin; Ernest Callenbach and Marilyn Schwartz, my editors; Peter Dreyer, who provided such a close and helpful reading of the manuscript; Paul Killiam; Hal Walker; Jay Leyda; Julius Edelman; Ray Foery; and my doctoral advisor, Stefan Sharff.

Introduction

"I think one should mention Griffith in every discussion about the cinema: everyone agrees, but everyone forgets, nonetheless,"[1] says Jean-Luc Godard, stating a problem with reputation: the revered one tends to fade into the mists of the very history he is supposed to have created. Though D. W. Griffith has been cited in film histories as the "discoverer" or "inventor" of film techniques—a myth he helped create; although his work is cited with approval by such film artists as Sergei Eisenstein—who then felt the need to distance himself from Griffith's melodramatic techniques; although he was recognized by contemporaries as the "Belasco of the motion pictures"[2]—a comparison that conferred cultural legitimacy; although he is supposed to have been the first, everyone forgets.

In fact, we have come to a point in film history where the assertion that Griffith was no inventor is as commonplace as the idea that he discovered all of cinema. Many more films from the earliest period of filmmaking (1898–1907) are available for comparison and lend credibility to the suspicion that D. W. Griffith was in no pure sense a discoverer of early film techniques. It is clearer than ever before that when Griffith joined the Biograph Company in 1908, he was a neophyte, if a brilliantly gifted one.

By that time, filmmaking was already an international industry, with production companies such as Edison, Vitagraph, and Biograph in the United States vying for both artistic and technical preeminence in an ever-widening field of international contenders. By 1908 directors had already cut their film dramas into shots, intercut closer views into long shots, dissolved shots into each other, faded shots in and out, dollied in, tilted up and down, tracked with action, built coherent story-telling sequences and employed tinters to hand color each frame. In the face of all this activity, if Griffith's reputation had to rest on the number of techniques he introduced, he would be reduced to a footnote in film history.

But there may be a genuine first that can be claimed for Griffith's work, and it is on the basis of this "discovery" that his films merit special attention even in the context of all the new information we have about the early cinema. Current film theory is beginning to recognize that the film experience is some

1

kind of contract between the filmmaker, who constitutes meaningful signs in a film, and the viewer, who "decodes" these signs immediately during the film, or later, upon reflection. However, neither the nature of the signs nor the nature of the contract has been agreed upon. It is to this question that the work of D. W. Griffith speaks eloquently, suggesting that perhaps he should not be forgotten in our discussions about the cinema.

Griffith may have been the first filmmaker to think systematically about the relationship he wished to have with the viewers of his films. In his essay on youth in the cinema, he formulated the terms of that "contract" as follows:

> We sit in the twilight of the theater and in terms of youth, upon faces enlarged, we see thoughts that are personal to us, with the privilege of supplying our own words and messages as they fit our individual experiences in life.
> There we see truth in silence. Silence, then, becomes more eloquent than all the tongues of men.[3]

Certainly, the truth that Griffith wished to convey to his audiences is an amalgamation of a great number of cultural and aesthetic assumptions. Some of these notions were brought—distressingly unquestioned—from the post–Civil War Southern culture in which Griffith was brought up. Griffith's father fought in the Civil War, which figured prominently in many of Griffith's films. Furthermore, Griffith shared the genteel conceptions and unquestioned prejudices of the section of America in which he first learned to dream. Other ideas were formed in the regional American theater in which Griffith performed. Some of his attitudes were simply those of a man of great energy, convinced that he had a mark to make on the mind of the world.

But one of Griffith's most daring assumptions about the cinema was that he could make audiences "see thoughts" on the screen. Though Eisenstein would criticize Griffith for not going far enough into ideas—for remaining stalled at the level of parallel montage—Griffith's accomplishment remains radical in its own terms. He presented his narrative dramas to viewers beginning to demand new thrills to replace the simple shock of recognition they had received from the first magnified images of factory workers and speeding trains. In part, Griffith lulled his audiences with familiar stories from popular literature, theater, and penny-dreadful melodrama. In part, he dragged them breathless into a new relationship with the images he would present to them in the "twilight of the theater." He confronted his audiences, and continues to confront them, with films in which disarmingly "realistic" effects are based on alarmingly abstract construction.

Griffith made nearly five hundred films in the five years he worked for the American Mutoscope and Biograph Company, and he controlled all phases of production on these films. His Biograph period thus offers a unique opportunity to examine in depth the ebb and flow of experiment and structural formulation—a wonderful record of the process of learning to create cinema. In addition, the verbal silence of the films offers an opportunity to examine the effect of a narrative without a spoken text, to see the other levels of communication on which film may operate. Obviously, this requires a simplification even of the "normal" processes of viewing silent cinema that employed verbal and aural messages ranging from accompanying music to titles to actors standing behind the screen and actually reciting lines.[4] But if these very important elements can be set aside for the purposes of argument, then the Biograph films reveal the level of experience described by Maurice Merleau-Ponty in "Film and the New Psychology" when he says: "The perception of form, understood very broadly as structure, grouping or configuration, should be considered our spontaneous way of seeing."[5]

Griffith seems to have tried throughout his career to tap that immediate and spontaneous energy that an audience expends as its "natural way of seeing." In 1915 he wrote:

> [The motion picture audience] has the good old American faculty of wanting to be "shown" things. We don't "talk" about things happening, or describe the way a thing looks: we actually show it—vividly, completely, convincingly. It is the ever-present, realistic, actual now that "gets" the great American public, and nothing ever devised by the mind of man can show it like moving pictures.[6]

The uniqueness of Griffith's approach to the cinema is embodied in the form he found to capture the "realistic actual now." In this very early period, there was a basic awareness of the fact that the realism of the "actual now" in film images was a constructed and perceived event. Frank Woods, one of the most acute of the early film critics (and later a scenarist, title-writer, and apologist for Griffith), understood that in the cinema, "it is not pretended to us that we are looking at the real but at a photographic record of the real. This is so plausible to our sense of reason, that we accept it without question."[7] The fact that he was criticizing Griffith's *A Strange Meeting* in 1909 for a lack of smooth continuity, suggests that Woods had at least a rudimentary sense of the fact that this "plausibility" was based on the film's construction.[8] And Václav Tille, an early Czech critic, directly "criticized filmmakers who continue an action from one location to another 'without succeeding in linking together all the moments of a moving scene.'"[9]

In 1916 Hugo Munsterberg, a Harvard psychologist, approached the constructed reality of the film image from another perspective. He investigated the idea of persistence of vision, the phenomenon that makes continuous action from a set of still pictures: "The motion which (the viewer) sees, appears to be true motion, and yet it is created by his own mind . . . the essential condition is rather the *inner* mental activity which unites the separate phases of the ideas of connected action."[10]

The relevance of Munsterberg's observation here does not lie in the discussion of the phenomenon of persistence of vision, but in the emphasis his theory places on the activity of the viewer—the sense that the audience participates in the creation of the film event on a fundamental level. The extent to which early viewers noticed the plausibility of construction mentioned by Woods and Tille was summed up by Horace Kallen, who wrote in the *Harvard Monthly* in 1910 that "pantomime on the screen evoked a more vivid response [than pantomime on the stage], hypnotising the audience to breathlessly fill in the missing details." [11]

The illusion of reality created by plausible construction to take advantage of the audience's ability to fill in the missing details is exactly the strategy that Griffith refined in his Biograph period. Many factors are involved in creating the total "text" of the film, but audience participation has everything to do with the narrative and emotional impact of a Griffith film. Griffith had "only" to decide what "plausible" meant in terms of film "reality" and what "gaps" the audience had to fill in order to participate in his films.

Resistance, facilitation, tension, resolution, clarity, ambiguity, strong graphic orientation, lack of graphic orientation—all are aspects of the experience of Griffith's Biograph films and the basis from which the narrative effects emanate. Each shot, a separate entity, is made to contribute to the "world of the film" a coherent picture that is the sum of all the parts. As Griffith noted: "Literary ability . . . is not enough; the applicant for screenwriting must have a screen mind; he must be able to visualize clearly and consecutively. . . . When he writes 'Scene 1' he must mentally see it reaching out in unbroken continuity to 'Finis.'" [12] The fact that Griffith used no written script for *Birth of a Nation* gives eloquent testimony to his ability to follow his own advice. His Biograph work also demonstrates this unbroken continuity of thought and suggests that the experience of the whole film, as a chain of interacting shots, transcends every constituent element of construction. Acting, scenery, pictorial beauty, and, implicitly, sound and effective language, are subordinated to the total picture produced by the film.

Griffith's Biograph films demonstrate that he was one of the first filmmakers to achieve what the Russian theorist and filmmaker Lev Kuleshov describes as "that organizational moment during which the relationship of the parts to the materials and their organic and spatial connections are revealed [to the audience]." [13] Although he never even approached the experimental extremes envisioned by theorists such as Kuleshov, Griffith's Biograph films do exhibit an understanding of that "organizational moment" in which the impact and meaning of the film are realized by the audience. Munsterberg described the experience: "We are familiar with the illusions in which we believe we see something which only our imagination supplied. . . . Are we not also familiar with the experience of supplying by our fancy the associative image of a movement when only the starting point and end point are given, if a skillful suggestion influences our mind?"[14]

Griffith's brand of screen reality is characterized by spatial and temporal elisions, bridged by formal suggestions, that convince viewers that a continuity of screen action and screen narrative they perceive has, in fact, occurred on the screen before them. In his Biograph period, Griffith aimed at creating a concrete visual style that was basically narrative in thrust. As he progressed, his visual experiments resulted in a gradual process of redefinition. Action is redefined from the mere movement of bodies across the screen to the logically motivated motions of well-defined characters. The duration and impact of activity are determined by the cut. Continuity is identified with the control of the flow of the dramatic actions through largely discontinuous space, as well as with the generation of mental nuances and qualities created in affective links between shots.

Griffith relies on intercutting repeated images to make a clear and simple statement of relative positions in film space and film time that produces a feeling of character, emotion, and psychology. The effectiveness of Griffith's films begins to derive more and more often from the audience's feeling and perception of that "organizational moment" in which a relationship between space and space is transferred to a relationship between character and character. The audience is led to believe it knows what the people in the world of the film are thinking and feeling. Drama gradually assumes the qualities Frank Woods described as "deliberation and repose"—that is, of quietude and exactness in a medium that began its history with exuberant and generalized movement.

This process occurs in three basic areas of control: visibility within the composition of the shot; the order of the shots within the chain of shots; and the flow of physical and, eventually, emotional/psychological energy through the world of the film. During his entire Biograph period, Griffith was concerned to find spatial and affective relationships that would engage the audience's attention in the flow of the film and in the apprehension of the whole film as a self-contained "world."

In order to reach this goal, Griffith had to understand and confront the fact that the medium he worked in was neither the theater nor life, but a new form that bore a unique relationship to natural events. It is in the success of his struggle to discover the principles of cinematic organization that Griffith remains worthy of mention every time one discusses the cinema. The ideas he expressed in his films echo the yearnings of the nineteenth century. The way he expressed those ideas voiced the aspirations of the century to come.

A Basic Shot   1

Edwin S. Porter is commonly credited with being the first director to analyze a dramatic action into expressive bits (shots), and in standard film histories his *The Great Train Robbery* (Edison, 1903) has enduringly been cited as a seminal dramatic film.[1] Porter's currency with critics has declined over the years since *The Great Train Robbery* was "the most famous of all films,"[2] but this film does show Porter's feeling for the fact that film offered certain variables that could be altered to achieve various effects. The length of time an activity appeared on the screen; its course through the image; the camera's relationship to it; the relationship of the shot to preceding and succeeding shots—all are potential aspects of organization that allow the filmmaker to interfere with the implied realism of the film image. Porter was among the first filmmakers to show that film was simply not the real world, and that the real world need not determine the dimensions of the shot. What did determine those dimensions was by no means settled by the time Griffith began to make films in 1908.

The very definition of the shot in the early cinema was still very fluid, so much so that standard critical designations—long shot, medium shot, close-up—may actually produce a warped understanding of early structure. Up to this point early cinema has been analyzed in the context of its legacy instead of its history. It is as if Griffith and his contemporaries yearned to create the standard Hollywood film of the forties and had the intuitions of the standard Soviet film of the twenties, but somehow lacked the imagination to achieve either style.

In fact, early filmmakers, Griffith amongst them, were still sorting out the possibilities. For instance, Christy Cabanne, an actor and director under Griffith at Biograph, relates the range of shot designations to the human figure: head, bust, waist, knee, ankle-length; and, in another account, knee figure, waist figure, Bust, and Big Head.[3] The focus on the body as the definition of the shot's dimensions leads to Hollywood's typical construction, and to the conclusion that the talking face is the proper object of the camera's attention. Griffith himself wavered on the importance of words in the cinema. By 1934 he would shout "I want to hear words, words. I want words to come from the screen, beautiful words, like Shakespeare, like the Bible, so that moving pictures will *mean* something at last." [4] But ten years earlier he was "quite positive that when a century has passed, all thought of our so-called speaking pictures will have been abandoned." [5] This ambivalence suggests that Griffith's use of the "close-up" in his Biograph period cannot be taken for granted as a simple step in the evolution of "conventional" film syntax. Griffith arrived at the "Big Head" for his own purposes, and how he used it is crucial to understanding the shape of those chains of shots we have come to regard as typical of Griffith's style. Although Griffith's structures lead to Moscow as well as to Hollywood, his Biograph films are neither Russian nor Hollywood films. To clarify Griffith's position vis-à-vis those films that learned from his work, it is necessary to review some of the accomplishments that preceded his work.

Sources

For a while, the monumental naturalism of the film image was enough to enchant filmmaker and audience alike. There is something remarkably immediate about the very first films made by people such as the Lumières, Cecil Hepworth, and the Edison and Biograph cameramen. When people, motor cars, and trains hurry past the camera, reality slips past the bounds of the frame, in a sense that implies an aesthetic that would be consciously developed only much later by Jean Renoir and Max Ophuls. For the moment the frame is a *temporal* limit on the camera's glance—what is seen is what occurs before the camera "now." Action flies by and then disappears, establishing a "scene."

The sense of excitement generated by these first images was so strong that many versions of the same subject were produced. It is as if every early filmmaker had to capture a train rushing into a tunnel, waves breaking on a beach, automobiles coming toward the camera before the art could move on. To bear witness to the world of natural and commonplace events—even if these were staged for the camera—was an important aspect of early filmmaking.

On the other hand some of the first film subjects were simply recordings of vaudeville turns taken from the imagined position of the audience. Sandow the Strongman and the charming Leigh sisters made their appearances before Edison's camera performing in much the same way as they would have appeared on a real stage. Biograph's version of *Rip Van Winkle* was a straight recording of the famous Joseph Jefferson performance, and this film remained a popular catalogue item.[6] So strong was the impulse to record a dramatic event that obvious theatricalisms remained in early cinema long after filmmakers had begun to discover how to create dramatic effects using specifically cinematic methods. The years 1904–5 were splendid ones for the development of the chase as a specifically cinematic form—a form well understood at

Biograph, as evidenced by such films as *The Lost Child* (1904) and *Wife Wanted* (1907). Yet Biograph's *Tom, Tom the Piper's Son* (1905) and *Under the Apple Tree* (1907) seem deliberately anachronistic (even as early as this in the history of film grammar), so committed are they to presenting action enclosed in theatrical tableaus and painted scenery, as it might have been seen on a stage.

The relationship of film to its dramatic cousin, the theater, is a long and complex story. It is marked by film's envy of the theater's cultural legitimacy, as well as by a growing awareness that the cinema possessed certain dramatic advantages over the theater. Most important was the realization that melodrama, an enormously popular dramatic form, had come home in the film medium. "The essence of much melodrama was speed and mounting tension, qualities that required rapid transitions between scenes as well as special juxtapositions and skills in movement and change on stage."[7] In addition, melodrama "developed to guarantee unflagging interest by omitting the 'dead spots' of other drama, enlisting identifications with the performers and refining resources of suspense."[8] The nineteenth-century theater was desperate to present a stage large enough to encompass the breadth and sweep of the melodramas that enraptured audiences. The head-on view "from the audience" in cinema indicates a sensibility that regarded film as the answer to the nineteenth-century stage's appetite for melodramatic spectacle—a vision that saw the enlarged cinema image as the biggest stage in the world.

It is intriguing to contrast attempts to mount chases and railroad trains on the stage with the ability of film to make an impact by simply recording the real thing. Magnificent machines were devised to pivot scenery in such productions as Dion Boucicault's *The Shaughraun* (1875), and Steele McKay invented sliding and double elevator stages that suggested tilting and panning and prefigured the mobility of the camera in the cinema.[9] But the film medium naturally offered the semblance of reality so important to melodrama that "guised fantasy in the costume of naturalism."[10] In fact, the theatrical producers of the nineteenth century yearned for the very aspect of the early cinema that was its initial problem: Dion Boucicault's sets, for all their ingenious scenery, were attempting to achieve the very illusion of reality that early filmmakers had on their hands as a natural by-product of the focal length of their lenses.

Somewhere between the enclosure of the stage scene and the unruly street scene lay the rhetorical beginnings of film language. The development of film as a form of expression to some degree rested in establishing a sense of selection. Early exhibitors were the first "editors," combining documentary footage and dramatic reels with lantern slides, dance, and spoken narratives to make programs that traveled from meeting hall to meeting hall.[11] For instance, the assassination of President McKinley at the Pan American Exhibition of 1901 offered enterprising exhibitors a historic opportunity—a major contemporary event could be brought to audiences almost "instantaneously," and it could be dramatized. Such a program was reconstructed by Tom Gunning and Charles Musser at the Collective for Living Cinema in New York City a few years ago. Documentary footage of the exhibition shot by Edison's crews was followed first by lantern slides depicting the assassination, then by film of a theatrical tableau in which the character "Columbia" was shown mourning at a tomb honoring assassinated U.S. presidents, whose faces faded in and out of a central medallion in the monument. The entire program culminated in a theatrical recreation on film of the electrocution of McKinley's assassin, presented as "historically accurate." The easy transition from reality to recreation, from documentary presentation to "historically accurate" depiction, charts the history of the cinema, which is able to perform an event in all of these modes in order to extract the emotional essence from it.

It did not take early filmmakers long to recognize that the very processes of filmmaking could also radically alter the "performance" of actor and reality. Méliès' magic theater is only the most coherently inventive example of this recognition of the weird ambiguity that results when "magic" and "naturalism" meet in the cinema image. Filmmakers such as Cecil Hepworth in England were also captivated by the "magic" capabilities of the camera and used them to alter the "naturalism" of the cinema image radically. In *How It Feels to Be Run Over* Hepworth sends a car rushing toward the camera to simulate the "feeling" of being approached by a real vehicle—"magic" that consciously utilizes the kinetic thrill early audiences reportedly experienced in confronting the enlarged cinema image head-on.[12] In a later film, *That Fatal Sneeze* (1907), the explosive effects of a sneeze actually rock the frame itself, after various episodes occur in which the contents of the frame are laid in shambles by the sneezer (rooms are knocked apart; houses blown down). The reference to the camera's complicity in the screen event is even more pronounced in Williamson's *The Big Swallow* (1900), in which the camera and cameraman are "consumed" by the man they are filming. (A man who resists being filmed finally approaches the camera, his image growing in size until he is only a big open mouth; the screen goes black. Cut to a reverse of the cameraman and camera facing away from audience toppling back into the frame and into the blackness. Cut back to the extreme close-up of the open mouth, and the man backs away from the camera, enjoying his "meal").

When directors actually began to assemble film dramas around 1902-4, all of these early intuitions were brought to bear on the problems of narration—for narratives were clearly what the early filmgoing public wanted.[13] The development of the narrative film took place in an atmosphere of story-telling culture that seemed to cry out for the spectacular moving image. The theater's romance with melodrama has already been mentioned. In retrospect the great nineteenth-century novels also seem particularly cinematic in their detailed accounts of lives observed from panoramic to delicately intimate vantages. And Victorian writing in general seems to have remarkably "filmlike" qualities: "concerns with fragmenting exposition in terms of time sequence, with particularizing the images and their compositions, with the interjection of 'movement,' and with the externalization of memory into tangible, 'visible' experience." [14] There is a wealth of analogy to shot-by-shot construction to be found in comic strips such as Windsor McKay's *Little Nemo.* [15] And the number of visual toys that preceded the Cinematograph and the Vitascope all seem to strain toward the freedom of position and swiftness of movement that would become the hallmark of the cinema. All of the cinema's early associations with other forms of popular entertainment eventually would be recalled in charming amalgamation films such as *The Policeman's Tour of the World* (Pathé, 1906). This film shamelessly coopts documentary footage of Cairo, Calcutta, and Bombay, which might have been the subjects of travelogue programs in pre-Nickelodeon days. To round out the entertainment in *The Policeman's Tour of the World,* Pathé chorines perform a "native" dance in each new locale. A chase with its roots in the realist urge to have been "on the scene" that was the cinema's earliest delight, *The Policeman's Tour of the World* tips its hat to its former vaudeville associates, the dance and the documentary, even as it reaches for the next stage of cinema achievement, the construction of narrative continuity.

Before *The Policeman's Tour of the World* could even be assembled, filmmakers had to arrive at an idea of a unit of narrative construction. Some of the films Porter made after *The Great Train Robbery* suggest that the discovery of shot-by-shot construction did not guarantee the permanence of the idea. For all the precedents that can be cited, the definition of the shot was not self-evident or fixed. The early cinema had to start from "ground zero"—having to invent and reinvent the long shot, medium shot, and close-up that had already been suggested by the novel and the graphic arts of the time; having to discover the rush of activity out on the streets before it could translate that energy into drama; having to revel in its own technical marvelousness before it could settle down to express the thoughts that were so important to Griffith.

"The Edison people believed that the integrity of the continuous action film was a matter of commercial option. As Porter described it, the long film was merely a 'series of scenes' or 'really an aggregation of several series of negative impressions' that were used 'to produce a positive film upon a single long continuous strip.' Each series deliberately constituted one independent photograph.'" [16] Porter was arguing a commercial point here that actually pertains to the integrity of each strip of film—the idea was to establish each series of frames as a continuous image for purposes of copyright. But this commercial sense also prompted Edison to release his films as single takes that lent themselves to a creative arrangement of parts such as the Pan American

Exhibition program. This practice suggests that there were industrial and financial reasons for the sensibility that regarded the "single shot in an isolated manner, as complete unto itself." [17]

In fact, there was a powerful sense of enclosure in the shot in early cinema. Generally, early films can be formally characterized by their tendency to let the entirety of an action play itself out in a scene-space, whether the subject is consciously narrative or documentary. This practice can be related to the earlier sense of "situation" in the theater, "where action is wrought to a climax when actors strike attitudes and form what they call a 'picture,' during the exhibition of which a pause takes place; after which action is renewed, not continued." [18] A. Nicholas Vardac notes that originally "action-tableaux . . . were simply used as the photographically realistic versions of the same material that audiences were accustomed to viewing on the stage." [19] But, certainly, this "one-shot" sensibility would also have had its precedent in setting the camera up to witness a "reality." And in the earliest films, the length of the strip of film limited the filmmaker's view of an event.

Between the McKinley program and *The Policeman's Tour of the World,* an aesthetic of construction was forming based on the perception of the strip of film as a shot—a discrete unit of construction having some relationship to other units of the film. In order to understand this early formal attitude, it is useful to consider the recent revisionist view of Edwin S. Porter's film *The Life of an American Fireman* (Edison, 1903).

In 1979 Charles Musser reported his evidence that the print of *The Life of an American Fireman* that had been circulated for so long had actually been altered to conform to the rules of "continuity cutting" that obtain in cinema today. For instance, between shots 8 and 9 (an interior to exterior transition) the action was probably repeated, causing a temporal overlap between the shots instead of a smooth "match" of continuous activity. It seems that this overlap was intentional, especially when one finds that other films of the period (Biograph's *The Firebug* [1905] among them) exhibit a similar phenomenon. This "overlap" or repetition of action could be regarded as a "mistake." Or it could be regarded as evidence of an aesthetic choice made by early filmmakers, based on a different perception of the function of the shot. As formulated by André Gaudréault, based on Musser's research, that choice could be stated as follows: "In a general way, early filmmakers were more or less consciously considering each shot as an autonomous, self-reliant unit; the shot's objective is to present not a small *temporal* segment of the action but rather the totality of an action unfolding in an homogenous space." [20]

Commercial and aesthetic reasoning, then, could describe and rationalize the overlapping shots in Porter's *The Life of an American Fireman* and Biograph's *The Firebug.* But the implications of such an attitude become particularly important when considering the early history of continuity cutting. The existence of overlapping shots suggests an interim stage in the construction of a dramatic sequence.

The conventions of continuity cutting are like the conventions of perspective in painting—they exist to provide the comforting assurance that the representation is realistic. In classic continuity, the spatial and temporal "gap" between two cuts is smoothed by matches in direction and angle that belie the fact that a spatial and temporal break has occurred. The logic of continuity is broadly the perceived logic of geography. Overlapping or repeating the action between two shots challenges the audience because it exposes the reality of the film as an artifice, a creation based on assembly. As a conscious choice, overlapping action emphasizes the independence of one shot from the next; as an artifact of film history, overlapping shots indicate a point at which "spatial anchorage [prevails] over temporal logic. Stability, persistence, and uniqueness of point of view remain so important that they supersede anachronism." [21]

How does one analyze the continuity that is created between "autonomonous, self-reliant, homogenous" units? Early cinema abounds with examples of ostensible close-ups and long shots (Biograph's *The Widow and the Only Man* [1904] making notable use of the "conversational" mid-shot) that suggest the conventional units of film grammar. The tendency to date has been to apply the "master-shot" aesthetic indiscriminately to a series of films—Griffith's included—in which the relationship between shots is not necessarily based on any such master scene. Any analysis of early forms must consider whether we need new terms to discuss the relationship between shots that are not based on master scenes—long shots, medium shots and close-ups that cannot be equated with theater scenes and yet function as formally as master shots.

The Boundaries of the Shot

By the time Griffith began to make films in 1908, the general stability of the narrative, broken into shots, had been established. But the early units of construction retained a stubborn integrity. The camera tends to maintain a passive attitude toward the action once it has assumed a vantage point—in some cases using quite radical angles, such as the "foot level" view of passing pedestrians in G. A. Smith's *Story Told by Feet Only* (1900). The early satisfaction with watching activities from a single vantage—*Comic Faces* (Smith, 1898), for instance, in which a man makes faces at the camera; or *A Quick Shave and Brush Up* (Smith, 1900), in which a man performs his morning toilette for the camera—seems to remain once stories are attempted. For instance, in Williamson's *Fire* (1900), an early version of the fireman-to-the-rescue scenario, the camera is positioned at the firehouse door. The first fire truck comes out of the firehouse and exits left. Then the camera patiently waits while a second fire truck backs out of the frame to the right and reenters to exit left for the end of the shot. From the viewpoint of dramatic economy, things improve a great deal in 1903 with *Firemen to the Rescue,* Cecil Hepworth's version of the tale. Hepworth dispenses with the dramatic sweeping action provided by firetrucks and opts for a dramatic mid-shot of two firemen clinging to a ladder breaking into a burning building with axes to save an imperiled mother and child. There are two locations in *Firemen to the Rescue,* an exterior and an interior. Hepworth treats each as a separate "scene," letting the action play itself out before he cuts. In *That Fatal Sneeze* (Hepworth, 1907) progressing versions of a joke are developed within the frame. A naughty child administers sneezing powder to his elder in revenge for enduring the stuff himself. The victim proceeds to demolish his room with sneezing. When he ventures out onto the street, his sneezes create similar mayhem, and he collects a trail of enraged citizens as he blows up houses with his sneezing. The comic situation builds and becomes progressively exaggerated and more amazing until (with the help of a camera trick) the sneezer himself explodes.

In *That Fatal Sneeze* there is an absolute coincidence between the amount of information possessed by the character and the audience: both experience each newly exaggerated version of the basic comic situation as the story unfolds. The action within the frame is therefore emphasized, and the connections between shots are less crucial—each new shot exists to provide a new context (provisionally we may regard it as a "stage") for each new version of the escalating joke, a sneeze so explosive that it finally blows the sneezer to smithereens. But the comedy escalates by invention—it is a witty marriage of comic business with camera "magic" that generates excitement within the frame. Even though there is a nominal chase in the film, the resolution of the situation is not identified with the resolution of the chase: the sneezer never is caught and is stopped by a device (he appears to explode), not by his pursuers.

Among the many British filmmakers, Hepworth presents an interesting case in point, because his films exhibit those features that are most often considered "developments"—his work often has a fine sense of continuity based on the flow of activity from shot to shot; he may have been the first to create tension by repeating shots in sequence to indicate that a character is "returning" "home," and by the same token using the accumulation of spaces to indicate "how long" it will take him to get there. Hepworth has a flare for amplifying dramatic action (e.g., using horses, trains, cars), and yet he often abandons chasing to elaborate or pursue a joke that remains shot-bound until it moves to a new "stage" to perform the next comic turn. And when he is making this kind of film, Hepworth is not too careful about matching action between shots. So there is a clear indication that *That Fatal Sneeze* is not just an early stab at comic chasing gone wrong, but a form derived from the concerns of the filmmaker, who was capable of inventing the "rules" and observed them when he chose to. Although Hepworth values action, he is quite happy developing it within the frame, where he can take advantage of the considerable inventory of special effects he created to amaze and amuse his audiences.

The Biograph Company made a series of splendid chase films in the period before Griffith arrived. Wherever they learned the form (there is some evidence for British invention of chase rhetoric),[22] the Biograph inclination to action and comic mayhem creates films in which the chase is not aborted (as it is in some of the films of Hepworth and Williamson) but displayed in all of its chaotic fervor. The best of these films—*The Escaped Lunatic* (1904), *The Lost Child* (1904), *Wanted, a Dog* (1905), and *Wife Wanted* (1907)—show a firm grasp of continuity cutting, quite often matching action from shot to shot very smoothly. The comedy is closely married to the action that is propelling itself from shot to shot. Escalation becomes acceleration—the chase is not a device that hypes the joke, it is the vehicle of the joke. The inventiveness of the filmmaker is concerned with creating original "business" within the body of the chase, but the action also hurls the characters through the frame and at the cut where it might be possible to generate effects from construction. This suggests that the comic situation is a nuance—the form could stand equally well to generate tension in a drama.

But this more conventional picture of continuity is not fully realized in the Biograph chases. Although the situation is more dynamically "cinematic," chasing figures tend to use up one space and then go on to the next one. There is little intercutting and almost no sense of constructing a single location from a number of different angles and distances. The subject-to-camera relationship is varied only by the approach of pursuer and pursued toward the camera. These early Biograph films rarely display the sense of repeated images that Hepworth recognized—except to indicate a return to zero that ends the chase. It is as if events are created within shots to simulate the "natural" spontaneity of a flood or of a train passing the camera. There is a sense that the camera is there as a "witness" to an event in its entirety—the entirety in this case being the full diagonal extent of the image as people run from background to foreground. When it comes to constructing a narrative film, the camera attitude remains passive, and when the action overflows the frame, the camera's eye is dragged along with it. This effect can become quite unnerving as pans append spaces to shots that are used to establish dramatic locations. Such is the case in Biograph's *The Moonshiners* (1904). The camera pans left and right in the opening shot to include more bits of space until the action becomes quite disordered with all of the "ells" that have been added on to the establishing space.

Griffith essentially adopted this spectator's view of the shot. Many of the qualities of these early Biograph chases also appear in his early work, such as the "trailing pans" in *The Barbarian, Ingomar* (1908). The basic set-ups are usually not cut up into a series of related angles and subject-to-camera distances, and when close-ups, medium shots, and long shots emerge as deliberate units of construction, they are marked by that early sense of self-containment that Musser finds in *The Life of an American Fireman*. Whether Griffith's work finally arrives at the master-shot aesthetic (and there is some evidence of this kind of construction in his later Biograph films), any analysis of Griffith's contribution to the cinema must first consider how totally he radicalized the "passive" camera attitude with his growing awareness of the function of the "bounded" shot in the construction of dramas.

Basic Units of Construction

Already in 1910 Frank Woods was defining the uniqueness of the cinema as its "semblance of reality," and insisting that this semblance depended on maintaining the integrity of the image. Woods claimed that the realist illusion of film depended on the internal coherence of the film "world" and on the audience's ability to separate itself from the self-sufficient "other" world of the screen event. He inveighed particularly against the use of theatricalisms such as the "aside," the glance that directly sought the audience's eye. Quite the contrary of extending the frame, a look or leer directed away from the rest of the image implied, in Woods' thinking, a second audience beyond the camera, one that supplanted the position of the audience in the movie theater.[23] But implicit in this criticism is the assertion that the glance "aside" called attention to the artifice of filmmaking and therefore broke the illusion of the self-sufficient, self-contained reality of the screen world.

The eternal validity of Woods' theory notwithstanding, his concept of cinematic coherence is tailor-made to describe Griffith's imaginative apprehension of dramatic space as a unified field creating a coherent effect. Griffith's interest in staging for dramatic impact is indicated in the stage directions to the two plays he wrote before coming to the Biograph Company. *The Fool and the Girl* (1907), Griffith's first play, received only a short run, and his more ambitious *War* (1908) was never produced at all. Both of these plays, however, provide evidence of the fact that from the beginning Griffith's imagination, though as spectacular as Boucicault's, was incompatible with theatrical space and closer to the realization of Woods' theories about the integrity of the film world.

In *The Fool and the Girl* Griffith filled the stage with characters moving about a whirling dancing señorita. When they closed in on her figure, they integrated its movement in a composition of flashing activity. The flickering play of attention across the surface of the resulting moving "image" unified the activity of the scene into one dramatic effect. In *War* morris dancers occupied the center of the stage, and their collective energies drew the scene together and inward.[24] Both staging plans suggest Griffith's feeling for the concentration of the dramatic image and the same sensibility that was happy to unify theatrical space with the centripetal force of a dance felt completely at home in a medium in which unity and coherence could be built in a self-contained format through which activity, like the señorita's dance, would flow from one center of attention to another until "closing up so that she is lost in a picture in order to keep away from the idea of the dance being a specialty." [25]

Such "specialties" had already made their appearances in films. In *Professional Jealousy* (Biograph, 1907) a fully staged "Russian" dance vies for dramatic attention with the backstage antics of two feuding actresses. As is common in Biograph films, the situation soon degenerates into hair-pulling mayhem. Both Biograph's *The Chicken Thief* (1904) and Edison's *The Watermelon Patch* (1905) stop dead in the middle of the action for an interlude during which blacks tap-dance. The Pathé chorus girls of *The Policeman's Tour of the World* indicate that the practice was international. Quite the contrary of including vaudeville material or any such "specialty" on the screen, Griffith concentrated on organization, resisting any effect that would draw attention to the artifice of filmmaking and spoil the internal coherence of the frame, thus challenging the realistic impression of the film event. The resulting economy of style manifested itself in a number of ways.

Although Griffith has a reputation for innovation, and apparently was an experimenter on the set, his Biograph films are notably conservative in respect to many of the technical capabilities of the camera that were already taken for granted by 1908. More remarkable are the number of technical effects that did not appear in Griffith's Biograph films. For instance, the dissolves that captivated Edwin S. Porter and Georges Méliès are seldom used by Griffith in this period. Griffith absolutely avoided the trick photography that Hepworth used to such delightful effect. An image matted into the screen of a movie theater in the one-shot film *Those Awful Hats* (1909) and the reverse motion of *The Curtain Pole* (1908) are exceptions to Griffith's general practice. The mattes used in pre-Griffith films such as *As Seen through a Telescope* (Smith, 1900), *The Big Swallow* (Williamson, 1900), and *Grandpa's Looking Glass* (Biograph, c. 1901) to produce rudimentary close-ups appear in Griffith's second film, *The Redman and the Child* (1908), to simulate a "close-up" view seen through a telescope. Thereafter, the use of the matte becomes less and less frequent. Close-ups of objects, a fairly common screen event by 1907, were abandoned in general practice by Griffith after 1909. The cut-in and -out on the axis appears in Griffith's sixth film, *The Greaser's Gauntlet* (1908), and is the most persistent technical "effect" to remain in Griffith's canon. As Sam Landers, an assistant at Biograph, put it, "Griffith was not strong for trick stuff . . . [he] used effects only for drama." [26]

Griffith also displayed an ambivalence to close-ups of actors. He seems to have wanted a closer view of the actor's face in an almost magical "soul-catching" sense. [27] "Why not move a camera up close and show an actor's full face?" Griffith asked in a discussion reported by Mack Sennett. "That would reveal his emotions, give him a chance to show what he was thinking." [28] But there were technical problems and front-office qualms to be overcome. Billy Bitzer, the cameraman with whom Griffith did the major part of his work, generally used a lens of short length. This means that when focused, the lens produced "infinity," an image of great depth of field in which the image was clear and distinct from the extreme background to a knees-up figure in the foreground. Furthermore, there seems to have been a desire to maintain "good" focus that made the production of the close-up something of an aesthetic battle between Griffith and Bitzer. Griffith's basic conservatism caused him to reject Bitzer's experimental close-ups (in which "the background was out of focus and only the central figure in sharp focus") as "too distracting." Griffith felt that too much attention was drawn to the fuzzy background. "Griffith . . . told Bitzer to find some way of giving him a piece of film with only the actor in it." [29] Except for the magnification of detail, for which a black background was used to minimize the blurring of the background, the Biograph Company policy also rejected such a shallow field as a pictorial mistake. [30] There is some evidence that Bitzer himself regarded such images as unprofessional, although Griffith and Bitzer seem comfortable with the "racked" focus of later Griffith Biograph films such as *A Corner in Wheat* (1909), *The Musketeers of Pig Alley* (1912), and *The House of Darkness* (1913), in which the background is deliberately thrown out of focus as a character moves from background to foreground.

General industrial practices also affected Griffith's decisions. Kemp Niver relates that it was "Griffith's habit, starting with his very first film and continuing throughout his career [to shoot] all the action pertaining to the story regardless of its sequence in the film from one camera position before proceeding to another." [31]

Shooting all the action "on one side of the door" before proceeding to the other side to film all the action that took place there was simply economical. And this habit persisted at least until 1911, as is demonstrated by the print of *The Transformation of Mike* (1911), a Griffith Biograph film currently distributed by the Museum of Modern Art in "production" and "release" versions. But economy also shows in the remarkably small number of set-ups in each of the Biograph films. In the earlier years, it is possible that the smallness of the Biograph Studio itself argued against elaborate sets and multiple set-ups. In addition, the camera was bulky and difficult to move around. The Biograph executives had Griffith on a very tight shooting schedule (especially once his films became popular), and they may have insisted on limiting the number of set-ups to save time and money in the field as well as in the studio. There is evidence that these executives were notably parsimonious. [32] They frowned on wasting footage (which was admittedly still quite expensive) on "experiments." [33] This insistence on economy put a premium on speed and militated against breaking a basic camera-position into a number of different angles. Pre-Griffith Biograph films also generally have this air of haste about them—of all the early studios, Biograph's work is the most consistently done in long-shot, with a premium placed on action and a general lack of interest in the special effects that make other studios (such as Vitagraph) seem innovative. But the intriguing fact is that even the very late Griffith Biograph films still have a very small ratio of set-ups to total number of shots, though Griffith was often filming in California by then and was out of the confines of the studio and beyond the close scrutiny of the Biograph officers.

Griffith's natural reticence combined with industrial conditions to utilize the very set-up that had been the camera's vantage point all along—the autonomous unit that had functioned as a staging area for completed dramatic actions. The same camera set-up appears a number of times in a Griffith Biograph film with no *technical* change in dimension and no change in angle (although the placement of characters in relation to depth of field may sometimes temporarily give the impression of a technical change). Moreover, these spaces do not demonstrably overlap. They seem to be discrete units of the world of the film, often specifically bounded by doors, walls, entrances, exits, or natural features that seem to separate one space from another. Griffith used the autonomous set-up because he recognized the potential freedom offered by the inherent discontinuity of such a shot. In "The New Stage Supplants the Old," he radiates the confidence of an artist working in a revolutionary medium:

> For it is clear to me that not only can a producer express any old-stage idea on the new stage at least as effectively as could be done on the old stage, but more effectively. . . . I can open a play with so simple a thing as a glimpse of a rose, or a glimpse of a beautiful picture; and in a flash, I can take the audience from the banks of the Euphrates in Biblical times down to Medieval France, or down to the story of a little girl today.[34]

Griffith is referring to *Intolerance,* his boldest attempt to confirm the contract he had made with his audiences. But the terms of this agreement were set in the Biograph period.

In general, internal evidence suggests that Griffith extracted long shots, medium shots, and close-ups from the deep field given naturally by the technology with which he worked. Even as Griffith isolated various planes of action as separate units of construction (foreground as close-up; background as long shot), he retained his feeling for composition of the image in depth as a means of securing the attention of the audience within the chain of shots and ensuring the visibility of pertinent facts of the drama.

The shots themselves remain discontinuous, discrete units of construction. Eisenstein makes note of the "alternating" ideological layers in Griffith's films and concludes that "this society, perceived *only as a contrast between the haves and the have-nots,* is reflected in the consciousness of Griffith no deeper than the image of an intricate race between two parallel lines." [35] One does not have to agree with Eisenstein's ideological arguments to concur that Griffith's preference for melodrama, with its clear distinctions between good and evil, could have led to this kind of construction. But this line of reasoning also indicates the attractiveness of a distinctively familiar, distinctly bounded shot that would reinforce the sense of comparison and contrast in the narrative. The uniqueness of Griffith's use of these kinds of shots is that he understood that they must be made to connect. The relationship between discontinuous spaces is always more mysterious than the relationship between the master shot and its allied mid-shots and close-ups, because the relationship between such spaces is confirmed *only* by construction. The audience rarely sees that one bit of space (mid-shot) is a continuous part of a larger space (master shot). In other words, in Griffith's hands the "autonomous" set-up functions in an entirely new way. A unit of construction emerges that can be characterized by its *integrity;* the *frequency* of its appearance in the film; and, most important, by its *interrelationship* with other shots in the constructed chain. These connections are created either by activity, which flows from one shot to another, or by the juxtaposition of shots (one follows another in the chain) suggesting that the two shots bear some crucial relationship to each other. This system of construction convinces the audience of the reality of the world of the film by clearly focusing their attention within the frame and minimizing the "shock" of cutting by utilizing binding activity between shots.

Griffith enclosed a space in a frame and composed the elements of the image to guide the audience's attention through the world of the film. In his system of construction, continuous activity was the energy that bound shots together, and a limited number of set-ups were used to create patterns of repetition, and thus familiarity, on which the audience could rely for orientation in the flow of the film. Eventually, Griffith helped create the kind of filmmaking that Lev Kuleshov characterizes as "American": "solving the complexity of scenes by shooting only that element of movement without which at any given moment a necessary vital action could not occur, and the camera is placed in such a perspective in nature that the theme of any given moment itself reaches and is recognized by the viewers in the quickest, simplest and most comprehensive form. [36]

During his Biograph period, Griffith had to gain control of the growth of the screen image from long shot to close-up, and he wanted to preserve the organic relationship of these parts to the "theme" of the "given moment" in the film. His first major constructive decision was to decrease the number of people performing activities and increase the number of ways in which an activity might be performed. He very quickly picked up Porter's intuition that a filmmaker could freely interfere with the implied naturalism of the continuity of an action, and set about the task of managing the matrix of that continuity, depth of field. Griffith was not inclined to cut into a basic set-up once it was established in a chain of shots, because he relied on the recognizability of the basic set-up to provide one of the major cues of orientation in the film. Changes of angles and dimension seemed initially disturbing to the coherence produced by the repetition of a familiar view. This conservative attitude was only very slowly challenged by a developing sense of option in composition that eventually made depth of field a choice rather than an imposition on Griffith's work.

Visibility within the Frame
The Diagonal: Planes
of Action in Depth

The diagonal sweep of characters toward the camera in a chase is one of the best examples of the state of the image between 1905 and 1908. It can be found in films made at Edison and the Danish Nordisk Studios as well as in British and Biograph chases. Activity originates in the background of the shot and advances along a diagonal path through the image. Although there was no way to indicate that one position in this line of activity was more expressive or important than any other, the exterior diagonal offered several advantages. It was a large stage. A great deal of comic or dramatic business could be played out in the scope of the diagonal, and special effects such as the huge trick leaps across the lake in Biograph's *Wife Wanted* (1907) could be played for all they were worth. The raw activity of the running image was enhanced by the sweeping arc it described through all planes of action, therefore unifying a deep field of view. In turn, activity run through this deep field revealed the possibility of the dramatic impact of various subject-to-camera relationships. Activity was forcefully thrust toward the camera as a character ran toward the foreground, and a magnified image was projected toward the next shot as the character passed nearest the camera before the cut.

Griffith was greatly taken by the dynamic growth of characters from small to giant as they swept past the camera along the diagonal. In *Where the Breakers Roar* (1908) this dynamic sweep of activity provides the dramatic contrast to the two introductory shots of the film, the first controlled by the architecture of garden trellises, the second a peaceful, sunlit, diagonal to lateral passage from left to right, medium long shot, through the frame. The diagonal provides a wonderful stage on which to place the film's madman, who steals Alice, the heroine, and leads everyone on a chase. In shot 9 the eye-engaging sweep of activity toward the camera is even slightly curved in the frame to prolong the drama of the madman chasing Alice. The magnified faces of the madman and the heroine burst past the camera just before the cut to provide the graphic punctuation mark to an image organized around the effect of the maximum physical activity that the shot could contain without being crowded with runners.

The Zulu's Heart (1908) is one of the earliest films to indicate that Griffith was beginning to pay attention to the frame as a series of expressive layers, planes of action potential in the diagonal sweep of activity. In shot one a Zulu chief is presented mourning for his dead child in rigidly stylized gestures. Another warrior enters this long shot to call the Zulu chief to war against the Boer invaders. Instead of rampaging through the succeeding shot generally from right background to foreground, the Zulu band is moved very deliberately through shot 2. Griffith stops the action at three points along their diagonal passage through the frame. Each time they stop, the Zulus gesture fiercely to display their determination to destroy the settlers. In part, Griffith is staging both of these ceremonies to indulge his fascination with constructing imaginary social orders, complete with manners and mores—a fascination that continued throughout his Biograph period in such films as *Man's Genesis* (1912), *A Pueblo Legend* (1913), and *In Prehistoric Days* (1913), and more generally in films on Indian subjects. But the movement of the warriors through this shot is also reminiscent of the madman chasing the heroine in *Where the Breakers Roar*. Halting the action along the diagonal concentrates attention at "long shot," "medium shot," and "medium close-up" positions for a progressive magnification of the furious Zulus, until their menacing figures loom out over the audience just before they burst out of the frame at the cut. The situation itself may be melodramatic and overplayed, but the orderly progression of the figures from small to large lends a good deal of power to the action. The fact that Griffith particularized and encapsulated dramatic action in such a systematic way indicates that even in this, his twenty-first film, he searched for compositional possibilities in the frame in depth rather than relying on effects or business. The diagonal helped to reveal the impact of figures on the planes of action implicit in the deep and undifferentiated field of the early image.

The structural breakthrough along the diagonal occurred with the recognition of the foremost plane as an independent compositional area, a discovery first made along the diagonal in exteriors. *The Ingrate* (late 1908) ends with a close view of the reunited husband and wife that is developed from a diagonal passage of their canoe toward the foreground through the concluding frame of the film. *The Ingrate* indicates the solution that Griffith would find along the diagonal to approaching the foreground without violating the realism of the film. Although the close-up is implied in this shot, the last moment of *The Ingrate* also projects the image forward into the space "in front of the screen" that Griffith would explore in later films.

In shot 8 of *In Old Kentucky* (1909) a foreground "close-up" is developed from a continuous and uninterrupted line of activity that starts in the background (with the entry of both pursued and pursuers, who describe a diagonal through the frame), and stops in the foreground. Instead of having the characters run out of this shot, Griffith stages a dramatic resolution in the foreground of shot 8: brothers recognize each other as pursuer and pursued. After this dramatic revelation, shot 8 is resolved by having both groups return to the background on the diagonal for an exit screen right. The effect of a close-up has thereby been interjected into the race, although no cut occurs. In *In Old Kentucky* Griffith exploits the "traditional" extension of the chase diagonal toward the foreground and the cut, producing a dramatic climax in a burst of graphic energy before the figures resume their physical activity, receding into the background of the shot to continue the chase.

In later films of his Biograph period, the diagonal sweeps of activity through the frame were left mainly in remnant. As cutting replaced running as Griffith's definition of screen action, the diagonal became less and less extensive, activity often being extended through the frame in segments over many cuts. It is possible to see pieces of the chase diagonal resurfacing in the later films as quasi-medium close-ups, which are not, however, developed directly from a line of activity extended from back to foreground. As if he were taking advantage of the last magnified statement of the actor's presence before the cut, Griffith simply places characters in the foreground positions that they would have attained if they had run the diagonal. The jealous lover in *Love in the Hills* (1911) does not bother to chase his rival through successive shots along diagonals. Griffith simply places him at the right foreground position as if the chase had already been run. Valuable screen time is not wasted in running around. The country lover is poised at the cut to bar the leftward "matched" movement of his city rival into the heroine's frame. The jealous lover therefore makes the foreground position a barrier to progression along the diagonal and stops his rivals from attaining the goal they desire: to cross over the cut to claim the young woman. Griffith was able to make narrative and structural tension identical.

As intercutting supplants running as the generator of energy in Griffith's films, the diagonal is immobilized in two ways. In the later Biograph films, the diagonal becomes a graphic mark inscribed across the screen as a line of Indians, cowboys, or Civil War soldiers. The dynamism of actually running along the diagonal is transformed into a crisscross pattern of opposing lines created by intercutting shots in battle sequences such as the one between Indians and white settlers in *The Battle at Elderbush Gulch* (1913). On the other hand, observing the effect of the active image as it moved through various stages of magnification along the diagonal was one way Griffith may have become aware of how the frame could opt for one plane of action over another— that is, could be a long shot as opposed to a close-up. Once Griffith began to cut into the continuity of the diagonal, the implications of the last shot of *The Ingrate* and shot 9 of *In Old Kentucky* were realized in the independent close-up.

Lateral Balances

The integration of large images (medium close-ups and close-ups) into the chain of shots depended to a great extent on Griffith's confidence that such a practice would not damage the integrity of the world of the film. Even after the "close-up" was "discovered" at the end of the diagonal, Griffith persisted in controlling the frame with internal devices rather than cutting to close-ups.

In Griffith's early Biograph films, the dimensions of the foreground and background were medium long shot and long shot. Gradually, the background became longer (extreme long shot), and the foreground closer (knees-up figure), with the full figure occupying the middle distances in the frame. The general compositional impulse in his Biograph period is for Griffith to integrate the actor's body into the depth of the frame so as to dramatically utilize the relationships among the range of graphic sizes available naturally in the image in depth. The more surely Griffith learned to place figures within the frame, the closer he came to employing actual long shots, mid-shots, and close-ups as deliberately chosen units of construction.

The most characteristic mise-en-scène in a Griffith Biograph film results from an attempt to strike a balance between the mass of the actors' bodies and depth of field, especially when large foreground figures are counter-weighted with background activity performed by small background figures. Because he delayed cutting into the basic set-up until late in his Biograph period, Griffith was forced to deal with the simple fact that actor heights could balance and unbalance the frame. Kemp Niver notes that in the very early Griffith Biograph film *For Love of Gold* (1908), the camera had to be tilted to accommodate the height of the actor who was rising in the frame.[37] Indeed, as Griffith assembled his excellent repertory group of actors, the disparity of actor heights became an acute problem of composition in the frame in depth. There are stories of Mary Pickford being put in built-up shoes so that she and Arthur Johnson, a very tall person, could comfortably occupy the same frame.[38] Arthur Johnson more suitably fit into compositions with the more substantial and mature Marion Leonard, but as Griffith moved toward a tighter organization of the frame, accommodations for actor heights resulted in increasingly peculiar arrangements. In *Was Justice Served?* (1909) the entire courtroom in shot 11 appears at an unsettling angle that only balances out when James Kirkwood, another tall actor, stands up. In the few films specifically dealing with children, precocious mid-shots are actually nothing more than space pared down to the dimensions of a child, a practice with precedent in pre-Griffith Biograph films, which sometimes began with mid-shots in "limbo" to introduce the main characters (e.g., *Truants,* 1907). In *I Did It, Mama* (1909) the shots occupied by both adults and children are composed in the familiar interior medium long shots.

As the foremost plane of action is used in the composition of interiors, shots begin to be composed to accommodate the full standing figure, so that the seated actor is almost lost off the bottom of the frame, as are Kate Bruce in *Gold Is Not All* (1910), Mary Pickford in *The Broken Locket* (1909), and especially Mae Marsh in *Brutality* (1912). To correct for this loss of volume, Griffith often placed the camera at the level of the figure seated in the foreground, so that the standing figure (often in the mid-ground, often knees-up) is seen from below. But the composition of almost every two-shot is a compromise among the values of order and balance, the number of planes of action in use and the size of the actors in the image. All these had to be considered in producing maximum visibility in the basic set-up, which would not vary over the course of the film.

In *In Old Kentucky* the central frame, in general, can be seen as a conjunction of two axes—the progression from foreground to background (mainly in the chases) and the lateral organization of figures across the surface of the screen (mainly interiors.) Often the middle of the frame is deemphasized by the importance of an entrance or exit in the foreground or background, which is linked to the cut to create the continuity of the film's activity. The drama at the center of the frame is often forced to share the spotlight with another center of attention, as is seen in the emotional tableau that ends the film. In the last shot of *In Old Kentucky* the viewer's eye is drawn away from the centrally played scene of reconciliation between brothers who have fought on opposite sides in the Civil War. To the left of the group stands a young woman crying in sympathy. The viewer's gaze is returned to the center of the frame when she raises her head to cheer. Griffith is rarely content to concentrate the effect of the shot or sequence of shots at one point only, and even in this tableau, he insists that a relationship between combined positions within the shot make the dramatic impact.

The practice of multiple staging was a standard of melodrama. Vardac mentions Boucicault's *Forbidden Fruit* (London, 1880) in which "two adjoining rooms as well as the intervening corridor are put upon the stage . . . [so that] cross-cutting between parallel lines of action could be managed without scene waits." [39] There are many more theatrical precedents that can be cited. Of course, Griffith did not bring multiple staging to film. In Biograph's *Yale Laundry* (1907), the establishing scene places the audience behind a laundry counter, facing a window that fronts on a busy street. At one point a screen is set up in the left foreground of this interior. The screen blocks out the street view to make a private little alcove where naughty undergraduates in drag play laundry maid to their lecherous professor's advances.

In Griffith's Biograph films curtains or screens were often used to break up the space of an interior where a cut might be called for but no cut was possible. In *The Heart of Oyama* (1908), for instance, a screen hides Oyama's tortured lover from her sight and divides the interior into two significant areas of activity: Oyama's background and her lover's foreground. In *The Tavern-keeper's Daughter* (1908) a young woman pursued by a rapist ducks behind a convenient curtain at the back of the set, an action that divides the shot into background and foreground areas of interest, if not very plausibly, because we can hardly believe that the flimsy curtain is enough to conceal her. In *Confidence* (1909) a young doctor joins his sweetheart in front of a screen that blocks out the right side of the shot-in-depth and creates for the two a smaller playing area in the foreground more specifically tailored to the volume of the characters who occupy it and to the more intimate drama of the love story. It is Griffith's more serious version of the flirtation scene in *Yale Laundry*. A similar screened-off area occurs in *With Her Card* (1909) and as late as *Through Darkened Vales* (1911) to effectively alter the size of the shot without the agency of a cut.

In later cases, the placement of the screen pushes the activity in the shot to the foreground to display it more prominently by simply masking off space extraneous to the action. There are only two shots in *As the Bells Rang Out* (1910). In both rooms a portion of the playing area is masked at some time. The erection of a bridal bower in one shot alters that space; a background screen hiding the police who arrive during the wedding to arrest the father of the bride alters the dimensions of the second shot. One of the amazing qualities of depth of field is that such masking can radically alter the weight of the image in the frame and affect the dynamic flow of activity from shot to shot, whether the mask be a screen, bower, or the actor advancing toward the camera. By manipulating mise-en-scène alone, Griffith created a range of subject-to-camera relationships that went far beyond the possibilities of nineteenth-century staging. Depth of field is the potential Griffith always has hidden behind his multiple sets. The scene did not have to be changed, the camera did not even have to be reset to create the dynamic feeling that a space has been expanded or contracted. Yet the sense of orientation is preserved: when someone moves aside in the frame, the viewer recognizes that the basic set-up has been present all along.

Related to the curtain and the screen is an actual split screen that Griffith employed early in his Biograph period. This is another version of an established theater practice. "In [Edward] Fitzball's *Jonathan Bradford* (Surrey [Theatre], 1833) four apartments are organized on two floors. . . . The play's action progresses from one apartment to another or sometimes occurs simultaneously." Such a staging plan saves set-changing time, achieves rapid and economic action, and creates a sense of parallelism.[40] In Biograph's *At the Cross-roads of Life* (1908) the image is vertically split into two areas by the central placement of a dressing table mirror. Essentially, this kind of placement echoes the multiple stage set. Griffith, who was deeply interested in developing paral-lel action, briefly experimented with the simple division of the image. The split screen is used in *The Devil* (1908), *An Awful Moment* (1908), *The Girls and Daddy* (1908), and *Those Boys* (1909). In each film, one image contains an interior set in cross section, so that activity on both sides of the wall can be seen simultaneously. In *The Honor of Thieves* (1908) Griffith even pans across the split set, abolishing the conventions of screen realism for the immediacy of the theatrical convention. In all cases the object is suspense. The audience knows something that has yet to be revealed to one of the characters in the film, and the coincidence of audience and character knowledge is the dramatic resolution of the scene and of the structure. This is accomplished when the character passes from one side of the wall to another. But the split screen produced a spatial anomaly ultimately at cross-purposes to Griffith's structural goals. A house in cross section is an artifice that contradicts the realist illusion of the screen event and ruins the resolution of the two different positions on opposite sides of the wall. It revealed too much to the audience too soon. Gradually, the screen or wall separating the two interior areas combined in one shot was simply replaced by the cut between two rooms.

The split screen, however, did not simply disappear. The process of ab-straction at work in Griffith's Biograph period transformed many devices that were originally used in a "literal" way. The split screen, at first physically functional and substantial, was slowly reintegrated into the frame as a graphic mark with a structural function. One of the most stunning permutations of the split screen occurs in the desert setting of *The Female of the Species* (1912).

The sequence in question begins with shot 9. Three women stand in a space that is vertically split by a post marking a grave. This post divides the frame actively, if asymmetrically—the widow's sister stands to the right of the grave marker; the grieving wife and the other young woman stand to the left. As the interior split frame would eventually do, this uneasily balanced image is also rent asunder by the cut. The widow's sister moves out of the shot to the right, to occupy shot 10. The other young woman moves to the left (shot 11) to oc-cupy shot 12, leaving the widow to mourn in fury at the grave (shot 13). It is very difficult not to feel that the spatial relationship between these three shots is now *left, center* and *right,* although in fact the audience does not really know where the two companions have moved in relation to the widow. The audience perceives that the companions have moved away on a lateral because they exit right and left midframe and because each woman looks "toward" the central image of mourning from her respective shot. The result is a complex composite space centered in a split frame (the set-up of shot 9, repeated), but also composed of three graphically associated spaces separated from the cen-tral frame by cuts.

Her mourning finished, the widow calls her sister back from the right. This woman exits her space, but when the central image is repeated, the exit is not yet completed by a reentry. The viewer is first directed leftward to the second woman, who also exits her space. Only at shot 20 (set-up of shot 9) do both of the companions reenter the central space together, restoring the three-shot at once. The sequence is completed when the women leave the shot, exiting right through the foreground, in front of the grave-marker that originally split the frame. The sister who is plotting to destroy the other young woman is left trailing out at the cut.

It is the very ambiguity of the positions of the companions in respect to the center that creates an undercurrent of nervous energy in this sequence of shots from *The Female of the Species*. Moreover, Griffith is able to manage a double resolution of the sequence. First, the separation imposed by the cuts is resolved when both companions reenter the shot at once; secondly, the division of the frame by the grave-marker is abolished when the women exit the foreground. The tension of the dramatic situation depends on the shifting spatial relationships between these three women. The sister maliciously tries to convince the widow that the other woman was responsible for her husband's death, and to generate the tension of the situation, the splitting and resolution of these exteriors is very carefully handled. The dramatic rhythm of *The Female of the Species* is created by splintering this group of women. In shots 22 and 25 a similar lateral is set up. From shot 24 to 35 these two set-ups are intercut. The grief-crazed widow attacks the innocent companion, who becomes isolated "to the right" in a shot where she awaits further violence instigated by the villainess, who slyly places an axe in the widow's hand. This situation is balanced between two positions for twelve shots before the widow leaves her space, but does not harm the innocent woman. The group is reconstituted in shot 39 and travels toward the camera once again. Each time the three are rejoined in the "central" shot, the audience feels a measure of relief, as well as the renewed tension in the group that will lead to the next splitting off into separate shots. This is a direct result of cutting between spaces and requiring the audience to imagine the implications of the relationship indicated in the structure.

The Panorama

The transformation of the split screen, its utilization as a graphic mark rather than a real barrier, indicates a process by which Griffith isolated the variables of composition in the basic image and experimented with them to realize a dramatic impact. Eventually, the enlarged figure of the actor would be boldly juxtaposed to the panoramic sweep of hills and valleys that began to occupy the depths of Griffith's shots. After 1909 the California landscape itself provided part of the scenic inspiration in Griffith's films, for Griffith escaped the austerity of the New York studio and the confinement to interior work imposed by winter weather in the East by convincing the company to send him to the perennial sunshine of California. The films made in California show an abundance of vistas and pictorial settings that reflect the more varied terrain Griffith found out West.

However, Griffith's interest in the compositional possibilities of the panorama began in the East. Dramas produced in striking natural settings are the closest Griffith's work comes to a deliberate attempt to compose obviously pretty pictures. In *The Planter's Wife* (1908) a panoramic background of rocks and cliffs provides a breathtaking setting in a long shot where a wife broods on her unhappiness and meets her lover. The panorama is more structurally important in *The Greaser's Gauntlet* (1908). In this film the panoramic shot appears first and last. The Greaser leaves this shot to enter the world and returns to it from his adventures. This long shot is used as a tonal unit, enclosing the activity of the film and retarding the accelerated rhythm of the cutting that brings *The Greaser's Gauntlet* to its dramatic and narrative climax. In *Fisher Folks* (1911), a California film, the human element of the composition is more dramatically juxtaposed to the panorama, but the shot is still used for its tonal quality, creating a point of contemplative quiet, after which a film develops in which all the characters incessantly pursue one another and battle for position in the frame.

In *1776, or The Hessian Renegades* (1909) Griffith explored the panorama as a combination of scene-setting and a source of shot variables. In shot 1, an exhausted Continental soldier runs toward the camera chased by Hessian soldiers. The set-up achieves the typical quasi–close-up effect. Then all vacate a shot of scenic beauty that approximates a long shot. In *The Mended Lute* (1909), Griffith actually cuts out on the axis to place the lovers amid the scenic beauty of rocks and waterfalls. In this film the panorama is also a distinct feature of composition in depth, and from this point on, the Indian village will be a standard composition extended into the frame from an enlarged foreground figure, usually placed to the right or left in the image. A line of tepees directs the eye to the background from the foreground character, often an Indian chief. This composition creates a midground "stage" for activity that resounds fore and back in the frame very formally, since the foreground is so tightly controlled by a point of attention that leads to a background center of activity. In *The Redman's View* (1909) the juxtaposition of foreground and background is even more pronounced. The opening village scene is similar to that in *The Mended Lute*, but shot 7 takes up the structural theme of extension from foreground to background by showing the Indian line of march as an extended arc fully occupying the frame from medium close-up to an extreme long shot. Such a composition is related to the immobilization of the arc run by the madman and the girl in *Where the Breakers Roar*. It also demonstrates that the panorama had become entrenched in the frame as a structural unit no longer dependent on the chase diagonal for a raison d'être.

In *The Indian Brothers* (1911) the murder of the chief is staged in the foreground position to counterpoint the approach of the rest of the tribe, still tiny figures in the background, rhythmically complementing foreground activities with no sacrifice of spatial realism. Extreme depth of field, especially when panoramic, provided spaces in the frame that were genuinely far enough away from the foreground to pass unnoticed by characters there. With this kind of staging Griffith achieved economy of expression, spatial realism, and visibility of all crucial business in the infinite space of the deep frame.

Controlling Attention with Technical Effects

With depth of field as a "given," Griffith proceeded to recognize the various planes of action in the basic shot, centers of attention upon which activity could be concentrated for a dramatic effect without the agency of a cut. The chase diagonal and panorama contributed their share to making the background visible as a long shot and the foreground visible as a medium close-up. Throughout Griffith's Biograph period this space-oriented definition of subject-to-camera relationships complemented the production of close-ups, medium shots, and long shots as discrete units of construction.

If the technical effects contributing to visibility within the frame have so far largely been ignored, it has been to emphasize this evidence of Griffith's regard for the image as an organic field of control. Although Griffith employed lighting effects, limited camera movements, and an occasional dissolve during his Biograph period, and many more effects would appear in his feature films, it is important to recall Sam Landers' comment that "Griffith was not strong on the trick stuff."[41] Landers also remembers Griffith's use of a foreground screen of bushes as a natural "mask," and this recollection seems generally to apply to Griffith's use of technical effects.[42] While it is simply false to assert that Griffith opted against technical means of concentrating attention within the frame, it also seems that Griffith's interest was captured by a technical effect such as a fade, close-up, or dissolve only after he had found it naturally in the frame in the process of composing an effective image. Nonetheless, technical effects did contribute to the compositional development of the basic set-up.

Lighting.   Griffith developed a limited number of lighting effects. Attribution for their invention seems to be a matter of memory. Billy Bitzer claims credit for the firelit effect that begins to appear in Griffith's films around 1909.[43] Other members of the Biograph team remember that Griffith did all the mood lighting.[44] Whoever was the source of the inspiration, the firelit family scene was one of the first attempts to create a mood through lighting. Light also began to stream through windows to give some depth and dimension to the canvas flats that made up the sets in the Biograph Studio. Lightning flashed in the windows of a house in *The Pirate's Gold* (1908). Thereafter, sunlight effects were used in *The Violinmaker of Cremona* (1909), *The Expiation* (1909), *The Restoration* (1909), and *Fisher Folks* (1911). The appearance of "sunlight" through a window was even used to simulate a fade-in in *Pippa Passes* (1909) to signal the beginning of the action of the film.

Griffith's most theatrical use of a lighting effect, his most conscious use of light as atmosphere, occurs in a group of films that are less admirable for their construction than for the tone set by their lighting. *Edgar Allen Poe* [*sic*] (1909) is such a film, impressive in the pre-expressionist harshness of the contrast between light and shadow in the shots. Some of the most stunning lighting effects of this "expressionist" type center on the figure of Marion Leonard for a time in 1909, when Griffith cast her as a destructive siren and created a gothic atmosphere around her that sets her apart from other Biograph leading ladies. Griffith would eventually concentrate sunlight with reverence and worship on his favorite versions of feminine nobility: the innocent virgin and the noble mother. While Florence Lawrence was still with the Biograph Company, Marion Leonard could always be the city woman to her country sweetheart, the vamp to her madonna.

But with Lawrence gone to the IMP Company in 1909, Griffith's favorite female figure faded from his films to let Marion Leonard (who looked singularly silly in Indian costumes) take the stage. Her well-developed female figure, with substantial chest and full hips, placed her securely in a city setting of corsets and champagne, and in fact the life-wise Leonard persona, urban and urbane, temporarily produced a new tone in Griffith Biograph films. A series of marital disaster films centered specifically on her. Her children die, and in *Through the Breakers* (1909) it is even her fault—Griffith's ultimate indictment of a woman. Light collects around this monstrous and destructive figure. In *Fools of Fate* (1909) Leonard stands on the sun-dappled porch of a home in which her husband's suicide will later be revealed to her in the garish half-light cast by a lantern. In *His Lost Love* (1909) Griffith put Marion Leonard, who is breaking up her sister's home, at the organ in a church, and again the light streams down. In *The Expiation* (1909) the husband again commits suicide, and Leonard seems genuinely consumed with neurotic guilt, partly because Griffith places her in a close atmosphere of light and shadow. Shot 10 is a darkened interior, highlighted by unnaturally bright light streaming through a window. *The Expiation* is notable for a funereal gothic atmosphere that connects it with all those semi-mystical movie convents that are imbued with a strange sensuality born of the realization that women can be attractive and alluring in flowing habits and fluttering veils, especially if those outfits are exaggerated a bit with a few extra yards of material so as to put them just past the penitential. In *The Expiation* Griffith seems simply to have indulged in stage setting, reaching for an atmosphere of convents by moonlight in a film that is structurally unimpressive. This film is one of the few in which such theatricalism is so apparent. When the same material reappears in *Death's Marathon* (1913), with Blanche Sweet in the role of the wife, the dramatic effect of the husband's suicide is created in tense passages of intercutting.

Candlelight and flashlight also appear in *Fate's Interception* and *The Burglar's Dilemma* (both 1912), but on the whole Griffith tended to use natural light, heightening women's hair into haloes with the aid of reflectors. In 1948 E. Goodman quoted Griffith in a magazine article entitled "Flashback to Griffith":

> What the modern movie lacks is beauty—the beauty of moving wind in the trees, the little movements in a beautiful flowing of the blossoms in the trees . . . they have forgotten that no still painting—the greatest ever, was anything but a pallid still picture. But the moving picture! . . . the moving picture is beautiful, the moving of wind on beautiful trees is more beautiful than a painting.[45]

Panning.   In the absence of an opportunity to vary the basic set-up more radically, Griffith availed himself of the opportunity to pan. When linked with an action, the pan enhanced and magnified the activity in a shot with the momentum of the camera's movement. In *The Barbarian, Ingomar* (1908) the pan is a rudimentary stage-expanding device: it extends the opening walk of shot 1. This pan echoes the numerous camera movements in earlier films in which the camera simply stays with action that is temporarily straying out of the frame, although in *The Barbarian, Ingomar* this movement through the garden also precedes the more conventionally developed running activity of the film. By *The Ingrate* (1908) the pan is used to create a moment of pastoral tranquility before the dramatic running activity of the film begins.

As with other devices, the pan was quickly integrated into the flow of shots. In *The Call of the Wild* (1909) Griffith uses a pan to slowly reveal the proximity of the Indian to the woman he wishes to kidnap. But generally Griffith distrusted the moving camera to reveal dramatic action.[46] In the main, he was not very interested in the spatial ambiguity offered by either the deep frame or the moving camera. That is why his work with composition in depth cannot really be equated with a "deep focus" aesthetic. Griffith's project, his goal, required him to define and specify spaces, and the resulting images are generally concrete, specified, and bounded. Griffith's illusion of reality is firmly tied to ellipsis as a strategy, and he very creatively and consciously manipulates the breaks between spaces rather than the continuity of a single shot. The most memorable camera movements in his Biograph films thus have a tonal function.

The pan across the valley in *The Country Doctor* (1909) paces the beginning of this film and lends scope to the feeling of philosophical detachment stated in the static panorama that Griffith had used to frame *The Greaser's Gauntlet* (1908). The exterior space in *The Country Doctor* is made all the more formidable by the pan that moves across it. Instead of beginning the film by immediately identifying the threat to the principal characters, as he had done in earlier films, Griffith used the pan in *The Country Doctor* to internalize the activity graphically, to frame the film with a dispassionate moment and a quiet, almost architectural movement, to which the running activity of the film is contrasted. The pan in *The Country Doctor* is the film's source of energy and its final statement, bringing the world of the film around full circle to resolve all the spaces after the drama has ended. Its restatement at the end of the film restores a familiar image, but has the effect of generality, of quite literal distance, from which the drama is extracted as a particular. Unlike the panorama in *The Greaser's Gauntlet,* the pan in *The Country Doctor* represents repose only in the general sense of disengagement, invoking the largeness of nature to overwhelm and not salve the intimate tragedy it encloses. Structurally, as a statement of continuous space, the pan in *The Country Doctor* serves as the rhythmical complement to the pattern of intercutting and continuous activity over discontinuous space in which the story is told. It completes the pattern—pan–family portrait–internal lateral passage from sick child to sick child–family portrait–pan—that is the structure of the film.

Panorama and panning camera movement are combined in *In Old Kentucky* to create a sense of geographical proximity in an atmosphere of infinite space, a shot both intimate and spectacular. A soldier stands guard before the background of a striking valley; the camera pans to the entry of a Confederate soldier. This pan concretely describes the distance between the soldier and the guard when the camera returns to the left and the Confederate is discovered. Unlike the panorama in *The Country Doctor,* there is nothing distant or ruminative about the combination of positions and the preparation for the ensuing chase in *In Old Kentucky.* The lateral quality of the pan in this film is a rhythmical contrast to the next shot, in which the brothers enter on a diagonal, approach the foreground to recognize each other, and exit the shot through the background.

Changes of Angle.   The question of angles and actual changes of camera position is partly a matter of terrain in Griffith's Biograph films and partly a technical matter of actually being able to manipulate the still somewhat unwieldy Biograph camera. It is clear as early as *The Barbarian, Ingomar* (1908) that Griffith was interested in changing angles: although there seems no particular structural reason in this film to do so, shot 2 represents a change of angle from the end of the pan in shot 1. Changes of angle also homogenize the frame to accommodate the disparity of actor heights as characters rise and sit down again.

Griffith filmed architecture at a consistently low angle beginning with *The Cardinal's Conspiracy* (1909), and he continued the practice in films such as *Swords and Hearts* (1911) and *When Kings Were Law* (1912). In general, the Biograph films became an abundance of vistas, actions caught from varying high and low angles—very rarely from the extremes of right and left—when Griffith began to work in California and the terrain dictated camera placement to some extent.

But usually these angles are not varied once they are presented, and in that, these shots are consistent with Griffith's general attitude toward the need for familiarity of composition in the basic set-up. Possibly, Griffith's movement of the camera was at first simply constrained by time limitations, tight production schedules, and the length of the one-reeler favored by the Biograph Company. Griffith remembered that period in an interview with Henry Stephen Gordon in 1916: "Those were the days of the half reels; we made two pictures a week. It was something of a struggle to get them out. . . . Why, often we have got a picture completed in two days. Now we take that much time or more just to decide what costumes we will use." [47]

But as Griffith began to rely on the familiarity and recognizability of the basic set-up as a point of reference in the world of the film, he may well have felt that the flexibility of cutting amongst too many changes in angle would be disruptive and disorienting in a sequence of shots each under a second in length. Later in his Biograph period, shots are presented at increasingly acute angles, the camera hovering over or crouching under a scene. Occasionally, as in *A Welcome Intruder* (1913), an angle is shifted laterally on a familiar image. Most generally, changes of angle are little adjustments to restore balance in the familiar composition.

Cutting on the Axis.   The most varied treatment of one basic space occurs with the cut-in or -out on the axis. This is a practice of shooting a closer view of the same set-up from the same angle—that is, cutting straight out of or straight into the basic space. It is not possible to regard Griffith's general development of a sequence incorporating a range of subject-to-camera relationships from the perspective of the later master shot, but it is important to take cutting on the axis into consideration, because Griffith exercised that option quite often.

Although the cut-in on the axis in *The Greaser's Gauntlet* (1908) also winds up the first sequence of activity, its utilitarian function is to display the passing of the gauntlet, the Greaser's pledge to the woman who has just saved his life. Most of Griffith's early cuts on the axis seem to have this purpose of emphasis. But this cut can also be seen as a rudimentary attempt to break into the organic integrity of the basic set-up in the same sense that Griffith would break into the flow of activity with a cut to produce shorter, more economical shots.

It was not long before the desire to emphasize began to have more direct structural consequences. The cut-in and -out on the axis began to control visibility in Griffith's films. In *The Sealed Room* (1909), for instance, the cut-in to the king walling up his faithless wife in shot 9 supplants the wider view of the throne room and concentrates the drama of the film in the impact of the intercutting between a medium long shot of the two guilty lovers suffocating and a quasi–mid-shot of the jealous king directing their immurement. The substance of this sequence is silly, but the methodical alternation of these shots of differing volumes actually produces a rather chilling effect. The dramatic impact is concentrated at the doorway, and this emphasizes the feeling of causality that normally results when two shots are intercut.

Cutting in and out on the axis varies from film to film in its structural purpose. In *The Cardinal's Conspiracy* cutting in on the axis seems to have no other purpose than emphasis and does not create a particularly complicated set of visual relationships. But the cut-in on the wife in the grieving sequence in *The Female of the Species* introduces the structural theme of a film in which the dramatic tension depends on the composite sense of space created in the relationship of one shot to another.

A corollary of cutting on the axis is pulling focus. Griffith occasionally experimented with this technical means of mechanically directing visibility within the image. Focus is pulled in the planting scene that opens *A Corner in Wheat* (1909): as the farmers sowing the wheat approach the camera, the background is thrown out of focus to keep the farmers' images sharp, a manipulation of the depth of the image that echoes the extension of the pastoral image through the pan in *The Country Doctor*. The repetition of this planting image at the end of *A Corner in Wheat* produces a similar effect of distance and enclosure.

In other cases, Griffith was interested in pulling focus to eliminate the depth of the image and emphasize the foreground figure. He creates a dynamic and forceful presence in the frame with the advance of the character toward the camera. This effect is used with the Snapper Kid in *The Musketeers of Pig Alley* (1912) and the madman in *The House of Darkness* (1913).

Background as Long Shot; Foreground as Close-up

The realization that the foreground and background could be independent variables seems to have come when the enlarged foreground image was blotting out more of the background in Griffith's compositions. In 1911 Griffith radically juxtaposed foreground and background in such films as *The Red-man's View,* and there is a constant search for perfect balance between increasingly larger foreground and smaller background images in the composition of the frame. The figurative move of the medium close-up from the corner of the chase diagonal to the center of the frame depended on an increasingly sophisticated attitude toward screen action.

When Griffith deliberately began to block out the background with large foreground figures, chains of shots appear in the films that utilize the rhythm of the alternation of long shot and mid-shot for dramatic effect.

The Golden Supper (1910) is a film more or less devoid of any striking thematic interest, but it contains fascinating indications that Griffith was beginning to manage the flow of activity through images that vary, medium shot to long shot, from cut to cut. In the sequence from shot 8 through shot 19, the relationship of the rejected suitor to a wedding procession is presented by referring his rather intimate and solitary mid-shot to the longer and wider shots of the procession of newlyweds and wedding guests who sweep through the frame toward and past the camera (shot 10), then ascend a dramatic flight of steps (shot 13). This passage is particularly interesting when compared to *The Vaquero's Vow* (1908), which uses essentially the same plot material, but in which the rejected suitor is forced to occupy a spatially ridiculous position, following on the heels of the wedding party, who are supposedly unaware of his presence. In *The Golden Supper* Griffith expresses the poignancy of the suitor's rejection by isolating him in a separate shot and utilizing the fact that intercutting often forces a mental as well as a physical relationship between two shots. In other words, Griffith gives the suitor a spatially probable and graphically "weighty" screen position in respect to the festive group and then, by intercutting, suggests that the audience knows what the poor fellow is feeling.

In the sequence of shots from 8 to 13 in *The Primal Call* (1911) the foreground of shot 8 splits from the background to form "wings" of related activity to the right and left in shots separated on a left-to-right lateral from shot 8 in much the same way as the shots of the companions were separated from the grieving widow's position in *The Female of the Species.* In the foreground of shot 8 in *The Primal Call* are a mother, her daughter, and the fellow who would like to marry the girl. The mother and daughter move off right to shot 9, a bench in a garden, to conduct the business of convincing the young woman to marry. In shot 10, a repeat of space 8, the suitor and a friend move off to the left. When the foreground is vacated, this space is focused at a medium long distance on a woman standing in the center background of the shot. Her plane of action has been delineated from the foreground by the placement of the main characters. When the men exit left, she follows. This movement left is echoed in shot 11 (set-up of shot 9 repeated) by the daughter's look left. While

the look is clearly not "realistic" (she gives no indication of having seen anything significant), the viewer's attention is directed to the left, where, one
feels, the suitor, the friend, and the mystery woman are coming together. Indeed, in shot 12, they are revealed standing together and the mystery of the
"other woman" is solved when we find that she is the suitor's abandoned
sweetheart.

The beauty of the combination of the foreground and background positions
that begins this sequence is that all the interested parties in the proposed marriage travel from specific points in the basic set-up and direct the audience's
attention to specific positions in an allied cluster of shots where narrative information is revealed. Every necessary element in the drama holds a secure
position that ensures that it will be as visible as it would be if Griffith had cut
the central shot into medium shots and close-ups. Griffith opts to maintain the
spatial integrity of the original set-up, utilizing the possibilities for graphic
variety inherent in depth of field. At the same time, he is able to spin a web of
information from a central point, and the total picture of three allied spaces is
held by the viewer, who experiences the exchange of information among them
as a total dramatic effect.

In the final stage of the analysis of the shot in depth, the separation of the
foreground and the background takes place by both mechanical and organic
means. In *The Indian Brothers* (1911) Griffith utilizes the full extent of the
depth of the field in the basic set-up for the main action and closes off the
frame from the back when he does not want or need the scope of depth of
field. The elimination of the background was an important step for Griffith
because it represents a significantly new attitude toward the openness of the
wide open spaces presented by earlier film images. The effects of this developing attitude toward composition can be seen in the second sequence of *The
Indian Brothers*. A renegade is banished from the Indian camp. He appears
next in shot 6, in which the background and the horizon are blocked by
weeds. He crouches in this shot, which seems "close" because all of the activity has been crowded up into the foreground. In addition, there is no geographical relationship between this shot and the shot of the Indian camp: the
renegade's exit from shot 5 (set-up 1, the camp, repeated) does not match his
entry into shot 6, and there is no graphic indication given to tell the viewer
how far these two spaces are from one another. But Griffith uses intercutting
of these two spaces (5 [1]–6 and 7 [1]–8) to create a relationship between the
renegade's position and the camp. This position is consolidated by emphasizing graphic contrasts. Griffith centers the effect of the relationship of 5–6 and
7–8 not on proximity (the understanding of how close the threat actually is),
but on the weight of the villain, poised at the boundary of the shot, ready to
burst out of the shot to the left. The release of the tension between these two
shots is effected when the renegade pops into the shot of the Indian village to

kill the chief. This dramatic action takes place in the foreground of a familiar image while in the deep background of the shot the tribe is already returning to the village.

If the argument so far may at least be taken as suggestive of a process of learning to see possibilities for composition in the nature of the early image, it must be granted that the long shot was not a simply utilized element of structure or a "given" merely because it was technically easy to produce depth of field. The long shot had to be "discovered" as a discrete structural unit just as much as did the close-up.

The utilization of the long shot as a discrete unit of construction occurs in *Through Darkened Vales* (1911). Action deliberately passes through the background, and only through the background, of a shot for one of the first times in Griffith's work.

Through Darkened Vales is a film constructed of a number of exchanges. First one, then the other of a pair of lovers goes blind. Each lover alternately occupies shots toward which the activity of the film is referred in intercutting and the histrionic blindings are connected in a structure that aims to resolve the separation of the lovers.

In the second narrative sequence of the film, Grace, her sight restored through the sacrifice of Dave, her admirer, is stationed at a window in her house, looking out. This space is familiar to the audience, and in this home interior, eventually pared down by a cut-in to a tight mid-shot, Grace's gaze is concentrated at the window. With its stability, this familiar image structurally complements Dave's blind "wandering" through a series of shots that lead to Grace, and this walk completes the pattern of left-right relationships that has been formed by the positions of the man and the woman throughout the film. Dave starts walking "toward" Grace from his house, clearly set on a path to the left that leads directly to her (fig. 1). The shots in this resolving sequence are much shorter than is the case with the intercutting in the rest of the film, and the image of the woman alternates with the image of the man in a two-to-one rhythm as he approaches her position. As the frame tightens around her from shots 31 to 33 (figs. 2, 4), there is a complementary background/foreground order in the sequence of Dave's walk (shots 32 and 34). In shot 32 (fig. 3) Griffith places the first simple long shot in a chain of shots that is not a chase. Dave simply walks through the background of shot 32 on a lateral from right to left and out of the frame. The importance of such a shot is that it demonstrates that the long shot could be a structural choice, a fact reflected in the overall shape of the sequence. The balance between the growth in volume of the characters, the equalization of the weights in the related shots of the sequence, is enhanced by the fact that Grace is at the window leaning "toward" Dave's approach. (This graphic affinity compares to the first sequence of the film, in which the young man is positioned in his shot with his back to the young woman's position in her shot.)

Everything in this sequence of *Through Darkened Vales* speaks resolution: the rhythm of the intercutting, the shot lengths, the related graphic positions, the symmetrical balance of the sequence in respect to the other sequences of the film, and, finally, the intercutting itself, which allows Griffith to stage the resolution of the dramatic action in graphic terms, alternating shots of differing volumes in successive shots until Grace rises from her chair at the window and breaks from the tight referent position to run out of her house to meet Dave at her gate (figs. 5–7). The audience's anticipation of this resolution and the satisfaction that is derived from it in dramatic effects is related to the pacing and shape given the young man's general leftward walk referred to the young woman's position, and her break from that position to run rightward to the young man in a much more open space.

Griffith's regard for the long shot as a structural unit is reflected in a few of the films of 1912 and 1913. In *Fate* (1912) Griffith cuts to a long shot of the exterior of a shack just before it blows up, creating a moment of wholeness and peacefulness for the audience in the midst of a multi-shot depiction of crisis. The long shot is combined with a high angle to create the "bird's-eye view" shots that appear in *Iola's Promise* (1912) in a sequence of fighting between settlers and Indians. In *The Battle at Elderbush Gulch* (1913) the bird's-eye view appears quite suddenly in the midst of a battle, the immediacy of which the audience has experienced in the combination of shots that describes the relationship between the tiny, embattled cabin and the Indian attack that swirls around it. In *The Battle at Elderbush Gulch* the overall pattern of crisscrossing diagonals presented in the intercutting of shots of the battle creates the matrix into which the bird's-eye view of the cabin is placed for a combination of the effects of immediacy and detachment reflected in *Fate* and *Iola's Promise.*

The use of the close-up for the magnification of dramatic detail occurs in many pre-Griffith films. A lady's shoe is tied in a vignetted close-up in Smith's *As Seen Through a Telescope* (1900), and thereafter everything from real spiders (Smith, c. 1900) to animated "love microbes" in *The Love Microbe* (Biograph, 1907) are seen in this telescopic/microscopic close-up view. In Griffith's Biograph films between 1908 and 1912, close-ups of objects appear in *The Fatal Hour* (a clock face), *Betrayed by a Hand Print* (a handprint), *The Sacrifice* (a comb and watch fob), *The Golden Louis* (money), *Sweet and Twenty* (a book title), and *Home Folks* (coins), to name a few.

Considering the incidence of close shots in these films and those made at Biograph before 1908, it is clear that it was not the close-up itself that company executives objected to. The most obvious difference between close-ups that magnified information in the frame and those that one might call structural (i.e., flowing with purpose from a previous shot and contributing to the total effect of the film) is that Griffith insisted on making close-ups of the human body, not coins or clock faces. This impulse to come closer to the expres-

Figs. 1–7. *Through Darkened Vales*
(1911)—Resolution (condensed)

1

sive human element of the drama involves the fragmentation of the image.
Griffith remembered the Biograph Company's response: " 'That will never do
at all,' objected the proprietors. 'The actors look as if they were swimming—
you can't have them float on, without legs or bodies!' But I persisted. . . .
Today the 'close-up' is essential to every Motion Picture, for the near view of
the actor's lineaments conveys intimate thought and emotion." [48]

This impulse to come close to the expressive human content of the drama
rather than emphasizing informational detail is already clear in *The Greaser's
Gauntlet* (1908) when Griffith cuts to a tighter shot of the Greaser and the
young woman rather than to a vignetted shot of the gauntlet, although the exchange of that object is the ostensible reason for the cut-in on the axis. In *The
Medicine Bottle* (1909) the cut-in on the axis is made to magnify the act of
pouring the fatal medicine. This is the kind of shot that must have disturbed
the Biograph "proprietors." The resistance was to chopping bodies into parts
without a mediating matte à la spyglass or telescope that would help the audience "understand" the relationship of the part to the whole. It is this idea that
Griffith attacked in earnest during his Biograph period, demonstrating that
the audience would accept a wide range of visual variation from the screen,
especially if accompanied by the proper cues for orientation. It was easy for
audiences to accept every "innovation" that Griffith offered without much resistance because Griffith's effects are so firmly set in the chain of shots that the
fresh and original seems palatable and natural—that is, realistic.

Linda Arvidson, Griffith's wife, remembered company resistance to what
she called the "first picture to have a *dramatic* close-up [*After Many Years*].
. . . When Mr. Griffith suggested a scene showing Annie Lee waiting . . . to
be followed by a scene of Enoch cast away . . . it was altogether too distracting." [49] This sequence is an example of the desire to create a total dramatic
effect toward which all the shots in the film contribute. A shot of the stranded

2

3

4

5

6

7

8   9

Figs. 8–10. *After Many Years*
(1908)—Portraits

10

sailor (fig. 8) holding a locket (shot 8) is intercut with a shot of his faithful
wife (shot 9) (fig. 9). Where one might have expected to see only the close-up
of an object—a picture in the locket—Griffith gives the woman herself. The
disorientation that the audience might have felt in the juxtaposition of the two
radically discontinuous shots of the husband and wife is minimized by the
familiarity of the image in which the wife stands. The location in which Annie
Lee stands has already appeared in shot 2 (fig. 10). The "new" image of Annie Lee is produced by a cut-in on the axis that tightens the familiar image
around her. While the actual operation of cutting in closer to Annie Lee is not
seen, the resonance between the real image of the wife and the kind of picture
one might find in a locket is felt by the viewer. The newer, closer shot contributes to the impact of the film, in which memory is one of the themes.

Griffith's concentration on the human figure, the silent face of which he
would make the proper object of the camera's scrutiny, is related to the effort
to reveal this *mental* realm of the film to the audience. In *The Last Deal*
(1909) a cut-in on the axis is made to the backs of gambling cardplayers. This

cut-in is placed in a balanced position in a sequence of shots into which Griffith has also integrated a "sympathetic" shot of the gambler's wife waiting at home. The sequence of shots from 6 to 12 contains three components: a, the long shot of the card game; b, the cut-in shot of the players; and c, the wife waiting at home. The sequence proceeds $a(b)c$ (b) $c(b)a$, the cut-in to the card game appearing in an orderly context that expresses both spatial and mental relationships. The sequence observes the principles most characteristic of Griffith's work: repetition and cyclical resolution, with the closer shots neatly sandwiched between shots of the wife and the full view of the card game. The final subject of the sequence is a set of relationships between the wife and her husband created by the fact that Griffith places the shot of the wife at (c) in a structurally significant position in a chain of shots that rises toward and falls away from the dramatic and graphic highlight of the sequence, the cut-in. The wife is given a place in the drama even though her position is clearly spatially discontinuous with the game in which her husband occupies center stage.

This reliance on the power of the relationship of a closer shot or cut-in to other shots in the sequence is nowhere so well illustrated as in the tonal difference of cut-ins on the watching heroine in *The Battle* (1911). The visual tone of the first sequence of this film is set by the physical relationship of the young woman to the battle she witnesses. The exterior shot of her house reveals that the battle lines are within sight of her house, although the position at the window inside her house from which she "watches" the battle does not match the angle that would be needed for her actually to see the event. The cut-in to her praying for his safety at this window focuses her concern on her beloved, who is engaged in the battle. As in *The Honor of His Family,* the young man's flight from the battle is finally set along her sight-line. The heroine's look "at" the proceedings is therefore coincident with that of the audience. Both are in touch with the information of the battle at the same time, because it is the woman's position at the window that confirms the viewers' sense that they know where the man will go.

In the second sequence of *The Battle,* Griffith uses a cut-in on the axis (shot 46) to change this relationship of the look of the audience to the look of the character within the film. This cut-in states a new spatial relationship between the heroine and the position of her lover, who has tried to run away and is going into battle once more to redeem his cowardly act of desertion. Her figure at the window turned right (shots 44 and 46) "frames" the image of the young man (shot 45) turning away from her now. The cut-in to the heroine tightens the shot around her, enclosing a private position in a room that will soon become public space with the entry of wounded soldiers from the battlefield.

In the second sequence, the young woman's personal space (her house) is split between public and private events as her connecting gaze is split between public and private events in sequence 1. In sequence 2 the film is no longer evenly divided between the heroine's gaze and her fiancé's activities. Her look no longer orients the audience in the world of the film in which the man will be redeemed. This sequence is punctuated by the woman's presence at the window twice: first from the longer position in her house (shots 60 and 64), and then from the tighter position (shot 89) created by the cut-in, where she is shown nearly in despair, sunk down by the window, but no longer looking through it. Owing to the spatial dislocation between the man and the woman (he no longer travels through shots along the line defined by the direction of her look), her position at the window becomes figurative instead of active—a hope rather than scrutiny. Consequently, a split develops between what the audience knows about the progress of the battle and her fiancé's fate and what the heroine knows about it. The film decidedly shifts away from her in this second sequence, and this shift is signaled by the cut-in on the axis and by the relationship of shots in the 44–45–46 sequence in which the direction of the woman's look is disengaged from any direct geographical relationship to the man's position.

Griffith also approached the fragile forward picture plane with considerable freedom and assurance. So comfortable was he with this area that he presented actors to it with no fear that this orientation of the actor's look toward the camera would ruin the illusion of the self-contained reality of the film world. In *The Yaqui Cur* (1913) a young Indian is beaten by his tribe for his Christian nonviolence. The young man staggers into a new shot and lurches forward toward the camera. This is one of the most ambiguous spatial moments in Griffith's work, because the gesture is so forcefully directed outward. But through long practice, Griffith had learned to endow his films with such spatial integrity, based on the network of connections between shots, that there is no question of this gesture being a theatrical aside rather than a moment of special intimacy. The boy's gesture does not try to catch the eye of the second "audience beyond the camera." Instead, it reflects Griffith's intuition that the frontal plane, as the extreme forward position on the screen, could also be used to suggest the organic extension of the space of the image directly out of the frame, reversing the perspectival vanishing point of the composition forward toward the audience. The boy's look in *The Yaqui Cur* is directed, not at the audience, but into the abstract space that mirrors the depth of the image. By the look, the shot becomes a temporary abstraction in the context of the film's activity, the moment of concentration and contemplation produced by the combination of the volume and position of the character in the frame.

In *Death's Marathon* (1913) the look directed out of the screen and the spatial ambiguity of the frontal plane are the structural subjects of an entire sequence of the film. *Death's Marathon* reduces the elements of Griffith's earlier Biograph films to the simplest set of structural components: a passage of intercutting mingled with a race to the rescue. Tension is created by cutting between the images of a man and his wife talking to each other by telephone while a continuous line of activity is described through the world of the film by a car racing from the woman to save the man.

The marvelous spatial ambiguity of the woman's gaze as she stands in the foremost plane is the conclusion of the Biograph history of the analysis of the frame in depth. The process of linkage begun in 1908 between spatially discontinuous images in *After Many Years* culminates in 1913 in *Death's Marathon* in a telephone call between a husband who is losing himself and a wife increasingly horrified by his description of his state of mind—a situation that the wife can only imagine, much as Annie Lee in *After Many Years* is forced to imagine the situation of Enoch Arden, her lost husband. The husband's position in *Death's Marathon* complements that of the wife, inasmuch as he gloats over her imagined reaction to the grisly suicide he promises to execute as she listens. The wife's look, directed out of the fragile frontal plane, creates a link with the image of her husband that reflects the fluctuation between the real and the imaginary in the film, between expectations and resolution, between anxiety and knowledge.

Griffith relies on the wife's look to create an imaginary vision of the event that will occur, and this vision complements the audience's actual witnessing of it. Intercutting sustains the dramatic disparity of positions between character and audience that characterizes Griffith's films. The narrative activity is therefore abstract and concrete in one and the same moment.

The wife occupies a specific physical position: she stands as really in her own parlor as Annie Lee in *After Many Years* stands on her front porch. From her position in the extreme foreground, the wife's look in *Death's Marathon* suggests that the room extends before her figure, an effect emphasized by the fact that she is presented frontally and her figure is curtailed by the frame— visible only from the knees up. But her position is also insular and visionary, and her look outward also functions as a graphic binder, flying across the cut and fixing her imaginary look in her husband's shot. The extreme foreground position is used to create a double sense of off-screen space through a look that flickers physically into imaginary continuous space and also creates a graphic link that builds continuity in the discontinuous spaces of the world of the film. Nothing in the wife's physical position suggests the actual sight of her husband, and in one sense her reactions are the externalization of the audience's anticipation of the husband's final action. This feeling is reinforced by the fact that, for once, the resolution of the tension between the shots of the sequence coincides for both character and audience: both the viewer and the wife experience the suicide at the same time. In shot 97 the wife's face tells the viewer that the threat has been carried out—the suicide's shot has been fired—although only the viewer gets the confirming body of the dead man in shot 98. Yet the wife's image cannot really be considered a reaction shot. The structural tension in this sequence hinges on the ambiguity of the extreme foreground position, which is simultaneously a concrete and abstract position. The look extending from it suggests extension beyond the frame in terms of the set and also in terms of the sequence of shots.

Griffith develops the extreme foreground position as the abstract limit of the frame—the position where the realist illusion of the world of the film is most fully extended as a bridge between all the potential spaces of the film.

Throughout his Biograph period, Griffith balanced the technical close-up and the close-up produced in deep space by the compositional movement of characters in the frame. It is typical of Griffith's work that he chooses neither one nor the other, but continues to use every constructive option he finds. Hence, one finds the close-up of a candle going out used metaphorically to signal a death in *The Massacre* (1912); a close-up to magnify a detail in *Death's Marathon* alongside the development of the frontal plane; and close-ups used in a complicated sequence of introductory shots in *The Mothering Heart* (1913), where Lillian Gish is introduced, characterized, and geographically placed in the world of the film by intercutting her image with the antics of puppies.

In sum, Griffith developed an aesthetic of depth of field in his Biograph period that laid the foundation for the shallow focus aesthetic he would explore in *Hearts of the World* (1918), *Broken Blossoms* (1919), and *Way Down East* (1924). While depth of field was a dominant characteristic of the basic space in his Biograph period, the range of image sizes was nonetheless various. If depth of field generally characterized the composition of the basic space, the desire to soften, emphasize, or vary the depth of the image called for experiments that placed specialized shots in the context of the total film. When long shots, medium shots, and medium close-ups finally appear as discrete units of structure, they represent the choice of one plane of action over another as the appropriate stage of activity in that particular unit of the sequence. In 1926 Griffith explained it this way:

> [A shot of a whole battlefield would be incomprehensible because] looking at real things, the human vision fastens itself upon a quick succession of small comprehensible incidents; and we form our eventual impressions, like a mosaic, out of such detail. . . . The director counterfeits the operation of the eye with his lens . . . and varies the length of shots to avoid the hypnotic effect.[50]

The problem with this observation is the temptation to extrapolate too far or too simply from it and conclude that Griffith only imagined how the physical eye would take in a sequence of activity and proceeded accordingly. But the sequence of varied subject-to-camera relationships that eventually resulted in long, medium, and medium-close shots intermingled in a chain resulted from a mind's-eye view rather than a physical one. Griffith begins to include the cut-in and -out on the axis in sequences of shots that are much too systematically constructed to represent anything but the most intuitive understanding of the physical processes of perception. His films are more nearly an artistic fabrication of what that process "must be like." When each shot is directly composed around a "small incident" in order to make that incident visible (or, to use Griffith's own term, "comprehensible") and cutting in and out on the axis is incorporated into sequences of such shots it is easier to see how Griffith understood the shifting of attention in the creation of the total film event.

For instance, in *The Girl and Her Trust* (1912) Griffith makes the chase sequence a drama of the gradual revelation of the relative positions of a handcar and a pursuing train. The handcar exits shot 96, but is picked up in shot 97, closer to the camera and remaining within the frame. As the camera tracks with the handcar for three shots (97, 99, 102), and the handcar does not exit these shots at any time, the audience is given no information about how far away the handcar is getting from the station, and the viewer is presented only with an image of speed and a feeling of gathering momentum (fig. 11). The thrust of this activity is "crossed" by intercutting shots of the hero's journey back to the station from his house (from right to left, then left to right) a spatial order that is known to the audience, and one that takes the hero rightward (fig. 12) in opposition to the handcar's general direction leftward. When the hero nears the station, matched looks form the only relationship between pursuer and pursued. Although the audience still does not know how far they have gone, the villains are obviously still within sight of the station area. When the hero hops on a train to begin pursuit at shot 103, Griffith injects two enormous images into the chain of shots: the exit of the train from shot 103 (fig. 13) fills the frame leftward; the reverse angle of the train's cab seen from directly behind the heads of the pursuers (fig. 14) mimics the closer view of the handcar in shot 95 and graphically matches the initial moment of pursuit to the initial moment of flight. Having graphically matched these two aspects of the chase (i.e., given them equal graphic positions in an equal number of shots), Griffith proceeds to match their positions relative to each other in the course of the chase. The movements of the handcar are at first echoed by the train, and their respective spaces are not continuously related as would be the case in a standard chase sequence in which pursuer flows into spaces vacated by the pursued. Griffith forms a relationship between the handcar and the train in *The Girl and Her Trust* by matching their directions in alternating shots and matching their graphic sizes: leftward long shot for leftward long shot (figs. 15–16); in complement, rightward track for rightward track (figs. 17–18). A cut-in to the handcar (fig. 19) brings it into better conformity with the mass of the train after the train has passed behind a barn. In an ensuing shot, rightward track is followed by rightward track (figs. 20–21) until shot 112 (fig. 22), when the train eventually turns toward the right background, away from the camera. From shot 113 the directions shift again, but this time in complementary three-shot groups: shot 113 (fig. 23) begins as a long shot of the

11   12

13   14

Figs. 11–31. *The Girl and Her Trust* (1912)—Train Chase (condensed)

handcar entering the right background and advancing toward the left foreground; shot 114 (fig. 24) is a cut-in to the girl on the handcar; shot 115 (fig. 25)
is a cut-out again for the handcar's exit from the image, going left. Shot 116
(fig. 26) is a long shot of the train entering left to right in a space that is not a
repeat of any of the series; 117 (fig. 27) is a reverse to a closer shot of the
engineers in the cab; shot 118 (fig. 28) is a repeat of set-up 116, with the train
proceeding to exit the right foreground. The resolution of these relative positions occurs in shot 119 (fig. 29), when the train finally enters a space just
vacated by the handcar. One of the bird's-eye views Griffith uses at comprehensive moments is employed here in the context of a chase. Shot 119 is an
extreme long shot from a high angle of the handcar entering right to exit left.
The train makes the same transit through the shot. In the next shot, a lateral
track (fig. 30), the two positions relative to each other are restated: the handcar travels right back to left fore, pursued only by the smoke from the train's
engine. The chase is finally resolved in shot 121 (fig. 31). The relative posi-

15

16

17

18

19

20

21

22

23

24

25

26

27

28

29

30

31

Figs. 32–42. *The Mothering Heart*
(1913)—Nightclub (condensed)

32

tions of the train and handcar are made completely clear by a dynamic reversal of direction (left to right) that is the graphic climax of the sequence, while the lateral organization of the frame simultaneously retards the momentum of the chase and prepares for the resolution: the villains are caught and the heroine is saved.

Apart from the sheer inventiveness and balance he brings to this sequence in *The Girl and Her Trust,* the film is a perfect example of Griffith's use of varying subject-to-camera relationships in his Biograph period. Although there is a range of shots in this sequence, the spaces themselves are generally still discrete, and the variety of the shots is used to express the tensions of the relationship between the contending forces in the chase as a structure. In the later *A Beast at Bay* (1912), Griffith uses similar reverses of direction and variations of graphic size to create a chase in which diagonal movements crisscross the screen first to the left foreground, then to the right, until the positions of chasing train and fleeing car are similarly resolved by the train's entry into the car's shot.

In *The Mothering Heart* (1913) Griffith finally presents something very like a "master-shot" sequence. He integrates a number of cut-ins on the axis into a sequence of shots that dramatically presents a flirtation. The range of subject-to-camera relationships in this sequence is dramatic in itself. The combination of the full, long shot of the nightclub with allied closer shots of specific areas of activity in it, constitutes a situation very close to the master-shot structure that would evolve in early Hollywood sound films.

A husband and wife enter a long shot that reveals the entire space of a nightclub, a large crowded room with a high ceiling and a gallery full of people in the background. Eventually, the couple will take their place in the right forecorner of the master shot, but Griffith gets them to that position by cutting into their approach (figs. 32–33). The first such allied shot is a cut-in on the figures of entertainers on a stage in the left background (fig. 34). The

33   34

expository segment of this sequence has already drawn the eye toward its resolution: attention is twice drawn to the left in reference to the dancers, so that
when the couple do reach the foreground (fig. 35) and the master scene closes
down around them (fig. 36) in the second segment of the sequence (shots
46–60), easy reference is made to the left foreground, where the husband's
eye has been drawn by the presence of the vamp. The rest of the sequence
describes the flirtation carried on in an exchange of naughty and alluring
looks between the husband and the vamp (figs. 36–42). The entertainment
drops out of the scene, having set the stage for the intercutting that takes place
between the positions in the left and right foreground. The order of shots demonstrates that Griffith approached both the flirtation and the use of a variety of
subject-to-camera relationships in the sequence in a very deliberate way.
There is nothing prosaic about his construction, because nothing is taken for
granted and every effect flows from the plan of the sequence.

All of the above sequences are based only in the most imaginative way on
the way "we form our eventual impressions" by taking in "a quick succession
of small comprehensible incidents," although each gives the same feeling of
immediacy and concreteness that seems a product of "natural" vision. Gradually, Griffith would move away from a line of activity that merely indicated
direction and proximity toward a more complex structure that used these factors to indicate the feeling, the sensation of the sequence. The basic units of
construction remained "bounded" until very late in his Biograph period, even
when they have the appearance of "long," "medium," and "close" shots. By
the time long, medium, and close views were integrated into the chain of shots
as distinct units of construction, Griffith was sure that these variations on the
depth of the image would not disrupt the integrity of the world of the film that
was first represented in that depth. All shots were made to contribute to
Griffith's structural end: to create the film's dramatic impact as a total, rather
than momentary, effect.

35

36

37

38

39

40

41 42

A Basic Line of Action   2

It is generally agreed that action is what the early film-going public wanted, though in the first films action did not have to occur in the form of a story at all. From about 1897 to 1904, the bulk of films produced fell into the "news, travelogue, and documentary" categories, with drama gaining precedence only by 1904.[1] But once the appetite for stories appeared, as was noted by the Kleine Optical Company in 1904, it was clear that those stories had to *move*. In an early exercise in industrial soul-searching, the Kleine Company developed the following criteria for future film productions: actual events are not as popular as staged ones; there must be excellence in photography; and action must be continuous—there "must be no lagging in the story."[2]

Many forms of activity made their way into Griffith's films for the same reason that explosions, car chases, and star ships appear in films today: they are simple, pure sources of visual excitement. Griffith used boats, barrels, canoes, horses, and cars to magnify, and thus enhance, the propulsion of the human body speeding through the frame. But the exploitation of these devices to construct dramatic action was no more self-evident than was the use of long shots, mid-shots, and close-ups.

An Accumulated Effect
Unfolding the Story

In films made before Griffith's tenure at Biograph, processions and chases were an attempt to organize activity in the frame. Although the passage of people across the entire face of the frame from one shot to another tended to be time-consuming, and offered only the dry continuity of serial order, it was nonetheless an early attempt to provide coherent forms that pointed raw activity *through* one shot and *toward* another.

As has been mentioned, there is a strong sense of boundary in the early shot. In some cases films give the impression of a faithful recording of an established performance, and the shot is totally equated with the theater scene, as, for example, in Biograph's *Under the Apple Tree* (1907) and Edi-

57

son's *The Scarecrow Pump* (1904). Even in films that show a precocious feeling for scene-construction, such as Biograph's *The Silver Wedding* (1906), the effect is not carried throughout the film. A "master shot" and its related "closer view" (a cut-in on the axis to show the robbers stealing wedding silver) are surrounded by shots that do not connect with it in any way.

In films made outside the studio, exterior shots show a strong preference for displaying the totality of activity, however long it takes. This results in overlapping action and trailing pans, which are sometimes used quite deliberately to preserve the unity of a dramatic space, as in Williamson's *Fire* (1900) and Biograph's *The Moonshiners* (1904). Even when there is running activity in a film, "business" within the frame often takes precedence over the relationship between the shots. Films such as Hepworth's *That Fatal Sneeze* (1907) and Williamson's *The Rival Cyclists* (1902) contain shots of pursuit that are never really developed into formal chases, because the situation within the shot is more important than the developing line of activity. In *That Fatal Sneeze* Hepworth is interested in special effects. In *The Rival Cyclists* pursuers chase the rival away (out of the film), which is how Williamson chose to resolve the story on the "correct" pair of lovers. In neither of these films are there particularly strong connections between shots. Even in films where there is a sense of spatial continuity (i.e., action is "matched" between shots), a favored piece of business determines the pace of the film. If the pursued climbs over a roof, everyone must climb over the roof (Biograph's *The Escaped Lunatic,* 1904). If the pursued dives into a culvert, everyone must follow (Biograph's *Nurse Wanted,* 1908). If the pursued is shown to leap a river by special effect (Biograph's *Wife Wanted,* 1907), the shot is worth a couple of minutes of screen time.

It must be said that this summary does not take the very best features of pre-Griffith filmmaking into account. The Biograph chases do have a wonderful sense of propulsion. Hepworth's *Rescued by Rover* has an economy and sleekness born of well-constructed continuity and succinctly imagined screen geography. But the bounded shot did generally drag on screen action because business was developed within the shot rather than in the totally imagined space of the film. For instance, in Biograph's *When Knights Were Bold* (1908), there is a clear equation between the shot and the scene. When the scene changes, there is a cut. *When Knights Were Bold* has five different set-ups and the length of each of these scene-shots varies only with the director's imaginative ability to invent enough business to keep the actors "on stage." Space is not explored, but rather exhausted by the numerous entrances and exits; parades and trap doors add pretexts for activity, until the space is finally discarded and replaced by another stage for succeeding activity. The dimensions of the scene-shot create an atmosphere of generalized activity and generalized characterization. Action remains centralized in a frame that confines itself in a box-set, and the possibilities of cutting to create continuity of action from shot to shot are not exploited. Continuity is based on succession, the fact that one shot follows another, and this further generalizes the dramatic impact of the film and inhibits the development of complex narrative and emotional effects.

Early processions in Griffith's own films are not the most fascinating or eye-catching forms of activity. The processions Griffith used in *The Vaquero's Vow* (1908) and *The Taming of a Shrew* (1908) might easily be translated to a theatrical stage. They represent only a rudimentary attempt to impose a formal pace on the activity passing through the image, as well as a way to fill the frame with orderly activity. The procession was generally used in interiors until Griffith brought it outside in *Where the Breakers Roar* (1908). The walk through the frame in this film is another version of the procession, but its measured sunny pace stands in dramatic contrast to the frantic chase that ends the film.

The paradigm for exterior action was the diagonal (although diagonal action was not absolute in exteriors). In most action films, especially in chases, activity is run from background to foreground through the entire diagonal extent of the frame, a somewhat more impressive trajectory than the lateral parading used in studio interiors. Exterior shots could therefore serve as the stages of sweeping and somewhat more dynamic activity. The important element in these early action sequences is that the diagonal from background to foreground—or vice versa, as in Hepworth's *Rescued by Rover* (1905) and *Black Beauty* (1906)—be run in order to make the entire frame visually active. Although the order of the action film—background to foreground and back again—created a certain sense of continuity between shots, continuous activity was the main concern, and sometimes only minimal care was given to creating exact "matches" between entrance and exit points from shot to shot that would indicate that the shots were even superficially joined by running activity. The feeling for matched action ebbs and flows through films made before 1908. Sometimes it is meticulous (Vitagraph's *Boy, Bust and Bath*, notably developing continuity cutting in an interior set-up in 1907); sometimes haphazard (Vitagraph's *The Mill Girl*, made the same year).

The Adventures of Dollie (1908), Griffith's first film, has this conventionally diagonal exterior structure. The barrel in which Dollie has been placed by her evil kidnappers falls into a river and seems to describe a reasonably direct course from shot to shot, suggesting that Griffith may have learned the rudiments of continuity from his experienced Biograph cameraman, Arthur Marvin (who reportedly was forced to wade into the stream repeatedly to get the shots Griffith wanted).[3] In any case, the illusion of continuous activity from shot to shot is created in *The Adventures of Dollie* by insuring that the barrel enters shot *b* in a reasonably connected way from shot *a*—that is, if it exits one shot through the foreground, it is picked up entering the next shot in the background. This is the simplest way to create continuity over the actually discontinuous spaces of the world of the film. The audience's attention is deflected from the cut's break in spatial continuousness by a constructed continuity of activity. If a reasonable connection from shot to shot is discerned, no "shock" is felt at the cut. The audience does not need this sort of reassurance to *understand* the story because it will take simple sequentiality, up to a point, as "reasonable" continuity. But the matching of action across cuts creates a fluidity that conveys a sense of easiness in the flow of the film that assures the audience that what it perceives is "realism." Continuity cutting adds sensation to sequential construction and causes the audience to *feel* the logic of the world of the film.

By 1908 a rudimentary chase form had developed. As mentioned above, action was run toward the camera through the entire diagonal extent of the frame. After the situation was set up in an introductory shot, pursuer followed pursued through shot after shot. Usually the pursued entered and defined the course through the shot, sometimes exiting before the pursuers entered, followed the same path, and took the same exit, which signified that they were on the right track. The chase is the form where it is most common to see attention given to "proper" continuity—that is, matching action from shot to shot to give a sense of spatial extension that establishes the chase as a continuous line of activity. The chase could be the subject of the entire film or could appear as a part of the larger situation. If the chase was the subject of the entire film, its resolution was sometimes a return to zero—a repetition of the first location in the film, and the resolution of the chase is identified with the resolution of the film.

Early chases attest to the desire for propulsion and magnitude. One had only to have groups of people running, skipping, and hopping across the screen to convey a dramatic situation. Dramatic terrain—hills, lakes, bridges, fences—provided the necessary variations on the theme of continuous activity. The drawbacks of this line of thought are obvious: dramatically, action for its own sake tends to be exciting at first, but diffuse and finally cloying. The negative aspects of Dollie's course down the river in the barrel are the generality of the shots and their time-consuming activity. The whole shot is devoted in a structural sense to making sure that the audience sees where the barrel is going in the shot. As in *When Knights Were Bold,* this is dramatically interesting only so long as interesting events are planned in the course of the barrel's trip. The drama is enhanced if the barrel nears the falls or heads for rocks or if the kidnapper discovers that it has fallen from his wagon and tries to recover it. Each of these plot possibilities could contribute to the dramatic intensity of the film. But Griffith could see dramatic potential in the *position of the shot within the chain of shots* that would shift the burden away from Dollie's position in the barrel and onto her position in the frame. Soon after *The Adventures of Dollie,* Griffith began to amalgamate the energy of running through the spaces of the film with the power of intercutting to create continuity rather than display continuous activity.

The idea of an accumulated effect is already present in 1898 in *The Burglar on the Roof,* a one-shot Vitagraph film into which pursuers pile to catch a thief. Moving from shot to shot, the accumulation of bodies in a chase provided a context in which to develop any number of bits of business within the body of the chase—as many as could be supported by the invention of the director, the momentum of the chase, and the length of one reel of film. The comic effect of accumulation depends on the gathering momentum of activity as the weight of more and more bodies is thrown into the chase and the spatial limits of the frame are strained to the breaking point with action and speed. The flow of bodies in and out of the frame was also controlled by the number and type of characters accumulated in the chase. By implication, the whole world would eventually speed through the progressively more frantic shots of the chase.

This structure gave the cinema its first experience of the coincidence of continuity with continuous activity—the production of pace from motion. *The Lost Child* (1904) is a good example of a pre-Griffith accumulation chase. In this film, an innocent stranger is suspected of kidnapping a child who gets "lost" by climbing into the kennel of the family dog. The suspect is chased by the distraught mother, who is eventually joined by the whole town. Activity is extended from background to foreground to exploit the spatial extent of the frame; it is stretched out purposely to display the line of pursuers and make the most of their comic business. An old man in a wheelchair, for instance, maniacally overcomes any obstacle posed by the changing terrain of the chase. The line of the chase heads for the camera, usually exiting the right forecorner of the frame until the suspect is caught, his parcels are examined, and the mistake is revealed in an explosion of the massed energies of the bodies of the chasers pouring into the resolving shot. Many variations on this situation were exploited by Biograph, including the famous *Personal* (1904), which was allegedly plagiarized by Edison as *How a French Nobleman Got a Wife through the New York "Personal" Columns* (Edison, 1904) and thus served as one of the rounds in the battle for dominance of the industry between the two companies.[4]

Griffith harnessed the energy of accumulation by constantly redefining what would be "accumulated" to create dramatic effects. *The Curtain Pole* (1908) carefully develops a pretext for the chase: the enraged reaction of the general citizenry of a small town to Mack Sennett's (mis)handling of an unwieldy curtain pole in a frame that never seems big enough to accommodate the pole and any other person or thing. As the frame becomes more and more crowded with chasers, the curtain pole simply becomes more of a menace. With each new shot, the audience begins to scan the image for the most vulnerable point (a window, a passing stranger) and waits for the impact. The comic effect accumulates from shot to shot, emanating from a clearly presented situation, amplified by the number of bodies that fill the frame. Unlike the very similar *Father Buys a Picture,* a British film made by the Rosie Company in 1909, *The Curtain Pole* takes fair care of continuity, so that the effect is accelerated as well as accumulated. The lesson of *The Curtain Pole* is fairly obvious: cutting a sequence into a series of shots, each of them deliberately pointed, becomes funnier and funnier if the audience is given cues that enable it to anticipate some specific action. Comedy becomes an effect created in the order of action in the order of shots.

The accumulation chase was not Griffith's only basis for this discovery, but once he did see the possibilities of the form, the chase was never the same. *Trying to Get Arrested* (1909) reflects this growing awareness of the possibilities of the chase as a structure, and is a marvelous visualization of a labored joke that was dragged along in an early Griffith comedy, *A Calamitous Elopement* (1908). In this earlier film the person everyone should pursue is literally hauled around in a trunk. An eloping couple actually take this trunk holding the crook to their honeymoon suite, where they are robbed. In *Trying to Get Arrested* Griffith demonstrates how easily the order of the chase can be exploited to get a joke like this moving. A tramp who wishes to spend a comfortable night in jail cannot lure the furious pursuers toward him. He winds up trailing behind them, carried along by the momentum of the chase "after" him that has become absurdly reversed. The persistent joke in this film is that all the chaotic energy in the chase is wasted from shot to shot. The tension is maintained by the tramp's hopeful presence at the rear of the line of "chasers." Above all, *Trying to Get Arrested* shows how funny it is to spring the "normal" comic tension of the accumulation chase. It is rather like the joke of putting someone in a tree to watch his pursuers chase one another around it. But the joke gains extension and momentum embodied in a chase, and derives its beauty from the shared awareness between pursued and audience, who know what the situation really is.

Trying to Get Arrested is the first of a number of "sprung" chases. In *They Would Elope* (1909) Griffith transforms the well-worn elopement story that had already appeared in Biograph's *The Elopement* (1907). The earlier film is a straight chase. In Griffith's version the young couple suppose that they are going to be pursued and expend a great deal of energy escaping from a family that has stayed at home to toast the elopement. As the young couple run through shot after shot "away" from their "pursuers," more and more people crowd into the shot of the family celebration. The comic disasters that befall the couple are intercut with the accumulation of people gathered to celebrate their "secret" marriage plans. The effect is delightfully ironic.

Refolding the Story

In the winter of 1908–9 Griffith sought to tailor the activity in the shot to the development of the sequence of shots—in other words, to cut into the real continuousness of an action. Although the span of activity would always determine the length of some shots in Griffith's films, those made in the winter of 1908–9 proved that, at least in theory, action did not have to play out its time in a shot before passing on to the next "stage." Significant dramatic activity could be tailored by the cut, because the dramatic effect was contained in the way a sequence of relationships was being built from shot to shot.

One way to describe the effect of intercutting between two shots is that the resulting structure challenges the normal direct relationship of cause to effect—that is, the assumption that an action has a direct objective. In a series of films made early in 1909, Griffith explored the effect of intercutting on the notion of dramatic causality and discovered that spatial, moral, and dramatic causality were linked and interrelated. The importance of *The Prussian Spy, The Medicine Bottle, The Deception, Lady Helen's Escapade,* and *I Did It, Mama* may not be immediately apparent. Except for *The Medicine Bottle,* these films are constructed of two primary set-ups that alternate *ababab* throughout the reel. But these films were one of the most important exercises that Griffith performed during his Biograph period in that they represent the beginning of the end of the tyranny of physical activity in Griffith's films.

His Ward's Love (1908) is of interest because, although it seems to be constructed of *abab* intercutting, it fails to achieve any accumulated dramatic effect in the process. In this film of ten shots, Griffith had not yet discovered how to interrupt an activity with a cut in order to extend the audience's interest into the next shot. People simply walk back and forth between two spaces. Actions are repeated, but imply nothing further than the most serial relationship between shots: first he walks, then he exits, then they meet, then he returns to the house, and so on. The activity in shot *a* has no consequence for that in shot *b*.

By *The Prussian Spy* a step has been taken. Made in the same cramped studio conditions as *His Ward's Love, The Prussian Spy* employs an infernal machine: a wardrobe with a trapdoor stands in shot *a;* shot *b* is of the attic the hero hopes to reach through the top of the wardrobe by means of the trapdoor. The business of the plot is for the heroine to detain the villain in *a* while her sweetheart rises to safety in *b.* When the audience is not viewing his actual struggles, the hero is present by implication in the efforts of the heroine and in the presence of the wardrobe at the back of shot *a.* How long will the woman remain cool enough to forestall the menacing villain who wishes to kill her beloved? Will the maidservant succeed in helping the hero into the attic? When will the villain actually go to the wardrobe? All these questions arise because, by interrupting the action with cuts, Griffith creates a sense of consequence between the shots. Intercutting set-ups *a* and *b,* the dramatic tension of the film is actually doubled as the attention of the viewer is productively split between two crucially related (but still discrete) spaces. The audience imagines the continuation of the action in shot *a* while the information in shot *b* is appearing on the screen.

This effect of increased mental involvement is even more apparent in *The Medicine Bottle.* The tension in this film is totally created, drama derived from the juxtaposition of three shots from which (essentially) no one enters or exits. There are three locations in this film—parlor, telephone exchange, and parlor—and the drama of the film arises from the anxiety produced when the shots are intercut. A mother has unwittingly left a bottle of poison rather than medicine at home. She goes to a party and discovers her error. She knows her child will administer this fatal stuff to her ailing grandmother. It is too late to run home. The mother tries to call the child, but all the young women in the telephone exchange are bored and inattentive on this particular day. Will the mother get through this center of resistance in time? The drama is created solely by cutting back and forth from one location to another, advancing the poison toward the grandmother, *while* the mother frantically calls *as* the telephone operators ignore the call. The sense of three simultaneously occurring activities is created by interrupting continuous activity with the cut, and the dramatic tension is consequently trebled. The drama is created as the audience cross-references the elements of the situation.

In *Jones and His New Neighbors* (1909) Griffith combines intercutting with spatial continuity to transform the accumulation chase. Griffith centers the comedy in the tension that builds at the point of access between two contested spaces: a doorway that connects two shots. Intercutting between these two spaces completely does away with the running activity that characterized the accumulation chase, and at the same time it throws new and dramatic emphasis on the *accumulation* itself. This accumulation acquires a double meaning in the Jones film. In the first place, the pursuers simply pile into the Joneses' hallway, crowding the space more and more with each cut back to it. A comic effect is built by juxtaposing this rapidly filling space with a relatively empty space, the Joneses' side of the door. The feeling created by intercutting is that something has got to give to equalize the pressure between these two spaces, and this expectation is underlined by the Joneses' naughty and foolish enjoyment of the storm brewing in their hallway. Without any undue physical effort, using two basic set-ups, Griffith captures the spirit of the chase and enlarges upon it by defining it in terms of one spatial goal: the rupture of the barrier between two unequally occupied spaces. An exquisite sort of pacing was for the first time determined by the filmmaker's control of the flow of activity from *a* to *b.*

The juxtaposition of shots invites the complicity of the audience in the creation of the film, especially if the relationship between shots is tightly controlled and nonexistent outside the film. Griffith finally established that it did not matter how much space the activity traversed as long as the connections between shots were strong and constant. The number of shots was not as significant as the strength of a line of activity and the points of connection between shots. Whether they saw it or not, the viewers would "continue" activity through the film if the suggestion of continuousness was planted strongly enough. Never for a moment do we doubt that the hero continues to ride to the rescue, even when Griffith cuts to the menaced heroine.

These seem to be basic discoveries. But Griffith's work is distinguished by his ability to manipulate a line of action against a passage of intercutting with a facility rarely matched by his contemporaries. The similarities between Griffith's *The Lonely Villa* (1909) and Pathé's *Physician of the Castle* (1908) may be the result of simple story-stealing by Griffith himself or by Mack Sennett, who is credited with the scenario. In any case the parallels between the films provide an opportunity to compare Griffith's sense of construction with that of a colleague of his working in France.

The plot is as follows: crooks descend on a lonely house and trick the father into leaving on a wild goose chase. The family and fortune are thus at the mercy of the thieves, who begin to break into the house. The father is recalled by the frantic mother's telephone call. He races to the rescue by car while the terrified family retreats from room to room before the advancing crooks. The father arrives just in the knick of time to save the family.

The Pathé film is rather loosely constructed. The house consists of two interiors that are not related spatially. This lack of a clear relationship means that the connection between the interior rooms offers the audience no constructed basis on which to judge how dire the threat of criminal penetration is. Neither the direction of action from one shot to another nor any other graphic clue gives any sense of orientation in the house. Consequently, the tension between the interior spaces is lost in the intercutting between these interiors and the shots of the father's return to the rescue. The picturesque terrain covered by the father in a car plunging down hillside roadways and careening around curves contributes nothing to the growing anxiety the audience is meant to feel about the safety of the family. Although the father's shots have a certain urgency and dynamic composition, they are not related to the interiors by any link stronger than serial order.

Griffith expresses the basic dramatic issues of *The Lonely Villa* in two succinct and interlocking suites of images: in a lateral set of three rooms (figs. 43, 44, 45), the family is pushed through successive doorways into new spaces by the advancing crooks, and this clearly defines the issue of spatial proximity in the interiors on a straight line; a simple diagonal line sweeping toward the

Figs. 43–45. *The Lonely Villa* (1909)—Siege
(condensed)

43

camera (figs. 46, 47, 48) describes the father's return to the home by horse
and wagon. The position of the family relative to the advancing crooks is referred to the image of the father rushing home. At each point, the audience is
actually asked to assess two situations, the father's and the family's, from the
perspective of their spatial relationship: How close are the thieves to the family? How far is the father from the house? The question "Will he be in time?"
is answered by understanding how the two positions relate. Expressing these
problems in two clear lines of activity clarifies the dramatic situation and
produces a dramatic impact, and this means that by 1909, in his first year of
filmmaking, Griffith was finding a way to generate dramatic tension from the
structure of the film.

The formal relationship of the parts only summarizes the structure of *The
Lonely Villa,* but that is exactly the point. If Griffith's Biograph films are examined as a body of work, a surprising number of such "summaries" emerge.
One of Griffith's most basic intuitions in *The Lonely Villa* was to build tension
between a diagonal and a lateral line of activity, growing from the repetition of
set-ups cross-referencing each other as they are intercut. So important is the
relationship created in the chain of shots that Griffith rejects the effect that the
Pathè director obviously considered one of the most dramatic devices in his
film. During the phone call that will bring the father back to the house, the
Pathè director inserts a closer view of the call. There is no corresponding
close-up in *The Lonely Villa.* There is no close-up of any of the action. While
his utilization of the close-up may have been limited by technical considera-
tions, it is also clear that such a shot was unnecessary to generate tension in
the structure Griffith devised to present the drama of *The Lonely Villa.* Instead, Griffith depends on *ab* intercutting to maintain the tension within the
phone call. The father suggests the mother shoot the burglars and must wait
while she finds that the gun will not fire. When the burglars cut the phone
wire, the race to the rescue begins.

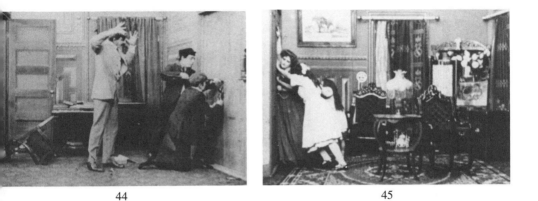

44   45

Griffith's contribution to the invention of cinematic narrative is rooted in this ability to take advantage of the atmosphere of speculation arising between shots, an effect especially powerful in his work because the master-shot relationship that fully reveals a space and then segments it is not often asserted in Biograph films. This means that discontinuity must be bridged. Ignoring for the moment that a certain inevitability was exerted by the standardized plots Griffith used, the basic principle of construction in Biograph films was to join two more or less random pieces of space and insist graphically that the juncture was logical, fluid, and *consequential.*

The creation of the feeling that action on the screen is motivated toward a point does not depend on the ability of the audience to predict the direction of the flow of the action through shots, nor does it depend on the order of the shots through which activity flows. But providing this kind of information opens the film to an infinite number of separate shots. The ultimate effect of this kind of structure can be found in the sense of directional probability created in *The Honor of His Family* (1909). A callow youth becomes frightened and runs from the battlefield in the Civil War. His proud father awaits him at home, sometimes stationed at the window straining for the first sight of his son returning in victory (fig. 49). Often he does no more than stand in the center of the image and say "my boy." But everything the son does is referred back to this shot (which appears nine times in the 25-shot film). Directionally the father's shot is the leftward terminus of the son's terrified flight from the battlefield (figs. 50–52). Although the son does not run an absolutely straight line home, there is a solid connection between his flight and the father's rightward gaze. Theoretically, no matter what terrain the son runs through, the audience has a clear, graphic expectation, if not assurance, that he is headed home as long as he continues to run left. Of course this expectation is also built on the plot. Dramatic logic and the sheer length of the reel combine to suggest that the son, frightened by the battle, is running home. But Griffith

Figs. 46–48. *The Lonely Villa* (1909)—Race to
the Rescue (condensed)

46

gives a clear and forceful indicator that this deduction is indeed the fact. The
viewer could be led to accept another terminus, but the link between the look
(the father at the window) and the line of activity (the son finally turning leftward in his run from the battle) indicates that the father's home is the most
graphically direct (and therefore dramatically satisfying) completion of the
son's flight (fig. 53).

It is the stability of this relationship that forms the basis of Griffith's most
successful dramatic effects. His dramas depend on the anticipation of resolution and the fulfillment of that anticipation. The clarity of expression in his
films and the splendid timing of dramatic and structural resolutions depend on
the idea that the audience's attention be concentrated on shots that maintain a
constant relationship in the course of the dramatic time of the film.

Access to the Shot

The juxtaposition of shots invites the complicity of the audience in the
creation of the film, especially if the relationship between shots is tightly controlled and nonexistent outside the film. Since unvarying set-ups create essentially discontinuous shots, access to the basic space is a crucial level of control
in the Biograph films. Griffith's sense of how a film must go together becomes
so firm in his Biograph period that his films seem very realistic and very natural. It seems that the shape of the film is directed by "reality," or at least the
requirements of a "realistic" plot. But this is not so. Reality is a consequence
of a Griffith film. The connections and relationships feel very natural because
usually the eye is deliberately led along very easy paths by the connections
between shots. But in fact one simply believes in the world of a Griffith Biograph film based on the way people move in and out of its spaces.

47   48

In notes to a Museum of Modern Art screening of Vitagraph's *A Tale of Two Cities* (1911), Eileen Bowser notes that the director, William Humphrey, showed

> a full use of the great sweep of the Dickens novel. There is little attempt to break scenes into component shots, but actors move into the depths of the set or approach very close to the camera to approximate a close-up. They make entrances and exits freely, even beside the camera instead of being limited to the stage right and left as they so often are in Biograph films of this time.[5]

Since Griffith was the major Biograph director of 1911, this statement indirectly refers to the fact that he never did a great deal of variation in interior spaces. But it would be incorrect to assume from this that Griffith limited action to a right-left lateral because he had adopted a proscenium model of the frame and could not break out of the confines of that stage-oriented ideal. In fact, the Vitagraph film is far more theatrical than anything Griffith did in 1911, the year he made *The Lonedale Operator,* with its conscious search for variation in matching action over the cut.

Griffith did take some time to get to the point of treating the limits of the frame with absolute freedom and to come to the conclusion that, like free-fall in space, orientation in the cinema can be totally dependent on relationships. Links between shots could therefore be made from any point on the perimeter of the image without damaging the credibility of its "realism."

The need for reliable connections between shots was too important to Griffith for him to take early risks with entering and exiting the frame. Activity is used to create the sense that the links between the shots are inevitable. The audience could then depend on the trace of activity across the frame to indicate the overall unity of the film, as demonstrated in *The Lonely Villa.* In this process the audience activities of speculation, prediction, anticipation, and resolution arise.

Figs. 49–53. *The Honor of His Family* (1909)— Flight (condensed)

49

The Central Entrance/Exit

Although there is quite a range of variation within the scope of almost five hundred Biograph films, Griffith began to gain access to the shot through the central entrance/exit. This central access to the shot recurs in interior compositions of 1908, Griffith's first year at Biograph. Some of these films have been discussed—in *The Greaser's Gauntlet,* for instance, characters enter and leave a barroom through an archway at the back of the set. In *Betrayed by a Handprint* and *The Call of the Wild,* the central entrance/exit provides the most functional access to interiors.

Since the viewer can see into the arch, an extra dimension of depth is added to the flat interior sets, and the ability to enter from the back of the set also lends some diagonal scope to the rather shallow studio interiors. But for all the central entrance/exit contributed to the composition of activity within the interior set-up, it is less clear in its connective suggestions, as is demonstrated by the interior structure of *Physician of the Castle.* Griffith gradually abandoned the central arch as a crucial entrance/exit point, but retained it as an alternate point of access to the shot.

In *The Hindoo Dagger* (1908) the main dramatic activity flows from side to side, from right to left through the interiors of the film. But the arch is retained as a secondary entrance/exit and provides at least a window-dressing of depth in the frame. By *The Lonely Villa,* the lateral suite of rooms—hallway, parlor, study—through which the family retreats as the crooks advance demonstrates a desire for a clear line of action from shot to shot. The central access, while still present as a compositional factor, is less important as an entrance/exit. By *In The Watches of the Night* (1909), the arched porch entrance forms a strong compositional feature on which the frame is extended through a pan across the front of a house.

50   51

52   53

The Cricket on the Hearth (1909) is somewhat turgid in execution and displays the hesitancy that sometimes gripped Griffith when he approached an important "literary" project. But the film displays the progress of Griffith's thoughts on the possibility of access to the shot to that date. The interiors of *The Cricket on the Hearth* are an interesting blend of all the options of interior mise-en-scène to that date. Central access appears in shots 4 and 6. In shot 4 a central door, which is the general entrance/exit, implies an exterior that is never shown. In shot 6 the arch is choral, serving no exit/entrance function at all, but having both the architectural and dramatic function of deepening the shot of the tavern. The sister's home is delineated in two interiors that are the most complex playing areas in the film. Shot 13 is the common room of the sister's inn, in which a stairway in the background functions as a compositional feature, diagonally breaking the surface of the image into two levels, though it provides no access to other spaces in the world of the film. The most functional entrance/exits of shot 13 are lateral and this connection between shots 13 and 14 creates the greatest sense of mobility projected from one interior shot to another, out of one frame and toward a specific goal in another. In *The Cricket on the Hearth* the archways and central doorways are negative points of access because they do not connect to other spaces in the world of the film. The arch represents a random sense of connection, and the viewer has to take the existence of succeeding spaces in the same film for granted, because the arch naturally offered no "after-image" of a logically connected screen world.

In *Sweet and Twenty* (1909) Griffith was finally able to connect the negative and difficult central access to the exterior of a house by setting up an exterior/interior repeated pattern of intercutting medium-long and long shots together. The relationship of the two spaces, porch and parlor, reflects Griffith's perception of the immediacy and straightforwardness of the lateral connection. Even though the central arch is a feature of the parlor, great care is taken to make activity flow through it into the shot from the right and back again. This clear right/left connection indicates how the porch leads into the rest of the film.

In early films, the entrance/exit is the only way Griffith had to signify the "world beyond the set," in much the same way that this doorway would function in a theater set. The crucial difference between early central doorways, in films such as *The Tavernkeeeeper's Daughter* (1908) and *The Lonely Villa,* and the lateral reorientation of activity through the arch with reference to a complementary shot, as in *Sweet and Twenty,* is that the early arch tends to stand for "the world beyond the set" and the lateral orientation refers to access to the "world beyond the shot." The arch or central entrance/exit gradually becomes a more and more formal aspect of composition. The lateral is used to lead into the world of the film.

The Lateral

It seems likely that Griffith straightened the line of action through the frame to create beeline connections between shots. In interiors, lateral movement (right to left or left to right) seems to be a "natural" connection between shots, which conveys the feeling that rooms adjoin. But the lateral was not the natural choice in early sets—many filmmakers used the highly visible central entrance/exit. And, considering the variety of architectural models, the lateral passage of activity through the frame is not even particularly realistic. But the interior lateral did prove a useful abstraction. The lateral used in interiors is direct—the most efficient passage through the frame—and the ease of "reading" this straight line convinces viewers that adjoining shots are "logically" connected. Furthermore, the lateral gave Griffith the opportunity to develop dramatic tension between shots on a natural boundary, the door.

The result of this logic is a suite of three rooms in which the pressure of the situation is gradually exerted until it reaches the pitch of crisis. The earliest attempt to create such a structure is in *An Awful Moment* (1908). A judge's room is separated by a hallway from the room in which his wife is assaulted. This film, like *The Fatal Hour,* makes use of an infernal device—the gypsy has tied a rifle beneath the wife's breast and set it to go off if the judge opens the door to her room. Essentially, the judge "races" to the rescue through this direct structure, but, in a typical plot twist, the "straight" path is ironically perilous. Griffith visualizes this situation in three spaces separated by cuts at doorways. The first break over the cut is safe; the second is not. The situation is not structurally resolved in *An Awful Moment.* Coincidentally, the baby wakes up and saves the mother. But the sense of three spaces, laid end to end, has been set as a tension-generating structure. In *The Guerilla* (1908) the imperiled heroine is forced from right to left through a set of rooms until the villain breaks down the doors to each and literally forces her to the wall at the far left—a clear signal that it is time for the hero to enter.

This "tryptich" appears again in *The Hindoo Dagger* (1908), this time with clear right and left boundary shots. The series of interiors is bounded on the left by the lover's jealous gaze through a window, and on the right is the bathroom, from which there is no exit for the faithless woman. In *The Hindoo Dagger* a murder melodrama is developed exclusively in the lateral suite of images (parlor-bedroom-bath), with no reference to a motivating frame (such as the gypsy's trial scene provides for *An Awful Moment*) or an allied line of activity (such as the hero's race to the rescue in *The Guerilla*). There is only one exterior shot in *The Hindoo Dagger,* and it suggests that the lateral is extended further to the left.

In *The Hindoo Dagger* Griffith uses the lateral passage through the rooms of the house to indicate the degree of peril in which the wife finds herself. Menaced in the parlor by her jealous husband, she can lock herself in the bathroom. The limits of her freedom though, are bounded on the left and right, and the lateral, side-to-side passage through the suite of images makes a simple and clear statement of position in spaces. The set-up keeps the audience in minute-to-minute touch with the position of one person in respect to another in respective shots. The structure indicates the extent to which pressure is being exerted by one character on another. In the course of lateral passage, great dramatic pressure builds at doorways because they become identified with cuts—the breaks at which one space yields to another space. The rhythm of pressure and release is built as space after space is invaded by a pursuer. Renewed pressure is exerted with the awareness that another exit has been closed off and the pursued is literally being cornered. When the rightward boundary of the tryptich in *The Hindoo Dagger* is reached, the climax of the drama occurs.

In *The Hindoo Dagger* this equals death for the wife, but the fact of the pressure in the structure is much more dramatic than the weak plot of the film. While the characters of *The Hindoo Dagger* are really quite vague, the dynamic of the drama is very clear. Two lateral movements to the right through a suite of rooms each results in tragedy for a faithless woman. Boundaries right and left confine the dramatic activity within a marked space, and the audience is presented with a condensed dramatic scheme in which the *position* of one character itself affects the fate of another.

This structure is crucial to *The Lonely Villa*. The besieged house is essentially a lateral suite of rooms, although this time the drama starts in the neutral center, in which pressure begins to build when the leftmost space, a hallway, is penetrated by the thieves. When the leftward door of the central room finally yields, Griffith renews the tension in the structure by introducing a new room to the right. This suite of three, a tryptich of peril, has the advantage of stating the dramatic issue of the siege as one of proximity, and that issue is presented clearly at all times to the audience on a straight, right-to-left line. The viewer may not know how close the father is to the lonely villa, because his journey home is an abstraction drawn through exteriors on dynamic diagonals that convey momentum instead of place. But the audience cannot miss the sense of urgency conveyed by the tension that grows between the lateral and diagonal lines of action in this film.

Jealousy and the Man (1909) is a film of only three locations: an interior, a yard, and a painting platform where a fellow and his friend go to work. The platform is actually at the end of one of those tryptich formations, although the movement through the film is not strictly lateral. But the painting platform is the rightward boundary of action in the world of the film, and the characters go ping-ponging back and forth between it and the parlor interior, producing a composite picture much like that provided along the lateral in interiors. Shot 7, the painting platform, also demonstrates the strength of the three-set-up-format, no matter how loosely it is stated from left to right and back again. The three-set-up structure allows Griffith to affix almost any space he wants to the preceding shots in *Jealousy and the Man*. What is required of shot 7 is that it be a terminus—a place where people finally go—while in reality it is an enormous imposition on the audience because there is such a tremendous ellipsis of time and space between the platform and the domestic parlor and the yard through which the characters pass to get to the platform. It could be blocks away and take a twenty-minute walk to get to the platform, but its immediate presence in the tryptich is plausible and unerring because it is so directionally reasonable. The viewer does not stop to think about how or why or where the platform "really" is, because it has a formal position and is therefore a plausible place to develop the business of the plot. The boldness of the placement of this shot and its radical nature never seem to become an issue.

As Griffith becomes surer of the kinds of connections that bind spaces together, he becomes more willing to vary the lateral model of entrances and exits. But the direct line of side-to-side lateral activity remains very strong. In

The Battle (1911) the coward runs so far back along his sweetheart's look toward the battlefield that in effect he reverses the general rightward orientation of the first sequence of the film. Overshooting the familiar room in which she has been waiting, he enters two entirely new spaces added to the house. To the left of the parlor, he travels straight into her bedroom and finally into a new exterior. The film is pivoted on this newly stated leftward-directed tryptich, and in the second half of the tale, the fiancé's redemption begins.

The lateral appears condensed in the garden scene of *The Primal Call* and as the structural premise of *The Female of the Species.* In *The God Within* (1912) portraits of motherhood frame the film's lateral walking activity (see pp. 114–15 below). The two young women at the ends of the lateral are compared: happy wife and abandoned girl. The death of the wife (fig. 80) and the death of the girl's newly born, illegitimate child (fig. 83) are the pretexts for the passage of the girl from one end of the iconically bound lateral to the other, where she becomes the wife-surrogate and finally achieves security. The interiors of this film stand at the poles of exterior traveling sequences, transcending the simple railroad car logic of the room in *The Hindoo Dagger,* but remaining rooted in the basic principle of tension and release that Griffith first explored in that film. By the time the lateral appears in *Judith of Bethulia* (1913), Griffith's last Biograph film, the lateral is a truly massive structure. Woven into the patterns of activity that unify that film is the purely abstract opposition-attraction built on a lateral between the shots of Judith, the furthest point right in the film, and the tent of Holofernes, the furthest point left traveled in the order of shots, over the plains of Bethulia.

The Diagonal

Action along the lateral was one of Griffith's earliest attempts to gain access to the shot in a logical way, and this line of action also made fine use of the potential of shot order. The audience received a coherent picture displayed in a suite of images clearly linked by a straight line of physical activity, or, as in the later films, a mental relationship.

Just as the diagonal displays the range of compositional possibilities inherent in the deep frame, so it represented the first organized thrust of activity out of the proscenium. Just as the diagonal utilized the compositional extent of the frame, it encompassed the maximum amount of activity that the frame could hold while it compressed that activity into a clear, and therefore dramatically meaningful, line. A crowd generally streaming through the frame would obviously be visually "louder" than a few people following the diagonal through the frame, but that loudness could also be chaotic and cacophonous.

As has been mentioned, the benefits of the diagonal were recognized long before Griffith made films. The angle toward the camera lent magnitude to the thrust of activity through the frame. Providing a fine display of activity, the diagonal was particularly effective at its ends, whether the thrust of activity was being exerted by running or walking bodies. This dynamism has to do with the character of the diagonal as a line that utilizes the illusion of depth presented by the film image and asserts a three-dimensional space on the flat screen. In addition, the image itself could grow dramatically along the diagonal, from a small figure in the background to a considerably magnified presence in the foreground as an actor approached the camera before bursting out of the frame at the cut. The diagonal is the early model for exteriors. The growth of the image along the diagonal is used at least as early as Biograph's *The Escaped Lunatic* (1904).

In exteriors the most provocative possibility along the diagonal was the potentially easy connection between left background and right foreground, clearly understood as continuous action maintained over the cut. Griffith had a keen awareness of the powerful thrust of activity out of the right or left foreground to continue the diagonal's extension over the cut and into the next shot. Once this connection between shots was perceived along the diagonal, the rudimentary unity of exteriors was established and the energy of the film flowed in an overall pattern.

For instance, the simple repetition of the diagonal by two people in succession suggests following or pursuit. This convention was part of the pre-Griffith chase structure and was adopted by Griffith in his early films. For instance, the power of *Money Mad* (1908), an otherwise overly histrionic film, derives principally from the structured pursuit that is created quite simply by having first one person, then another pass through a particular frame. The acting also suggests threat and peril, but the line of activity strung from shot to shot makes the drama an experience of tension and release—a physical sensation.

In *Where the Breakers Roar* (1908) the film's rhythm proceeds from the contrast between the diagonal-lateral orientation of the walk that begins the film (shots 1 and 2) and the diagonal sweep of action exploding past the camera (shot 9), which provides the graphic form for the boat chase (shots 11–15) traveling diagonally across an otherwise unbroken expanse of water. In *Where the Breakers Roar* action in the chase is "doubled" along the diagonal as it had been in *Money Mad*. The continuity of pursuit in shots 13 and 14 in *Where the Breakers Roar* is understood because the pursued travels through the shot, exits the frame completely, and is directly followed into that shot by pursuers who trace the same path along the diagonal and exit as their quarry exited, leaving an empty frame. In *Where the Breakers Roar* the activity, reliably flowing from shot to shot, is charged with the dynamism of the thrust along the diagonal, which, extended from shot to shot, is as "readable" a line of action as that of the interior lateral. In addition, Griffith was able to explore the effect of the magnified burst of the actor's presence passing the camera before the cut. When this effect appears again, as in *The Salvation Army Lass*

(1908), Griffith uses the line of a marching band advancing on and swinging past the camera to create a dynamic effect that was to mature in the classic images of soldiers swinging past cheering crowds in Griffith's epic visualizations of the Civil War.

So satisfactory was the combination of extension and intensification along the diagonal that it was eventually incorporated into interiors in 1910. The idea of projecting a line of activity was particularly important in interiors in which a number of possibilities of entering and exiting the frame was necessarily limited by the lateral "realism" of connecting shots on a straight line. But when cutting assumed its role in creating screen activity, Griffith realized that in each particular shot only relevant activity need be shown. Consequently, the diagonal, which had heretofore only been possible in exteriors, and had actually become ponderously time-consuming there by 1910, could be imported into the smaller interior spaces to give depth to the sets without sacrificing the speed of the dramatic action. Scaled down, the interior diagonal did not effect the fluency of passage in the film. It maintained the sense of connection created on the lateral, because its composition involved only a slight adjustment of the doorway points that defined the lateral. Doorways placed left back and right fore, as in *The Purgation* (1910) and *The Marked Time-Table* (1910), preserve the right and left exit points that orient the viewer from shot to shot, while breaking up the railroad-car feeling created by straight lateral passage between interior shots.

In the diagonal, therefore, Griffith found the qualities of clarity and dynamism. The figures of the actors grew from tiny to large, until the burst of graphic activity that resulted from the magnified image exiting the frame in the foreground at the cut. Because of the ease of "reading" such a line of activity from shot to shot, physical activity could be controlled within the shot and projected from shot to shot in a way that emphasized fluidity and created speed.

The transformation of the diagonal took place when Griffith became aware that action along the entire extent of such a path was time-consuming and too general, however well it lent scope to screen activity. Where earlier directors had invented endless business within the body of the chase along the diagonal, Griffith drastically curtailed first the number of chasers, then the extent of the diagonal itself. By 1910 Griffith had gradually cut the duration of action projected along the diagonal by relying on the entrance and exit points to imply the line itself. Pursuer and pursued were separated from each other and held apart until their presence in the final shot of a chase identified "catching" with the resolution of the structure. The increased use of intercutting to create relationships between shots affects the diagonal organization of the frame most extensively. Though Griffith was always to retain the diagonal for its power and impact, the length of its sweep through the frame was gradually curtailed in the interest of economy of expression.

Less is More: Economical
Structures Increase Activity
Cutting at the Entrance/Exit

Applying the narrative device of withholding resolution and not information, Griffith begins the chase in *Swords and Hearts* (1911) by withholding a space: although the Union soldiers are chasing the heroine, they are stopped in the chase order and kept from following the trail she lays out. These Union soldiers are temporarily halted in set-up 16. Five cuts back to them, held in this space while the heroine advances to new spaces, maximize the tension between the positions of pursuer and pursued by frustrating the flow of activity from one shot to another that normally signified chasing. The release of activity from the shot thus becomes an event in itself.

Griffith had begun constructing chases very simply on the principle that passage of the pursued out of the shot guaranteed the easy entry of the pursuers. In the chase sequence of *Swords and Hearts* Griffith experimented with withholding a space as a means of generating energy in the chase. There is an introduction of one shot of new material to advance the chase for every repeated shot (set-up 16) that holds the pursuers back. Griffith increased the *sense* of action in the sequence by controlling the tension at the frame boundary instead of increasing the amount of physical activity that flowed through the shot.

The process of construction that leads to this sequence in *Swords and Hearts* equates the burst of activity at the entrance/exit with the cut. The lateral logic of interior architecture, with its focus on doors, identifies cuts with the boundary of the frame. This identification persists in the films of 1908, and projects such as *An Awful Moment* and *The Hindoo Dagger* suggest that it is the break at the doorway, the cut, that is the significant dramatic action in the film, because this break represents the release of the tension that has been gathering between two centers of activity in separate shots. The cut identifies this dynamic structural process with plot information and creates a narrative statement.

The entrance or exit on a cut becomes useful exactly because it uses the frame as a barrier to control the flow and pace of the activity through the chain of shots. This engages the audience in a speculative activity about the shape of the world of the film. In *The Lonely Villa* the bounded frame yields to constant lateral assault on the doorways. The family is pushed from room to room as the thieves break down successive doors. The intuition is that dramatic pressure builds between two spaces in intercutting. Gradually, this pressure is equalized by a burst of activity through the doorway on the cut. *In the Window Recess* (1909) is a variation on this theme. In the course of this film, the audience's attention is divided between two points in the stable parlor frame: the right foreground entrance that leads to the window recess in which a convict hides and the central background entrance/exit through which friends and family pass. The situation recalls *An Awful Moment* with its "safe" and "perilous" doorway cuts. But in *In the Window Recess,* Griffith found a way to extend the audience's experience of the dramatic tension in the situation indefinitely. The central entrance/exit can promise no resolution—the comings and goings of old friends and potential helpers at this background point of access threaten the fragile stability between the right foreground entrance/exit and the shot of the window recess. The very entrance of the father at the familiar central entrance/exit, an easy indication of salvation in *The Lonely Villa,* is initially a threat to the foreground stability of the domestic interior in *In the Window Recess.* In maintaining the tension in the right forecorner in the many repetitions of the familiar parlor set-up, Griffith manages to transform the traditional siege-and-rescue format. The wife, far from seeking to communicate her peril and the danger posed to her child by the villain, only wishes to withhold information long enough to equalize the pressure exerted against the foreground by the villain's presence in the window recess. Of the twenty-three shots in this film, all but five exploit the fragile balance of pressures at the doorway between the parlor and the window recess.

The resolution of *The Usurer* (1910) takes place at a doorway. Griffith exerts pressure at the cut to externalize a largely metaphorical drama in one definitive action. The usurer is killed when one of his victims enters his office and, fainting from hunger, pushes closed the door to the vault where the usurer sits counting his filthy lucre. Unwittingly, the poor woman thus repays the usurer for his conscious oppression of his debtors, which has been established in passages of intercutting. Griffith saves the "geographical" connection between shots for the final dramatic activity of the film. This last sequence begins in shot 19, when the poor woman leaves her apartment. When Griffith cuts to the usurer's office, there is the expectation that the poor woman will enter. But her entry is momentarily delayed by the entrance of a relative of the usurer's (sister? wife?), continuing the direction of the poor woman's action to make the match over the cut. The usurer then enters the vault. Only after this business is done does the anticipated entrance of the poor woman occur, and she faints and pushes the door to the vault closed, knowing nothing of the usurer's presence there. The continuity that leads to this fateful moment is balanced by the sequence of shots 35–36–37, in which the usurer is shown inside the vault banging on the leftward door of the vault while his killer/victim, already having left his office in shot 32, appears at the rightward entrance/exit of her home, passing through quite easily and overtonally underscoring the usurer's inability to escape and her liberation from his evil.

The doorway did not necessarily have to be physically locked to represent a barrier between spaces and serve as a useful focus of the tension between shots. In *As the Bells Rang Out* (1910) nothing physically restrains the young bride from entering the parlor where her father is about to be arrested on her wedding day, although the proximity between the hallway in which she stands and the room where he waits is very strongly established—they adjoin. The contiguousness of these spaces is asserted by the passage of people through them, and the suspense generated in *As the Bells Rang Out* causes the audience to desire that the bride *not* cross the frame boundary—that information be withheld from her. This tension is heightened by the fact that the connection between spaces is an easy, fluid lateral. The bride could all too easily stray across the frame boundary/cut to discover her father's shameful plight.

Griffith began to rely on the suspense, anticipation, and drama generated from the fact that people are poised at the entrance/exit-cuts. The siege sequence in *The Girl and Her Trust* (1912) leads to a standoff at the doorway. Each party enters his or her respective shot: the girl locks herself in her office, slamming the door just as the villains finally break into the outer room where the strongbox is kept. This siege sequence had begun with looks intruding into the railroad station office and concludes with a series of entries and exits, made of very short shots in which people break down and slam doors before the actual siege sequence begins and tension again builds at the doorway/cut.

In *Brutality* (1912) Griffith uses the anticipation of a resolution between two spaces separated by a doorway to create a brooding, anxiety-ridden atmosphere in the same temperance plot that he had used in 1909 for *A Drunkard's Reformation*. *Brutality* even employs the temperance play to awaken the conscience of the erring husband as did the earlier film—the second half of *Brutality* is devoted to intercutting between the stage play of *Oliver Twist* and shots of the hero that suggest a growing self-awareness inspired by the play. But *Brutality* has a considerable prologue to this rather conventional resolution. Some thirty shots are all developed in spatially related pairs (set-ups 1 and 2; 11 and 12) in which the break out of the frame at the cut becomes increasingly ominous. The first pair of set-ups begins the film—a young man playfully courts a young woman. He enters and exits shot 1 right. She stands at the left, conversing with a friend, shyly noticing him. He enters shot 2 from the right and stands at the left. From this set-up he turns to look to the right background "at" the young woman, smiling, almost daring her to come over the cut to him. Facing the right foreground, she flirts with him. Finally, at shot 9 (set-up 2 repeated), the young man breaks into the young woman's set-up again through the right foreground and asks her to marry him. Only then does she enter shot 10 (set-up 2 repeated) with him to resolve the separation between shots that created the tension of the courtship.

By the alternation of set-ups that begins in shots 11 and 12, the opposing diagonals of set-ups 1 and 2 have been straightened to a beeline lateral connection between interiors. The breach of the cut by action implies a threat. The tone is still playful, but now hints of violence: the young wife throws her husband out of the kitchen; he raises his hand to her. By the time 11 and 12 are repeated at shots 24 through 30, the violence is open, and the playful tension of shots 1 and 2 has become grim and frightening discord. In shot 24, the husband actually does hit the wife, interestingly the initiation, not the culmination, of a sequence of intercutting between the parlor where she sits in fear and the kitchen where he retreats to pout and fume. Much as in *As the Bells Rang Out,* the audience is taught to fear the breach of the doorway. The burst of activity at the entrance/exit, identified with the precipitation of violence, makes the effect all the more vivid. When the husband finally emerges from his tantrum in the kitchen, he simply stands over the wife to resolve their separation, while the sense of danger generated in the structure hangs between them.

The versatility of tone available through creating tension at the boundary of the frame is based on the fact that intercutting forms a relationship between shots that suggests the exchange of some sort of energy. As *Brutality* illustrates, a sequence can express attraction or repulsion simply by adjusting the flow of the energy through the structure. When people are separated from each other by a cut, it is usually a very unstable situation—but it may be comic as well as tragic. In *Jones and His New Neighbors* (1909) the doorway becomes a dynamic possibility standing between two increasingly unbalanced shots. Angry neighbors fill the hallway; the Joneses listen to the gathering storm from the other side of the door. The audience, led to expect equalization between shots that are intercut, enjoys the film to the extent that the resolution can be anticipated, and the arrival of this moment in the Jones film depends only on the length of the reel itself and the number of people Griffith can pack into the Jones hallway before the barrier, the doorway/frame boundary, finally collapses from the weight of the congregation of bodies.

When the actual doorway was removed, the pressure at the entrance/exit was exerted more directly on the cut itself. This is the case with exterior action. For instance, *The Gibson Goddess* (1909) takes advantage of the boundary of the frame as a barrier and makes use of the burst of activity at the cut for comic effect. The goddess accumulates a crowd of admirers wherever she goes, and the humor of the film is built from the fact that each time she finds a new, empty, private space, that space is gradually invaded by amorous pursuers until the crush is unbearable. This modification of the accumulated effect focuses on the cut. The goddess wants to hold her position in the shot; she does not want to run. Each cut releases her into fresh, private space, and the frame stands as a potential barrier that is constantly violated by the invasion of her admirers.

In *The Gibson Goddess* the emphasis has been taken off the span of activity through the shots and shifted toward the dynamism of the cut. A similar situation arises in another comedy, *What's Your Hurry?* (1909). In this film the humor depends completely on the shock of an entrance into the frame. A young fellow is constantly surprised by his fiancée's father, who coincidentally turns up in each image the suitor has just entered. The young man begins to believe he is being pursued by a disapproving parent. The humor is located at the perimeter of the shot as the audience begins to scan the frame for the possible entry points of the "pursuer," identifying with the frightened suitor each time a "surprise" entry occurs. Although the entrance and exit points in *What's Your Hurry?* seem disjointed, they can be seen as loosely mapped spirals. The after-image of the film might be one of the young man running around in circles—a composite effect accomplished by having him run in and out of the frame at different points rather than having him travel through matched shots. In addition, the young man looks so disoriented and displaced because he cannot get into or hold his place in the frame. If the father is not there at the beginning of the shot, he will pop up. When the father is not there, the audience waits for him as the suitor does, uneasily. This pattern of anticipation and pay-off is the graphic counterpoint to the plot information that the father is in fact *not* chasing the young man and is totally perplexed by the latter's flight from each shot.

The type of spatial anticipation that serves as the basis of the comedy in *The Gibson Goddess* and *What's Your Hurry?* is the closest Griffith comes to developing his dramatic sense of irony into a mature comic view of the conspiracy of the universe against the characters of his films. In general, Griffith does not seem to have been able to get the necessary distance from his characters to stand for their being humiliated in any but the most serious way. Normally, comedy eludes Griffith. When the physical processes of the film turn "against" the hero or heroine, it is usually a tragic signal. Next to *The Curtain Pole* and *They Would Elope, What's Your Hurry?* is one of Griffith's more successful comedies because it is a formal project that manages to exploit spatial tension to make a disparity of information between characters comic. These comedies work because the anticipation of a resolution of conflict between characters could be exploited at the boundary of the frame in a comic plot as well as a tragic one.

As the examples above suggest, the interrelationship between shots that are intercut can be carried outside the motivating architecture of the domestic interior, and the same tension can be developed between the cut and the boundary of the frame. Freed from the doorway, intercutting exteriors presents Griffith's realization that tension is created by the fact of cutting itself. Controlling the flow of activity does not depend on the door or any other "real" barrier. Activity could be stopped effectively at the boundary of the frame itself and then released by the cut into the next shot.

In *The Primal Call* (1911) Griffith delays the resolution of the story with a passage of intercutting between the lovers. In previous films, the resolution would occur at the point when the lovers are joined in one space again after their separation in the crisis. In *The Primal Call* Griffith takes the time to

Figs. 54–60. *The Primal Call* (1911)—Seduc-
tion (sequential)

54

construct a resolution. The hero gets the heroine (fig. 54), then runs to a new
space with her (fig. 55), dumping her in it and running away to the set-up
where the chase sequence began for him (shot 44, a repeat of the set-up of
shot 39). There the hero makes a show of scorn (fig. 56). The point, of
course, is to make the heroine demonstrate her choice, a courtship situation
somewhat akin to that of *Brutality.* Griffith effects this little lovers' drama
over the cut in a sequence in which the heroine (shot 43) (fig. 57) and the hero
(shot 44/39) (fig. 58) are related to each other by shot order, by matched
looks, and by actions directed toward each other—all of which lead to a burst
of activity (she runs to him) (fig. 59) that finally negates the separation and
unites the lovers in one image (fig. 60).

In addition, Griffith had taken control of the flow of activity in this sequence to the extent of actually subordinating real duration to a pattern of shot
lengths. This sequence has a constructed rhythm, shot *b* occupying the screen
roughly one-third the time of shot *a. The Primal Call* represents an amalgamation of a number of devices present in Griffith's work for some time by
1911: intercutting *a* and *b;* the orientation of shots by look; entrance and exit
control; the strict graphic orientation of characters in discontinuous shots
to suggest proximity; and the last-minute reversal of direction in the final
matched cut. There is a new-found ability to control, not only the quality of
the relationship between the shots, but the length of the shots, imposing a
rhythm of presentation. The tension in the sequence of *The Primal Call* is
structurally identical with those of *The Prussian Spy* and *Jones and His New
Neighbors.* The impact is created with a burst of activity over the cut that
equalizes the pressure between shots. Tension collects at the boundary of the
frame because the audience, in contact with both spaces in the relationship,
continues the action in both spaces, perceiving them as simultaneous. This
awareness doubles the *sense* of the amount of activity or incident in a sequence. In one sense, the main difference between *The Primal Call* and the

55

56

57

58

59

60

earlier films is that the actual door between the two shots is missing and the frame itself stands as the barrier between the characters. But the result of this difference is a much more complex narrative in the space of the same short Biograph reel.

Variation of Graphic Size over the Cut

The bounded shot did not yield to the master view until late in Griffith's Biograph period. But within the scope of the basic set-up, he managed some effects by manipulating graphic size within the image and over the cut.

Because of cramped studio conditions, the staggering of entrances and exits and *ab* intercutting were the most advanced solutions Griffith found to opening up spatially restricted interior sets. It was much easier to achieve somewhat closer shots from a greater variety of angles in exterior work, and one of the first films to demonstrate the startling difference between exterior and interior mise-en-scènes is *The Voice of The Violin* (1909), with its juxtaposition of a rather tight shot of a young man on the steps of a brownstone, looking in a window, linked to a wider, frontal, still rather theatrical, shot of his sweetheart standing in the family parlor.

By *Sweet and Twenty* (1909) Griffith was exploiting this graphic difference in sizes from exterior to interior by intercutting the tighter view of the suitor on the porch with the conventional, mid-long view of the parlor in which his contrary girlfriend stands, refusing to let him into her house. The *abab* order of this sequence alternates between closed and open spaces until the young man finally breaches the doorway/cut to confront the young woman.

It was not until later in 1909, with *In the Window Recess,* that Griffith was able to achieve this rhythm solely in interiors. The dramatic tension develops between a loose, conventional interior (*a*) in which a frantic mother tries to chase everyone away from shot *b,* a tighter composition containing only the fugitive and his captive, the mother's little girl. The enlarged figure of the convict is always exerting a pressure at the boundary of the frame in the window recess and it is typical of Griffith that he could make this drama a spatial issue. The mother tries to maintain the equilibrium between the two spaces by chasing help away rather than seeking it. *In the Window Recess* becomes a tour de force, creating drama by combining intercutting with the burst of activity threatened at the doorway by the presence of a figure of enlarged graphic size.

Griffith never got "inside" the proscenium in interiors—for the most part the camera's view remained a frontal one. But when the diagonal was incorporated into interiors, a more complex playing area provided the opportunity to exploit the growth of the image as it was projected toward the camera along a limited diagonal.

In *The Purgation* (1910), the most visible position in the frame is no longer right or left of center in the middle distance of a full shot. People could

Figs. 61–66. *The Primal Call* (1911)—Abduction (sequential)

61

be placed in a variety of playing areas in a shot, and the range of subject-to-camera relationships is from full-knees-up in the foreground to medium long shot in the background. The whole room is potentially active. The rightward entrance/exit fills the frame with a figure that may recede into a medium long shot as the figure travels back into the frame. In *The Purgation* Griffith links tension at the doorway with the variation of graphic size over the cut to build momentum at the doorway for assault. As thieves approach the right foreground entrance/exit in a hotel hallway, intending to rob the heroine, they grow in size, and are poised against the doorway/frame boundary/cut with an increased graphic weight that focuses the burst of energy produced by images at the ends of diagonals in early exteriors.

At the end of *The Primal Call* Griffith sends the heroine and her worthless fiancé on a walk, during which the rough, but worthy, sailor will have a chance to rescue her and claim her for his own. A variation of size in a series of shots leads up to this dramatic climax. The variation of size in the series takes three shots in *The Primal Call* (shots 40–42), but is oddly reversed—starting with a rather close shot of the couple (40) effected by sending them to the left forecorner of the shot to magnify their exit from the frame (fig. 62). They travel through a looser shot (41), which ends in a medium close-up corner (fig. 64). Finally, having reversed directions on a diagonal (right to left/left to right), they travel into a third image, full-figure (fig. 66).

There are two interesting aspects of this successive opening of the frame in series. First of all, 40–42 takes place in the context of two shots that show the sailor (39 and 43). The dramatic duty of 40–42 is to transfer the heroine to the sailor's space, a process described above. The relationship between shot 39 (the sailor looks right) (fig. 61) and shot 40 (the heroine and her fiancé enter the shot and pass through it from right background to left foreground) is tense with spatial speculation (fig. 62). Where is the sailor? Does he see them? Is he close enough to do anything? Does she see him? While a clear graphic link is

62

63

64

65

66

implied by the sailor's glance, the immediate relationship between the couple and the sailor is not yet clear. Griffith expresses this relationship in the classic form of the chase: the sailor enters shot 40 in the background and follows their path through the shot (fig. 63). This action resolves the spatial ambiguity between shots 39 and 40, at least insofar as the viewer understands that the sailor is close enough to take steps in the heroine's direction. The relationship is at once clarified: he is on their trail, the dimensions of which successively open up as the sailor follows them through the next shot (figs. 64–65) and then actually raids the last opened image (fig. 66). He bursts in on the heroine and her fiancé, carrying her off to a new space (shot 43). He leaves her in this space, and the courtship described on pp. 82–85 concludes the film.

In *Iola's Promise* (1912) Griffith uses the successive variation in size in a more conventional series to introduce new characters into the body of the film. Griffith always took care to introduce new space in a context of old associations. Such is the case in *Iola's Promise*. The second sequence of the film begins with the juxtaposition of shots: in 28 Iola sits in a formal Indian composition, a village. She has been reunited with her tribe. In shot 29 the cowboy who nursed Iola back to health enters a new desert exterior from the right and stands center to read a letter from his beloved. In shot 30 Iola concludes the story of how she was saved by the cowboy, and these three shots therefore provide a concise summary of the film to that point, as well as a transition to the next sequence of the film, in which the wagon train carrying the cowboy's fiancée will be attacked by Iola's tribe. A three-shot transition is linked to a three-shot introduction of the wagon train. In shot 31 the wagon train is shown traveling from left to right. This is followed by a closer shot of the sweetheart, Dora, in her wagon traveling left to right. Shot 33 again shows the wagons passing by the camera left to right. One retains this image of the rhythm of the wagons passing—full, closer, full—throughout the ensuing battle sequence. The pattern is repeated in shots 44–45–46 and succeeded by a bird's-eye view of the battle between the wagon train and the attacking Indians. The full–closer–full pattern reappears in shots 52–53–54 (set-ups 44–45–46 repeated) and is succeeded by another slightly high angle of the fight. The rhythm of introduction becomes the basis for the structure of the entire action sequence of *Iola's Promise*.

Finally, in *The Painted Lady* (1912), the variation of size at the doorway and the fatality of the step through the doorway are combined for tragic results. The lady, a large figure in the right foreground close to the camera, steps out of the frame and through the doorway into a longer shot, where she mistakenly kills her lover. It is ironic that a position normally associated with felonious threats and criminal actions should be occupied by this gentle young woman. In a film that generally concentrates on spatial tension within the frame and is somewhat loose geographically, Griffith uses intercutting at the doorway with a concentration on graphic pressure at the cut to create a dramatic climax.

Camera Movement and the Cut

The combination of the burst of activity at the entrance/exit and the tension gathered at the boundary of the frame before the cut is eventually connected to camera movement, although the combination is only tentatively exercised in Griffith's Biograph films. While the pan following the Indian along the fence in *The Call of the Wild* (1908) is an inventive way to show proximity within the frame and makes use of the continuity of screen space as well as the continuousness of a dramatic action, this pan is structurally related to the "trailing" pans of earlier cinema and contributes nothing to the overall pattern of the film.

These "trailing" pans could be made to define a space. In *A Baby's Shoe* (1909) a destitute mother enters shot 2 on a panning movement that will bring her to the door of the rich family where she will abandon her child. Every time this space is repeated (shot 9, shot 14), the pan is restated to maintain the familiarity of the exterior image. In *In the Watches of the Night* (1909) a familiar image is extended through a pan. A poor man is turned away by a rich one. Denied at the doorway in sequence 1, the poor man forces entry through a window in sequence 2. The continuity between these two moments is stated in a pan across the rich man's porch, with its sweeping archways. In *The Voice of the Violin* (1909) a car trails a pan into shot 4a, revealing the exterior of a house. This continuous space will split along a cut into two shots bounded by doorways. A longer view of the exterior includes the door leading down to the basement, where villains plan to blow up the house. An allied cut-in on the axis closes in on the upper doorway and window, where the boy sees that his sweetheart is in danger. In effect, Griffith uses the pan to define a master space into which he cuts for a closer view.

These examples illustrate how circumscribed Griffith's camera movements were. They are generally confined within shots, and once used, they remain a part of the definition of that shot. The fluidity and grace that might have been gained from camera movement is usually achieved by managing the speed and magnitude of actions as they coincide.

In *Faithful* (1910) all of the sequences are constructed for breeze and easiness above all, for smooth passage through shots that give the impression of a complete place in which people move with facility and grace. Between shots 1 and 2, there is definite sense of spatial as well as directional continuity. This sense is not usually found in a Griffith Biograph film, where the expository shots usually express a dramatic opposition, an adversary relationship that defines the dramatic conflict. In *Faithful* Adonese's opening walk meets the momentum of an approaching car on a smooth, directionally logical cut. The walk is matched to the approaching speed of the car, and the film begins on a marvelously fluid movement that sets the light romantic tone of the story. Adonese gets into the car, which continues the action toward the exit from the expository sequence.

Adonese's meeting with his Dear Lady in the next sequence is a directional complement to his exit from the expository sequence. Having started from his house to the right and having continued that movement in the car, he leaves the car to enter her shot from the left, reversing directions to begin a new chain of shots.

In sequence 17–21 Adonese tries to lose Faithful, a gentle half-wit played with taste and subtlety by Mack Sennett. Every link between spaces in this sequence is a smooth continuity cut and makes the activity appear logically continuous, although the construction of the walk is purely cinematic. In the last sequence of the film, in which the Dear Lady is saved by Faithful, Griffith continues to find ways to enhance the flow of the activity. Faithful saves the Dear Lady from a burning building. This event gives Griffith the opportunity to swing fire equipment past the camera, utilizing the dramatic sweep of motion that had thrilled audiences as far back as Williamson's *Fire* (1900). In addition, the conventional sweep past the camera is used to echo the expository momentum, and the resolution of *Faithful* is thus structurally tied to the exposition.

Reversing over the Cut

The reverse of activity over the cut is often employed by Griffith for a rhythmical effect, and this device is related to the exploitation of the burst of activity at the boundary of the frame. The reverse angle is so dramatic because it presents the object of attention almost, but not quite, simultaneously from two radically different, spatially opposed positions. When shots are short, the reverse of the direction of activity over the cut can have the effect of a head whipping around, a moment of obvious kinetic power.

Some conventional reverse angles appear in Griffith's Biograph Films. In *Her Mother's Oath* (1913) the reverse is finally used for exposition. This suggests that Griffith finally began to see the reverse as a spatially revealing device as well as a way to generate tension, although a cut to the hero entering the church mediates the shift between complementary views (front and back) of the heroine seated in her pew. Generally, Griffith dynamically reverses direction at the cut. The separation of the lovers in *The Primal Call* resolves on a reverse of the young woman's position. She exits frame right and enters left to embrace her sailor, but over the cut she also turns away from the audience to maximize the impact of her burst into the frame (figs. 63, 64). The last moments of the chase in *The Girl and Her Trust* devolve on a reverse (fig. 31). Reverses in Griffith's Biograph work are interesting because they lend such a sense of visual rhythm and impact to sequences of shots.

In *The Broken Doll* (1910) Griffith unfolds a sequence of activity that leads to a sudden Indian attack on a white settlement. This sequence is particularly interesting because it contains a variation on the chase-and-siege format. Instead of concentrating on the static family menaced by the ferocious mob, Griffith concentrates on the drama of the mob's arrival. The Indian attack generally advances toward the right foreground for three shots, the first two of which are related to familiar images of the settlement at which the Indians might be expected to strike. The relationship of the line of the attack to the first of these familiar images, shot 22 (a repeat of the set-up in shot 4), is one of direct opposition. The Indians advance toward the camera in their shot and the settlers are shown in 22 (4) with their backs to the camera. In the combination of these two shots, the thrust of the Indian attack is effectively countered by the opposition of the image of the settlers, who actually have no knowledge of the Indian onslaught. The attack does not occur between these two shots, although the directional logic between them indicates that a connection might have been made. This pseudo-reverse of directions is followed by shot 23 (3) of the settlement closing up for the night, a fact signified as much by the fact that the Indian attack does not connect with this familiar space as by the content of the image, in which a family enters the house for the evening. For the resolution of the tension between the line of the attack and the spaces it potentially threatens, Griffith introduces a new image of the settlement (shot 24), in which two lovers say goodnight. The long-anticipated attack finally connects with this new image; the threat of violence is realized as the Indians break into the frame.

Griffith was able to foreshadow the large physical and visual impact of the Indian attack in *The Broken Doll* by interposing two quiet, but graphically probable, shots between the Indians and their actual point of impact. The pseudo-reverse is used to heighten the graphic tension between two spaces where the physical impact is implied and then withheld.

The reverse of the flow of the activity from shot to shot is used to create a more complex visual rhythm in *Swords and Hearts* (1911). The central action sequence of this film is a combination of a chase and a siege, but this time the two structures are not dramatically melded. In *Swords and Hearts* the chase and the siege are separated into two distinct movements, which combine the impact of the burst of action at the boundary of the frame with the reverse of action at the cut.

The chase sequence in *Swords and Hearts* can be considered to begin in shot 27, where the Union soldiers chasing the hero are successfully diverted to the track laid out by the faithful heroine, who convinces them that they are still tracking the hero. Griffith reverses activity from shot to shot in this chase sequence to create dramatic tension from the contrasting directions in the body of the chase, an effect created at the cut, as well as with an accumulated pattern of crisscrossing diagonals. From shots 28 to 34, the activity proceeds from left background to right foreground across the frame. At shot 35, there is a reversal of direction: Jennie rides toward the left foreground exit of shot 34. A magnified image, she turns to the back of the frame to shoot at her pur-

67

68

69

70

71

72

73

74

Figs. 67–74. *Swords and Hearts* (1911)—Chase (condensed)

suers, then rides out of the shot to appear in shot 35, at the right foreground corner, a similarly magnified image riding to a mid-shot position in the frame before starting to turn left toward the camera to shoot at her pursuers. Griffith achieves a real visual burst of energy at this reversal. The juncture between shots 34 and 35 reverses the direction of the chase, and both shots are very short, which heightens the graphic impact of the cut. Furthermore, at this point Griffith changes the dynamic of the chase. Thus far, the chase has taken the classic form found in Griffith's early work: the pursued lay out the trail across the image and exit the frame; the pursuers retrace the trail before the cut and their exit to the new shot. But in *Swords and Hearts* Jennie exits shot 34 through the left foreground (fig. 67), and this exit is matched to her entry into shot 35 (fig. 68) through the right foreground. She rides to the center of the shot and begins to turn toward the camera, firing a gun. The Union pursuers are already in the set-up of shot 34 (shot 36) riding toward the left foreground, where one of the soldiers is shot (fig. 69). Griffith cuts back to the set-up of shot 35 (shot 37), where Jennie sits astride her horse in a tight foreground composition, firing her gun. She turns to ride toward the left background (fig. 70). The cut back to 34 (shot 38) shows the Union soldiers advancing toward the foreground exit once more (fig. 71). At this point, Griffith departs from the classical form of the chase. The set-ups of 34 and 35 are alternated until the girl has advanced, but her pursuers are held "in place" in the order of shots. The diagonals of 34 and 35 crisscross to create a cumulative effect of opposition that is underscored by the opposing positions of characters poised to confront each other at the cut. Intercutting 34 and 35 also complicates the relationship of pursuer and pursued. As the chase continues, Jennie's pursuers are stopped at a point two shots "away" from her in the order of the chase. Although they do exit set-up 34, they never effect her reverse of direction at the entry of set-up 35. At the reverse, Griffith prolongs the suspense of the chase in a new way: through intercutting he holds the flow of activity at the boundary of the frame. To end the sequence, Griffith reverses Jennie's direction on the diagonals twice more. In shot 39 she enters the left foreground and rides to the right background (fig. 72). In shot 40, she rides to the right foreground, a magnified image, and executes a tight turn to sit in the mid-ground of the frame looking toward the right foreground "out" of the shot (fig. 73). The look implies an immediate distance, which the viewer can only judge in a graphic way: the repetition of direction, trace, and entrance by pursuers and pursued into and through the shots in order indicates that she is "safe." The Union pursuers are chased from set-up 34 (shot 41) by Confederate soldiers, who enter from the right background (fig. 74). Finally, Jennie slides to the left out of a space that feels "far away" from her pursuers.

The disengagement of the parties in the chase in *Swords and Hearts* is intercut with a repeat of the familiar image of the parlor in the hero's home. The sequence 40–44 intermingles shots of the chase order (Jennie; the Union

75

76

77

78

79

Figs. 75–79. *Swords and Hearts* (1911)—Siege (condensed)

soldiers; the parlor; Jennie; the parlor) until the energy generated by the activity in the chase sequence is transferred to the next dramatic locale, the besieged mansion. The siege in *Swords and Hearts* begins to brew in this transition from sequence to sequence, during which the old father of the hero is warned of the coming trouble by the faithful family retainer. The siege is actually launched in shot 48: marauders break out of a space that is directionally related to the repeat of the mansion exterior as first seen in shot 1. This is one of the two views of the house given in the film and has the advantage of offering a fuller, more frontal view of the mansion, a more extended diagonal on which to launch the marauders' assault, which flows into the familiar image from the left. These men pour onto the porch and begin to break down the door (fig. 75). Between this familiar porch and the parlor, Griffith interposes a hallway (fig. 76), a space never seen before, although people have traveled between porch and parlor earlier in the film. This hallway instantly conveys the sense of "innermost" to the parlor, where the father will retreat (fig. 77). The exterior and parlor doors become two barriers, two points of impact, as the marauders try to get into the house to steal the father's fortune in gold.

The rhythm of the siege, with its successive door barriers, takes up the rhythm of the chase, with its successive reverses. The transition from the porch in shot 48 (1) to the hallway in shot 49 is graphically heightened in two ways: the relatively open space of shot 48 (1) is drastically curtailed in the transition to 49, a much tighter space. In addition, the direction of the activity is changed from left-right to right-left. When this transition from exterior to interior is repeated at 51–52, it takes place in two very short shots that give the activity of breaking into the house an extra graphic kick.

There follows a sequence of intercutting between the hallway and the parlor for six shots, the attempt to break into the innermost part of the house, with tension gathering at the boundary of the frame/doorway (figs. 78, 79). This passage is intensified by gunfire and smoke, which really do nothing other than activate an already exciting opposition of shots with extra visual "noise," somewhat akin to the roomfuls of furniture broken in barroom brawls where rapid cutting is combined with physical activity to heighten the sense of excitement in an action sequence. An interesting comparison to this method of generating screen excitement is offered by the fights in many foreign films in which men fall in an angry embrace that usually looks much more desperately futile than the satisfying punches and resolving impacts of American movie fistfights, which had their beginnings in sequences such as the chase and siege in *Swords and Hearts*. The dramatic secret that Griffith found in this film was that the point of impact had to be clarified. Whether by barrier or changes in direction from cut to cut, Griffith became very careful to signal the points of impact in action sequences in order to generate dramatic energy.

The turning point in Griffith's career, and a turning point in film history, was the realization that the continuity and impact of action are *created* in the cinema. This redefinition of screen activity was one of Griffith's most impressive contributions to the art of making films. His Biograph films make extensive use of the "bounded" shot—frontal views not analyzed into master shot and related angles—and Griffith remains "outside" the proscenium to the extent that the camera rarely provides a 360-degree perspective on any particular space.

Nonetheless, within the restrictions of this spatial attitude, Griffith did come to a realization that the cut created the shot as a unit of construction that not only conveyed information but imposed a mode of perception on the information given on the screen. Searching for a "reasonable" motivation for dramatic action, Griffith arrived at an understanding of the radical effect of the cut in terms of four basic principles: that shots are units of construction; that set-ups are repeatable; that continuous action can be extended over deliberately discontinuous space; and that the transformation of activity into a visual and narrative process takes place in the relationship between shots. Griffith himself put it this way:

> I found that picture-makers were following as best they could the theory of the stage. A story was to be told in pictures, and it was told in regular stage progression; it is bad stage technique to repeat; it would be bad stage technique to have an actor show only his face; there are infinite numbers of things we do in pictures that would be absurdities on the stage, and I decided that to do with the camera only what was done on the stage was equally absurd.[6]

Griffith learned that interference with the implied realism of the film image, the hacking of the world into pieces, would induce audiences to witness a drama as a process of accumulation and transformation. The effect is admirably summarized in Frank Woods' phrase "deliberation and repose," and is the source of much of the power of a series of films that would otherwise seem dreary and clichéd because of the repetition of melodramatic plots. There is a point early in 1909 when one feels Griffith's ideas of construction shifting toward the visualization of action in terms of shots directing the plot, and away from lengthy shots determined by the duration of an action directed by the plot. Griffith quickly reaches for the determination of the duration of action by the cut and extends the impact of that cut into the next shot. This awareness is founded on the discovery of the power of the relationship between shots. If by 1912–13 Griffith could be praised for having revolutionized acting, it was owing to the fact that physical activity had increasingly become calmer and more restrained in his films, while improved patterns of cutting and construction produced the *feeling* of physical and mental excitement. The scope of the plot increased from film to film, while actions themselves became simplified and direct. Griffith's contribution to the development of screen action was the creation of excitement through the audience's apprehension of the relationship between shots, as well as from the enjoyment of the activity that occurred within those shots. The viewer is forced to make the connections that transform ostensible melodramas into emotionally rich environments.

Basic Structures 3

When Griffith stopped at the familiar and bounded set-up as his unit of construction and rather stolidly maintained it against the claims of the moving camera and the device of breaking up the master shot, he created a radical spatial situation: he joined two pieces of more or less discontinuous space and insisted that the connection was logical. Sergei Eisenstein points out how well this method served Griffith's melodramatic material. The inherent duality of melodrama opposes good and evil; rich and poor; static and active, and this can be related to Griffith's "model of parallel montage [where] one [story line] emotionally heightens the tension and drama of the other." [1]

It is true that the structural methods Griffith developed served the material he worked with. His Biograph films are not Soviet films with their "play of *juxtaposed detail-shots,* which in themselves are immutable and even un-related" [2] When spatial continuity is an issue in his films, Griffith always joins two shots with the assurance that the viewer will take them as adjoining. Nonetheless, as units of construction, the shots Griffith worked with were spa-tially discontinuous. There tends to be a minimal sense of "real" spatial ex-tension beyond the frame and a preference for deliberately constructed spatial relationships. In Griffith's Biograph films, shots are *made* to connect.

Griffith valued those aspects of the cinema that re-presented the form and feeling of the world around him. Because he also preferred to use discon-tinuous shots (which subdivide and analyze "reality"), however, he had to be very careful to map out the world of the film in the semblance of "reality."

In the course of his Biograph period Griffith developed a very keen under-standing of the importance of indicators in what was actually an extremely sketchy and fragmented depiction of the world in which the dramatic action occurs. The first solution to creating a realist illusion in discontinuous space is the establishment of a clear line of activity. The line that was plotted across the screen in the early chases was an extremely powerful unifier. The simple thrust of activity across the face of the image provided maximum visibility within the shot and led the audience directly to the next space. Movement it-self asserts the "real" link between discontinuous spaces and convinces the

99

viewer that the shots are related according to a "geography" (i.e., that they fit together in a recognizably orderly way).

Once the trace of activity, with its entrance and exit points, is set in the composition, repetition and shot order combine to form the second level of control. The repetition of basic set-ups produces familiar images, which control the dramatic energy in Griffith's films. Repeated patterns of shots impose a pattern on Griffith's films from which the audience learns to ask questions and make predictions about dramatic events—"How soon?" "How far?" "How close?"—even though this audience activity is, by and large, not consciously analytical.

Griffith's accomplishment was to realize such dramatic goals in structural terms. He understood that a composite narrative picture could arise from the sum of the graphic clues. This composite might be called a sense of "place." Place in his Biograph films appears in a cluster of crucially related, but actually discontinuous, views. Although the spaces of the film are related by their sequence within it, they may in fact have that relationship nowhere else. The audience must rely on the filmmaker's directions to decipher the dimensions of a world created in this way—there is no other map of the world of the film but that provided by the filmmaker, even though the resulting film looks as though it is determined by the "realities" of the drama.

The use of repeated and discontinuous images opened up another realm of action in Griffith's films—that of mental cross-references. In *After Many Years* (1908) Griffith is able to clearly present a story in fourteen minutes that incorporates a long time span and develops in two different places. Griffith takes the emphasis off physical activity in this film and demonstrates that *waiting* can also be a dramatic activity if the film can be located in the thoughts of the characters.

Griffith once observed that every foot of film is important in telling a story.[3] It is not possible to overstate the importance of planning and order in a Griffith film—the audience is never left without a visual thread to follow as the world of the film is created before it. The sense that the film is an accumulated effect sets Griffith's films most completely apart from the work of his many talented contemporaries who excelled in the direction of acting or the invention of mise-en-scènes. Considered thematically, Griffith's Biograph films are repetitive. Seldom sumptuous, they are visually obsessed with the manipulation of the interrelationships between shots evolving into sequences. Neither acting nor composition is minimized in Griffith's work, but both of these aspects of narrative drama are subordinated to an overall structure in which the dramatic effect accumulates from shot to shot along a line of activity. Each foot of film in Griffith's work contributes to the unified effect of these interlocking structures.

Building Locales

Shots related in a stable chain define "locale." They give the audience a concrete sense of place, the experience of which leads to the narrative nuances of the story. An important step was taken almost instinctively when early filmmakers propelled activity from one shot to another to create screen "geography." Action run down the diagonal toward the cut and matched to a similar line of action in the following shot gives at least a rudimentary sense of coherence to early films. Matched action suggests that all the shots belong to the same "world." But in these early films, action also tended to use up spaces and then discard them, which emphasized the succession of spaces rather than the accumulation of dramatic effect. Some exceptions to this generalization appear in the films of James Williamson, Cecil Hepworth, and the Biograph Company.

Williamson's films contain some of the earliest examples of repeated shots that establish a sense of familiar location in the world of the film. In shot 1 of *The Soldier's Return* (1902) a soldier comes home from the war to find that his mother has moved into an old age home. In shot 2 he walks back into the frame up a steep street. In shot 3, which is very lengthy, he finds his mother. Shot 4 repeats the set-up of 2 as the man leads his mother down the street. Shot 5 repeats 1 as the mother is brought home again. The film is very simple: the drama is expressed in the shape of a walk away from and a return home. The symmetry of the structure (*abcba*) intuitively underscores the narrative resolution.

Signaling resolution by returning to "zero"—the introductory shot, or the shot where a chase began—is used in a few pre-Griffith films. At the beginning of the chase in *The Escaped Lunatic* (Biograph, 1904) the camera pans right with the lunatic as he escapes from an asylum. At the end of the chase, the lunatic enters a "new" shot that becomes a return "home" when the camera pans left with the action, revealing the asylum exterior. Biograph's *Nurse Wanted* (1908) returns the chase to a man's house (shown in a number of different views), where he tries to find refuge from the aggressive women who strenuously chase him in order to nurse him. In Williamson's endearing *Two Little Waifs* (1907) the end of the first sequence is signaled by a return to the introductory shot of a mansion.

The most systematic use of repeated images to create a sense of location within a film appears in the work of Cecil Hepworth. In *Black Beauty* (1906) Hepworth uses a pan to send Black Beauty and his master off on a journey. This movement is truly expository: Hepworth begins the film with a close shot in which master and horse are introduced; then he cuts out on the axis and pans with horse and rider as they leave the yard and ride away from the camera, back into the frame. The dramatic action occurs in the woods, where the master is attacked and robbed. When Black Beauty escapes from the thugs who rob his master, he travels through a repeated forest image and then returns down the street, where Hepworth repeats pan and the cut on the axis, underscoring the resolution of the first sequence with a symmetrical restatement of familiar spaces. In addition, Hepworth has found a way to allude to the time it takes Black Beauty to gallop back home and to make it a dramatic issue.

In *Rescued by Rover* (1905) Hepworth was even more emphatic in the repetition of a familiar sequence of images. Rover, the faithful family dog, tracks down a child stolen by gypsies. Hepworth sends Rover through a window and then down two streets and across a stream before the dog arrives at the cottage where the child has been taken. When Rover returns home, he travels through three of these images—over the stream, up the street, through the window. He drags his master down the street and over the stream to the cottage. There may be slight variations in these sequences, since Hepworth reshot *Rescued by Rover* when the negatives wore out through duplication,[4] but the important fact is that he was able to indicate a number of dramatic issues to the audience by establishing a locale—the way home—over a number of shots. From the order of the shots, the audience can understand that Rover is returning home, and that he is leading his master to the kidnapped child. Hepworth is also able to create a sense of urgency and suspense. The run takes a certain amount of time—the dog must traverse the entire length of a familiar series of spaces, which indicates that he is going "all the way" back home, and must bring his master "all the way" back to the gypsies' cottage before the child is harmed. Finally, these repeated sequences depict Rover's cleverness in finding the child and his determination to save the little one, eliciting the admiration that is the essence of any story about a beloved pet.

The process of creating dramatic expectations can be based on the audience's feeling for the pattern of a film. In Griffith's films intercutting is used to suggest that lines of action such as Rover's race to the rescue cross-reference one another. This is how Griffith creates the affective dimension of his films. In order to convey this more complicated sense of narrative, Griffith combined a created sense of geography with repeated sequences of images to interrelate locations with shots on which audiences could base their dramatic expectations.

As has been seen, the diagonal line of activity makes a clear dynamic statement across the frame, lending magnitude to the image that speeds along it toward the camera and across the cut. The lateral, the secure frame-based line of activity, creates tension from the frustration and release of activity at the cut. As a composite impression is made of two or more shots, the lateral appears to be a straight line that promises direct access from shot to shot. Both the diagonal and the lateral lead the eye of the viewer over cuts to ease the potential discomfort that might be experienced with the actual discontinuity of the world of the film. This is why the orientation of activity through the frame almost never varies in a Griffith Biograph film. When set-ups are repeated, activity is run back and forth along the original path, with its definitive entrance and exit point. In interiors, doorways emphasize the architectural "realism" of these connections. The tracing and retracing of activity through a sequence of shots is one of the major efforts Griffith makes to define place for the audience specifically in film terms.

The Lonely Villa (1909) is not just the combination of a siege with a race to the rescue. The juxtaposition of diagonal to lateral occurs as a structural scheme from which narrative results arise. The energy of this film is specifically related to the formal opposition of diagonal mobility to lateral crowding, with the secure positions of characters in the lateral creating the sense of diagonal placement (i.e., one feels the father's position racing home chiefly in respect to how close the thieves are coming to his family). Thereafter, it becomes possible to describe Griffith's films in terms of their structures as well as their plots. *Just Gold* (1913), for instance, juxtaposes two laterals—one ranging out from a house, one ranging out across a trackless desert. Neither locale is more "real" than the other in a documentary sense. If anything, the pastoral exteriors of the home are even more loosely joined than are the arid stretches of the desert. But in the combination of these two chains of shots, the audience gains an understanding of "where" in the film each character stands. The heart-breaking simplicity of the loyal friend's tragically fruitless drive "straight" through the exterior spaces of *Death's Marathon* (1913) contrasts with the tense intercutting between the images of the estranged couple, linked to each other only by shot order and a fragile telephone connection.

The extent to which "realism" is accepted in series of shots that are in fact a rather abstract assertion of "locale" depends on Griffith's ability to impose a created continuity in a series of spaces that are no more than provisionally contiguous. One might not be able to reconstruct any one place in a Griffith Biograph film, but one retains an absolute sense of how to get from one point to another in it. For instance Griffith can create the feeling that the furthest extension of activity along a line is related to the resolution of the film, an effect that is found in *Her Terrible Ordeal* (1909). Jack, who knows that Alice is locked in a bank vault, stands in the farthest region of a film that has been generally extended to the left through a sequence of shots. The father, who originally extended spaces in that direction, and whom Jack has gone to fetch, is back in the office, but he cannot free Alice because he does not know she is there. The irony of the father's return to the office without the proper information is obvious, as is the helplessness of the hero, who stands on the outskirts of the film, unable to save his beloved. This is the point of highest tension in *Her Terrible Ordeal* and works because the coincidence of information between characters and audience is so ironically out of whack—a situation embodied in the fact that the father and the boy are in the "wrong" places in the

world of the film. Returning from the farthest reaches of the film to effect a
resolution must be accomplished by the right person, and finally both the person who knows her plight and the person who carries the key to the vault are
manipulated back "to the right" to the heroine's rescue.

The combination of the race to the rescue with a stable point toward which
it rushes is a fixture in Griffith's canon of structures. It is worth reemphasizing
that the relationship of the line of the race to the rescue with the position of
the person in danger is totally abstract. One wonders that audiences got the
point—especially since Griffith accelerated the rate of "cross-cutting" and
separated the lines of action more drastically from each other (as in the train
and handcar chase in *The Girl and Her Trust*). Yet the power of intercutting is
such that the viewer takes each successive shot of a car intercut with a waiting
figure as coming "nearer," even as late as *Death's Marathon* (1913), although
there is no objective reason to do so.

Why this should work at all is clearer in later films, where the car enters a
series of familiar images that the viewer has come to know as "the way to"
the locale in peril (as is the case in *Her Terrible Ordeal*). Maintaining the
locale offers an opportunity to engage the audience in answering the question
"where" in very concrete terms. When a logical geography is conspicuously
absent, as in the Pathé film *Physician of the Castle* and in Griffith's own *The
Cord of Life* (1908), the sense of "toward" must be borne by the fact that
these shots of racing are at least sequentially related to the shots in peril. Any
effort to clarify that order is a refinement on the basic idea that suddenly acquires narrative details.

Cutting on action, then, involves a range of directorial choices somewhat
more complex than simply matching activity from shot to shot. By insisting
that activity is continuous and smoothing its transition from shot to shot, the
director conveys specific information to the audience about the dimensions of
the world of the film. He indicates that place or position mean something very
specific, that location is *consequential*. The audience judges certain shots to
be "next to" others, certain shots to be the outward boundaries of the world of
the film. If the designations "right" and "left" are meaningful, the audience
may feel that activity in one shot flows to or occurs to the right of or to the left
of preceding and succeeding shots, whether these directional indicators have
any meaning in realistic terms or not.

In *The Medicine Bottle* (1909) there are only three units: a room in which a
bottle of poison has been exchanged for a bottle of medicine due to be admin-
istered to a sick granny; a parlor where the mother discovers the mix-up while
visiting friends; and the telephone exchange, where the crucial connection
must be made through a rather lazy crew of telephone operators. This is already a significant variation on the race to the rescue, because instead of rushing home, the mother stays in place, deciding to call the little girl and warn
her not to administer the poison. The intercutting between these three spaces

involves no orienting activity at all, quite a unique situation in so early a film. Intercutting takes over from physical activity to provide the energy of the film, and both the pace of the activity and the pace at which information is revealed to the audience are created by the rhythm of the intercutting. The question "where" is very interesting in this very formal, very curtailed structure because one cannot really resist the feeling that the telephone exchange comes *between* the mother and the child, even if this impression is only the product of the shot order and has no reference in reality at all. This sense of place is the overtonal effect of the relationship between the shots and clearly creates the essential dramatic tension of the film. *The Medicine Bottle* shows that locale in film was beginning to have a completely new definition, which did not necessarily have anything to do with extending space through walking or chasing.

The Medicine Bottle is a fairly simple example of the construction of a dramatic effect by means of radical spatial discontinuity. The film makes the telephone exchange, a space that could apply equally well to any number of films about telephone calling, including a comedy, a crucial link between the more highly specified spaces of the mother and the child. In this way Griffith is able to make a drama of the exchange of information in the same way that he makes drama of the exchange of positions in *Her Terrible Ordeal*. It is this abstract link of communication that determines the relationship between three shots of absolutely discontinuous spaces, and for the first time Griffith was able to make a whole film in which shot order, irrespective of "realistic" geography, was the key to the film's meaning.

The Banker's Daughters (1910) is a kind of "camera" version of *The Lonely Villa:* the idea of the penetration of the home by burglars remains essentially the same as in the earlier film, but without the liberating car chase. In fact, *The Banker's Daughters* harks back to *The Medicine Bottle* in the way that the situation is set up and in the use of the telephone to convey a sense of suspense. This kind of film, especially if stripped of the exterior line of action, depends very heavily on manipulating the audience's attention by yielding or withholding the image that the audience feels to be next in the shot order.

In *The Usurer* (1910) there are three modes of relationship between the usurer and the people he exploits. The first is a physical and directional mode. A mother with a sick child actually leaves her locale and travels to the office of the usurer, a journey made on a straight line to the right. Fainting against a desk in the usurer's office, this woman pushes that desk up against the door of the safe in which the usurer has gone to count his money. Unwittingly, she kills the man. Hers is the only physically active relationship to the usurer in the film, and her location can be described as "to the left of" and "next to" the usurer. The second mode of relationship is a figurative one. A father, distraught with debt, kills himself because of the usurer's hard-heartedness. His place in the film can be described as the position of his image—"where in the chain of shots" or the "shot next to the shot" of the usurer dying in the vault—a juxtaposition that functions as a sort of memento mori. The third mode of relationship is more concrete than the figurative sequence, but does not have any physical, directional link to the locale of the usurer. The shots of a young couple working after hours to pay back their debt to the usurer have the same causal relationship to the shots of the usurer as do the others in the film—he is the reason for their anxiety. But their place in the film is more generally sequential. They appear "then" or "next in the story," specifically when they realize that they are a happy family independently of, but right after, the usurer's death, about which they know nothing.

In *When a Man Loves* (1910) Griffith attempts to create drama from the identification of people with the spaces they occupy. Briefly, this is the story of a young couple who wish to be alone. As is standard with this type of story in Griffith's Biograph films, the father objects, but this time he proposes his own candidate for his daughter's hand. The hero and heroine plan to elope, but when the hero climbs the ladder to the heroine's window, he finds the rival suitor installed in her room. The heroine has been locked away by her father. This "displacement" of the heroine by the rival suitor is the premise of the comedy. The audience knows a surprise is in store for the young man, the exterior shot of whom leads directly to the wrong person. The disparity between the supposed position of the heroine (her accessible bedroom) and her actual position (locked away one room to the right of her bedroom), objectifies the dramatic problem of the film in the kind of lateral structure that first appeared in 1908 in such films as *An Awful Moment* and *The Hindoo Dagger* to provide a surprise or an impact beyond the door-cut. Who cares if the couple elopes? That drama is simply a matter of piling them into a car and taking them through a couple of shots to the fortuitously placed minister. As will be the case in almost all of Griffith's finest films, the humor and charm of *When a Man Loves* is derived from the structure far more than from the material. Griffith perpetuates a comedy of mistaken identities by constructing a situation of erroneous positions. Cutting back and forth, Griffith sets up the proper order of the world: the heroine's bedroom yields to the hero's entry. But when the heroine is displaced and the rival suitor is put in her room, the world of the film is disturbed. Eventually the complications that arise from this exchange of positions are worked out by restoring everyone to his or her proper *place* in the elopement order. This situation is very close to the stage farces in which the comedy arises from the fact that everyone is in the wrong place at the wrong time. Griffith's accomplishment is to have defined "place" in specifically cinematic terms—that is, as shot order. If the three spaces of *When a Man Loves* are considered a unit, the hero is furthest left and the heroine furthest right, with the rival suitor placed "between" them. Although Griffith is working with geographical proximity in *When a Man Loves,* the dramatic tension is built in a structural situation that recalls *The Medicine Bottle*—used in this case to generate comedy rather than drama.

The Unseen Enemy

The ability to create a sense of place helped Griffith solve one of the most persistent problems in his films—the placement of the unseen enemy. This figure haunts the world of Griffith's Biograph films, spying on innocent families, peeking into windows, seeking out hidden fortunes, following faithless wives, husbands, and sweethearts. The watcher-lurkers are usually, but not necessarily, villains. Structurally, they embody the problem of conveying information in the world of the film, since the structural theme of so many of Griffith's films is the coincidence of what the audience knows with the awareness of the characters in the film.

Very simply, the unseen enemy is a way to create tension by suggesting that something perilous exists in the film about which the hero or heroine will have to learn in order to escape with life and honor. The figure of the watcher-lurker conveys this to the audience because it clearly externalizes the threat to the hero or heroine. The process of finding out the truth is the subject of the film.

The problem was to make this figure plausible in terms of film space. In early Griffith Biograph films such as *The Adventures of Dollie, After Many Years, Money Mad,* and *A Rural Elopement* (all made in 1908), the standard solution is to place the unseen enemy a few paces off and pretend that the foreground characters simply do not see him. This sometimes makes the unconscious assertion that people in silent films are deaf and results in such inanities as the lurker practically breathing down the dressing gown of the stolidly oblivious victim, as in *The Girls and Daddy* (1908). The placement of the watcher-lurker poses a serious attack on the illusion of reality that Griffith wished to maintain in his films. A holdover from theater staging, and certainly a convenience, the problem of the unseen enemy is a spatial one. On stage, one may have to accept a panorama in which six feet between pursuer and pursued may stand for sixty yards. As a stage convention, the watcher-lurker stretches credibility but engages the imagination. One accepts the convention because theater, an artifice exercised in limited space, allows such devices.

Six feet on the screen is a much more specific distance. We understand the world to be the stage of screen action, and a character gesticulating wildly six feet behind his supposedly oblivious victim may be supposed to be as mad as she is deaf. The position is an anomaly in the illusion granted to the realistic film. One wonders why the girl in *The Cricket on the Hearth* does not turn around and suspects that it is because the film would then simply end there, and as a result would be undramatic and flat.

The watcher-lurker mars one of Griffith's very best early films, *After Many Years* (1908), the version of Tennyson's "Enoch Arden" so often cited for its innovative "close-up" of Annie Lee. The shipwrecked Enoch, returned home, believes he has confirmed his worst suspicions that Annie Lee has been unfaithful to him in his absence. He follows closely behind her and her "lover" as they stroll up a street. This situation is constructed to take advantage of the disparity of information between the viewer and Enoch. The audience knows that he is wrong, and that Annie Lee is just out walking with a family friend and has not given in to the latter's persistent requests that she give Enoch up for dead. But Enoch does not know, and the fact that this situation must be squeezed into one shot for the sake of economy forces him into a ridiculous screen position that spoils his position in the drama.

Griffith's first solution to this early problem of placement was to cut. Instead of slicing into the basic set-up, however, he provided the lurker with a space by which this figure could be related to his objective without violating the spatial integrity of the basic set-up. One of the best examples of a film in which this intuition results in a specific structure is *In the Window Recess* (1909). As has been discussed, this variation on the conventional story of the besieged family requires the menaced wife to frantically turn away all potential aid, including policemen and her husband, because an escaped criminal is holding her daughter hostage. This man is not crouched behind a potted palm, but "in a window recess" to screen right, to which the audience is referred by the intercutting.

By physically removing the watcher-lurker from his prey's space, Griffith gains a number of dramatic advantages. Tension builds at the doorway that links the two spaces and the audience can be made to anticipate the lurker's intrusion into the frame as a dramatic event. Furthermore, Griffith achieves a very similar effect to that of Enoch following Annie Lee in *After Many Years:* in *In the Window Recess* the lurker is still present in every cut back to the mother because he is implied in every action she performs to turn the neighbors, policemen, and her husband out of the room. Now, however, the imagination of the audience is split between her efforts and a continued interest in the convict's activity beyond the doorway. It is less important that the mother's frantic looks toward the right-foreground doorway convey her "seeing" the convict. What is important is that her looks serve as a point of reference that creates the presence of the watcher-lurker beyond the doorway more really than his presence behind the potted palm in the same frame with her could ever do.

Intercutting to solve the placement of the unseen enemy in its turn suggested new uses for the character, new forms in which it could function dramatically. Both the Wheat King in *A Corner in Wheat* and the usurer in *The*

Usurer (both 1909) represent more sophisticated manifestations of the unseen enemy, the watcher-lurker who threatens the well-being of the characters in the film. The intercutting that relates these megalomaniacs to their victims does not utilize so direct a connection as a doorway. In fact, they never see the people whose lives they threaten. They stalk them down through the film surely, but allegorically, because intercutting indicates to the audience that there is a cause-and-effect relationship between the actions of these men and the ruined lives of the other people in the film. The Wheat King and the usurer are implied in each frame of suffering and anxiety, but the whole picture of human misery caused by their rapacity and hedonism is held only by the viewer making associations between the shots of the film.

Griffith's solution to the problem of the watcher-lurker was threefold: to remove him physically from his victim's space; to recreate his presence there by implication; and to provide him with a spatially probable position from which to operate. The definition of "spatially probable" was to vary from film to film. Of importance here is the fact that Griffith's first impulse in solving the problem of visibility was to provide a new space that anchored the character in a definite place in the world of the film. Intercutting related this place to the other locales in the film.

The watcher-lurker went from a theatrical melodramatic device to a pretext for constructive intercutting and finally to a graphic pointer or indicator in the composition of the frame, a series of steps that many of the devices already mentioned (such as the diagonal and the arch) also followed.

The unseen enemy was still spatially anomolous in the films of 1911 and 1912. In *As It Is In Life* (1910) the father lurks at the scene of his daughter's courtship. Even as late as *The House of Darkness* (1913), in which Griffith is experimenting with shallow focus and other alterations of the image, he still asks the audience to assume that the imperiled woman is either too hard of hearing or playing the piano too loudly to hear a lunatic climb through her window and take a place nearly at her elbow from which to spy and leer. In the context of the realist illusion of film, one could be generous and accept this placement of the figure as metaphorical, but Griffith's insistence on concrete images and events indicates that such allowances are out of the question.

In its final transformation, the figure of the watcher-lurker objectifies the intermingling of concrete and abstract, of composition and construction, that characterizes Griffith's best films. In *Love in the Hills* (1911), for instance, Griffith constructs a scene in which all the lovers of the story are brought together in one location, yet held apart by intercutting. The sequence in question begins with shot 36, a panorama in which a frame of bushes delineates the left foreground as a specific playing area. A country suitor enters and occupies this left fore position. The second country suitor is picked up in motion in the right foreground of a woodland exterior (shot 38). He exits this shot to the left and his action is matched to the entry of a pair of lovers into shot 39.

They travel right to left in the background of an exterior shot that is also masked in the foreground, so that when the second country suitor also enters this shot from the right, he occupies the foreground position to spy on the lovers unseen as the shot becomes horizontally split into two complementary planes of activity. The lovers enter shot 40 (a repeat of set-up 37), in which the first suitor has already concealed himself under a bush in the left foreground. As the lovers look and gesture to the left, it is clear that they do not see this concealed suitor, for nothing in their actions indicates such a recognition. But their gestures do lead to a cut-in on the axis to the first suitor: shot 41 is a magnification of the foreground position and closes this area around the first suitor, hiding him "behind" the cut. This cut relates the first country suitor to the master scene, and the audience can forget that the lovers in motion leftward may unwittingly trip over this man. More important is the fact that this mid-shot with the first suitor looking right introduces the second suitor in a new position, the previously undisclosed space of shot 42, which remains related to the preceding shots only by the second suitor's look left. It is quite obvious from their actions that neither of the two country suitors sees the other; nor do the lovers see either of the suitors. It is just as clear that when the girl starts nervously in shot 43 (37) and looks around, she is responding to the concentration of attention that is pointed at her from right and left, without being aware of why she should be so uncomfortable in this "central" position in the shot order.

If this scene in *Love in the Hills* is understood as a stage in the solution of the problem of the placement of the unseen enemy, it clearly takes advantage of two structural discoveries that Griffith had already made: (1) that the action could be generated from intercutting as long as (2) appropriate indicators of position cemented the sequence together. In *Love in the Hills* Griffith was able to exploit the structural potential of the figure of the watcher-lurker: the fact that this character objectifies the disparity of information between the audience and the characters in the film. The audience wants the unconscious hero or heroine to wake up and recognize the threat posed by the lurker. The result is the generation of anticipation, expectation, and dramatic suspense. The ease with which the audience assembles the three spaces in *Love in the Hills* and instantly interprets the exchange of information that occurs within them is because of the care with which Griffith establishes the graphic relationship among the three shots, making sure that lines of sight seem "natural" even though the space is discontinuous. This easiness is also a tribute to the fact that Griffith had found an expression as economical as the original position of the watcher-lurker (which after all stated the case quite clearly), while overcoming the spatial absurdity of the character's original screen position.

Finally, the character of the watcher-lurker did not always have to be menacing, and Griffith even learned to play with the spatial implausibility of the follower. In *Fisher Folks* (1911), from the moment two lovers quarrel and split up, a secondary lover is on the scene, standing center frame, unseen by the rejected young woman he would gladly comfort, and whose attention he craves. As she pursues her old lover from shot to shot, the hopeful second suitor follows along. There are few shots he does not enter right behind her. Her residual presence in each shot is created by his look, which follows this young woman throughout the film and reinforces the very strong visual bonds that are flung across cuts in *Fisher Folks.* The figure of the doleful suitor is part watcher-lurker in his dogged pursuit of the young woman, but Griffith now uses the conventional following position ironically: the suitor wants nothing so much as to be *seen,* but he occupies an "invisible" screen position.

The Observer: Linking by Look

Directing the look created visibility, and Griffith explored the look from the viewpoints of the character and the audience. Griffith was especially inventive and bold in the use of the look to direct attention within the shot, to direct attention into the shot, and to project these sightlines across the cut into succeeding shots. Long before he brought the camera close enough to witness their ultimate dramatic poignancy, Griffith realized that looks, as graphic entities, were active. Eventually, Griffith came to rely on the look flung across the cut to weld sequences together and produce emotional overtones in the combination of shots that were not "geographically" related. Looking, like the diagonal, like the basic set-up, like discontinuity, like depth of field, is characteristic of Griffith's Biograph work. That Griffith eventually equated the look with attention does not rule out the fact that the object of attention will eventually occupy the same frame as the looker. Griffith first gained an acquaintance with the look as an abstraction that was useful in binding the world of the film. The more "natural" connection between observer and observed does not occur until later in his Biograph period.

As the stage directions of his plays suggest, Griffith was a fan of the well-populated dramatic image. But populations of early films could quickly become mobs pelting through chases or milling about aimlessly in films such as *When Knights Were Bold.* Griffith achieved a choral resonance from the population of his images by exploiting their potential as active observers of the drama. In a narrative sense, these characters "extend the frame" by suggesting the number of other stories that exist in the world of the film. Structurally, their placement suggests that the unity of the film may be built of patterns of thoughts, desires, and hopes as well as patterns of activity.

Observers are a group of people related to the action of the film by the fact that they see it from within the world of the film. These are a remarkably discreet group of presences within the frame, whose involvement ranges from complete uninterest to minor participation in the action of the plot. Most important, observers establish the sight-lines within the frame and help to direct the attention of the viewer in the deep space of the image. One such fellow sits at the side of the road taken by the prodigal to the big city and big trouble in *The Modern Prodigal* (1910). This observer thus serves as a portent of, and ironic comment on, the prodigal's descent and shameful escape from the city that shimmers in the background of shot 2. By the observer's presence, Griffith calls a witness to the fact that a whole "chapter" of a story has passed in the space of a single shot, broken by a title indicating that time has passed.

Beyond the narrative significance of the observer is his or her structural significance. The placement of the observer serves as an index to Griffith's identification of various screen positions as discreet but visible. The observer must be integrated into the mise-en-scène to render the service of his or her look, but must also remain a tonal element in the frame. The discreet observer is usually moved into areas in the frame upon which Griffith feels he can rely. This character thus indicates how Griffith carved out areas of visibility from the deep field.

When discreet observers are physically active, they often work to amplify action occurring in the frame. In these cases, Griffith is always careful to control the population of the frame with a strong graphic plan so that bodies do not create aimless activity. In *The Adventures of Dollie* (1908) two fisher-boys travel the same diagonal that organizes the action toward the foreground of shot 2. The fisher-boys merely extend the diagonal far back into the frame and provide a secondary center of interest to complement the mid-ground left entrance of the gypsy who will steal Dollie from her parents. In the same film, an observer is picked up in transit during the chase after the gypsy, amplifying the momentum of the chase with the extra weight of one more body to burst out of the foreground of the shot before the pursuers pour into the ensuing shot of the gypsy camp.

After he discovered that cutting could take the place of running action in a film, Griffith rarely piles observers into the frame. These combinations of observer and activity in *The Adventures of Dollie* reflect an early instinctive attempt to supplant raw physical activity with more carefully motivated action, although the inclusion of the stranger in the chase also takes advantage of the process of accumulation by which the chase often made its impact.

The Arch

One of Griffith's most enduring graphic plans for the observer was the arch. The construction of an arched space at the back of the set lent a much-needed dimension to the limited studio space and functioned much better as an element of composition than it did as an element of structure. Griffith often used the arch to contain the chorus, and a tension is created in the frame between areas of activity and areas of observation. The "other world" of people and events in the film could be bounded by an arch, a use that was retained as late as the ballroom scene in *Intolerance* (1916).

In *The Lonely Villa* (1909) Griffith explores the tension between the foreground playing area and the arch, which is spatially related to, but emotionally unconnected with, the events that are played out before it. The father takes the mother's frantic phone call for help in a hotel lobby containing an arched space. The intercutting between the mother and the father is slowly amplified by reference to the figures in the arch. Each cut back to the father reveals that another uninterested observer has been lured from the detachment of the arched space by the developing drama. Every time Griffith cuts back to the hotel lobby, another fellow is wandering out, vaguely alarmed, wondering what is going on. Gradually, the background arch and the foreground playing area are bridged by this activity, and Griffith uses the sheer press of bodies around the father to magnify the sense of alarm he feels. What the accumulation of bodies over many shots in the chase tried to accomplish with running activity, Griffith achieved by combining intercutting with the accumulation of bodies in a gradually coalescing space.

The interest of the observer is not always so welcome in the frame. When the arch is employed in *The Voice of the Violin* (1909), it is occupied by a rather too observant maid, who accompanies her mistress to a violin lesson and constantly leaves her discreet position in the arch to interfere primly in the blossoming love affair between the girl and her young violin teacher. In this film, Griffith uses the arch to relate background to foreground comically and ironically. There are no cut-ins to the maid. The arch assures that she will be seen, although the activity she performs to unify the arched space with the foreground is all too intrusive and unwelcome.

In *The God Within* (1912) many observer positions combine to create the effect of constant scrutiny. A young woman becomes pregnant out of wedlock and is forced to seek refuge in the back room of a tavern, where her child is stillborn. Eventually, the grieving young woman is asked to nurse the newborn baby of another woman, who has died in childbirth. To enter the tavern, the young woman is forced to walk through the town's menfolk, congregated in a foreground position in the frame. In the tavern interior, the damning look emanates from the doorway/arch in the background of the shot. The doctor who delivers the living child to the young woman must also break through the crowded exterior foreground to enter the tavern. He, too, is caught in the accumulated effect of the link between exterior and interior. (figs. 80–83) In the exterior, attention is focused back into the shot from the crowded foreground. The more or less central arch/doorway of the interior concentrates attention on the foreground much as does the set-up in *The Voice of the Violin*. No other information about this interior is known beyond that busy doorway, which functions mainly as a funnel of observation and spotlights every entrance into and exit from the interior, just as the crowd in the exterior shot did. The arch

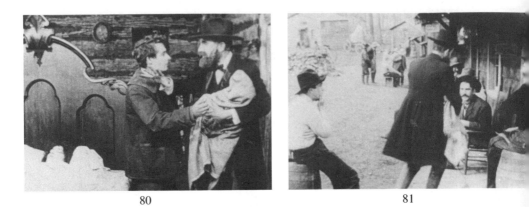

80   81

Figs. 80–83. *The God Within* (1912)—Lateral (sequential)

carries the scrutiny of the town's menfolk into the building with every entrance and exit, although none of these men actually comes into the building or out of the arch to confront the young woman or the doctor, as each passes from the exterior through the arched interior and further right into the back room, where the drama of motherhood is played out.

The observer's look in *The God Within* is transformed from a physical obstruction to a psychological burden as the judgmental look is passed from exterior to interior between the public world of the street and the very private space where the young woman retreats. Structurally, the arch reverses the observer's position in the film so that the look emanating from the arch is the mirror of the gaze directed back into the frame in the exterior. The direction of the observers' focus shifts eight times over the cut from exterior to interior and vice versa in *The God Within,* indicating that by 1912 Griffith could place the observer so surely that these minor characters had transcended their primitive narrative roles. The observer becomes an important device, placed so that no space is allowed to stagnate through the constant repetition required in Griffith's structures. The observer's look constantly refreshes space that might otherwise have been considered merely functional and transitional.

Looking over the Cut

Observers confirm the realism of the film. They focus the attention of the audience on the important information in the frame. Even the cut between exterior and interior in *The God Within* does not disturb the direct relationship between the observer and the object of his attention—quite the contrary. But even in 1908, Griffith began to see how totally this relationship could be *constructed,* how completely the viewer's imagination could be involved.

82   83

   In *The Feud and the Turkey* (1908) the look over the cut signals the cut and
gives graphic reinforcement to the directional force of the activity of breaking
through the boundary of the frame and obtaining the object of attention, the
turkey. This is a minor, but important, example of linking space by looks,
because Griffith does not ever show the object of attention from a matched
("realistic") angle. Pragmatically, this view would call for another camera
set-up to adjust sight-lines, and Griffith rarely had the time to waste on such
niceties. The porch where the turkey hung is also the staging area for the next
thrust of activity, and Griffith opts to maintain this generalized and omniscient
view of that space. But it is also true that the combination of the look with a
line of activity glosses over the disparity of angles between two basic set-ups
and reinforces the realism of the connection between them.
   The *Voice of the Violin* (1909) offers another example of the effect. In
this film Griffith cuts in on the axis of an exterior shot of a New York City
brownstone, thereby tightening the shot around the gaze of a young violinist
looking into an apartment window to see his beloved. He realizes that she
lives in the house he has promised to blow up. The flat studio interior of the
house is given a dimension of reality as it is linked to an exterior shot of a real
street, but more important is the fact that the window focuses the look that
smooths the spatial and angular disparity between these two spaces. When
analyzed separately, these two shots do not "go" together—the hero could not
possibly see the heroine from that angle. Their succession in the chain of shots
forces these two shots to form a unit, the exterior and interior of the same
house, and the look confirms that this perception is accurate.
   The window focuses a look that confirms the "realism" of the link between
two shots even when an analysis of angles, mise-en-scène, and spatial discontinuity between the shots argues against such an opinion. The construction
of *The Voice of the Violin* clearly tends toward the realistic look—the shock

the hero gets when he really sees his beloved in that house. Perhaps Griffith could not practically overcome the disparity of angle and mise-en-scène in this juxtaposition of exterior and interior. But his subsequent treatment of looking over cuts does not seek to solidify the reality of the observer's look over the cut. Rather, Griffith insists on using sight to create even more radically imaginative relationships between shots.

After Many Years (1908) presents the first striking experiment (discussed on p. 40 above). This image of the marooned Enoch is joined to the image of his wife, Annie Lee. Enoch is shown in shot 8, a repeat of the set-up of shot 5 (fig. 8), looking at a locket that presumably contains a picture of Annie Lee. But we do not get that photograph. Instead, Griffith presents the audience with a living portrait: the waist-up shot of Annie Lee looking out of her space, past the camera, waving (fig. 9). This connection cannot be accounted spatially real in any sense, but the conviction of a connection is absolute. Yet the image of the wife is ambiguous. Griffith sets her up in a deliberately closer view of a familiar image, but the audience is caught between interpretations. Is she a mental image representing the husband's memory as he looks at the locket? Is Annie Lee shown coincidentally with Enoch's gaze in parallel time to remind the audience of her faithfulness and constancy? Whether Griffith immediately understood the mechanics of this conjunction the first time he used it, or whether he did not, he never stopped exploring the power of its resonant effect. Two obviously discontinuous shots suddenly cross-reference one another in a cross-temporal, cross-spatial relationship that produces a mental activity: memory, thought.

In *The Salvation Army Lass* (1908) a young man knocks down the lass in shot 14 to stop her from following him. He exits shot 14 left and enters shot 15 right, a strong statement of spatial continuity made by matching directions over the cut. The surprise comes when the young man turns in shot 15 to look right, or "back" in the lass's direction. To press a point somewhat, this look is meant to signal activity, and it signals film activity—a cut back to the lass (shot 16, the set-up in 14 repeated) without any clear indication of the distance between the two shots. This interaction between 15 and 16 (14) blends the effects of *After Many Years* with those of *The Feud and the Turkey*. The look is felt to be a realistic link over the cut. But in the conjunction between the two shots, an aftereffect arises: the hint that this look "back" is also a mental image of the lass lying on the sidewalk, a memory invoked at the moment the young man is about to commit the crime that the lass tried to prevent. The alternative interpretation of the combination of three shots is that the young man is conscience-struck by the memory of his action, not the actual sight of the lass lying on the pavement, and returns to her on the basis of this moral twinge. This interpretation is the less strongly stated—one might call it a nuance. But with the use of the look as a link between shots characterized by discontinuity that nuance appears in Griffith's work, and visibility acquires a new definition: the audience can "see" what the character thinks as well as what the character does.

The theatrical window was one of the earliest indications that characters were coming from some real space, not just the rear of a set. In films such as *The Tavernkeeper's Daughter* (1908) an exterior could be suggested by having an "off-set" character look into a window to view the interior of the shot. In *A Drunkard's Reformation* (1909) Griffith acknowledges this stage convention. In the course of the temperance play that is part of *A Drunkard's Reformation,* one of the stage characters looks through a window "into" the set to view the events that are occurring on stage. But by 1909 Griffith had radically shifted the position of the watcher at the window, redefining the watcher's gaze in combination with the cut. Extended over the cut, the physical gaze through the window becomes "looking" and demonstrates that affective attention as well as physical links can unify the world of the film. Griffith discovered the power of the window as an opening that suggests spatial extension. He wedded that effect to the cinematic power of the link between the look and the cut that projects attention "across the miles" regardless of actual distances. By this means, Griffith gained control of both the physical and the affective aspects of attention.

The faithful wife in *A Drunkard's Reformation* is used to advance the action to succeeding shots, regardless of the reality of space or the passage of time. Her look out of the window of her parlor directs the viewer to the shot of the drunken father sitting in a beer hall—an image she sees only abstractly, in her imagination. Griffith accomplishes this effect in a five-shot sequence at the beginning of the film. The mother stands at the window waiting and watching for her husband, who is shown carousing in a saloon. This dramatic effect is not merely the aftershock of the juxtaposition of two shots between which a powerful connection has been made. It is reinforced with activity. The mother and child walk right to approach the window and look out (shots 1 and 2); the father is shown in the bar (3); the mother and daughter turn from the window and walk left (4, a repeat of the set-up of 1); the father echoes their movement by exiting the bar left background in 5 (3). Only in shot 6 (1) do all the characters physically occupy the same space for the first time.

In *A Drunkard's Reformation* Griffith confidently projected the look across the cut in a pattern of intercutting in which the shots were bound by a mental, rather than physical, probability. When the mother and daughter look right, in a direction that would "connect" their gaze with the figure of the father, the audience surely understands that the mother and child do not physically see him. When the combined looks of father and daughter later connect with a real object of attention, the temperance play, the effect of the sequence is that the audience understands what both characters "think" of the temperance melodrama. The look is such a strong graphic binder that, even over obviously discontinuous spaces, there is no doubt that the father is the object of attention in the first sequence as much as the stage play is in the second sequence—though in *A Drunkard's Reformation* there is no locket to sanction such an interpretation.

These looks create two strains of dramatic activity in *A Drunkard's Reformation*. The stage and film melodramas tell the same story, but the temperance play is built of physical violence and madness, while the violence of the film, particularly as it takes advantage of gazing and glancing, is much more psychological. Shot 6 (1) is the first point at which any physical violence is used to depict the father's debased condition. One of the most striking differences between *A Drunkard's Reformation* and the temperance play it encloses is that the dramatic emphasis is shifted from physical brutality to anxiety.

The placement of the wife at the window was a stepping stone to further developments in the binding of the world of the film with eye-beams. Although Griffith also sought to establish eye-contact at realistic angles in later films, from *A Drunkard's Reformation* onward he realized that this time- and space-bridging link by look is also powerful because sight-lines are so graphically convincing. While there are exceptions, the look is usually meant to be a definitive link between shots, a mark that creates continuity over discontinuity. Far from meaning an extension of any particular space, the look is used to give the definitive point of reference between related spaces.

When intercutting occurs between a "static" point and an allied line of activity, the function of the look becomes even more impressive. There is the feeling that the activity of the film is drawn along the sight-line almost as if the concentration of attention in the look were powerful enough to draw the person being thought of back to the thinker. *The Honor of His Family* (1909), *A Drunkard's Reformation* (1909), *Fisher Folks* (1911), and *Through Darkened Vales* (1911) all share this quality.

When the young woman in *The Battle* closes the door on the parade that passes her house at the beginning of the film, she weeps for the temporary loss of her beloved. It is the contrast between two looks—the public (crowd) and the private (girl), both of which the audience shares—that strikes and moves in the midst of the excitement of the film's first moments. This relationship between public and private, omniscient and sympathetic, viewing is the structural theme of *The Battle*. Exteriors where action occurs are constantly referred back to the expectant gaze of the young woman at the window, though no effort is made to adjust angles to simulate a more "realistic" view of the action.

The relationship between looks and the position of characters in respect to sight-lines is a constant structural theme of Griffith's Biograph period. The presence of affective relationships formed by looks waxes and wanes, but whether it is organizing principle or nuance, the importance of the look is attested to by its continued use. In *The Expiation* (1909), for instance, a man pens a letter to his beloved in shot 9. The cut to shot 10, the sweetheart, is signaled by the man's look left. The woman to whom the letter is addressed appears to the left in shot 10 and moves right "toward" the man's look. The relationship of sequentiality is the stronger link between these two shots: the audience understands them to come one after another and so belong together in the same film. But the look and the woman's movement toward it reinforce the serial relationship between the shots by suggesting that the cut occurs as the man thinks of the woman he has written to, and there is the implication in her movement that the thought is reciprocated.

The look in Griffith's films almost always resonates between concrete and abstract, a fact even more apparent when the look is not metaphorical or figurative, but attached to a real object. In *Simple Charity* (1910) much of the film's activity is created in the intercutting between shots of a young woman and an old couple she pities. Spatially, their positions are separated, though proximity is clear: she is in the hallway outside their apartment and there is a door between them. She looks at the closed door. Griffith cuts to the other side of the door where the old couple sit. Although the spatial relationship is not really in question, this connection employs the same abstraction Griffith used to extend the look "across the miles." The viewer believes that he knows what the young woman is thinking about the old folks.

In *A Plain Song* (1910) Edith is a lonely young woman kept from regular friendships by her duty to her parents, one of whom is blind. In the first sequence, shots 2–8, Edith stands in the open doorway of her house gazing right. A title, "Lonely," might have sufficed to express her mood, followed by her image at the door looking; young couples passing; she closing the door. But Griffith needed no title. (There is none in the 16mm film kept by the Library of Congress.) Griffith conveys that feeling of solitude in a sequence of shots. He places Edith in the doorway looking right (4); couples pass "before" her, though actually coming toward the camera in a line slightly angled through the frame to the left foreground (5); the young woman nods (6–4); and the street scene is repeated (7–5). The sequence returns to Edith (8–4) for a third time as she closes the door. Her moment of loneliness, a fact that might have been portrayed in one shot, is made into a drama of three distinct moments relayed by the direction of her look, until the composite relationship between the shots conveys the dimension as well as the fact of her situation.

Griffith was able to use windows to relate watchers more directly to ensuing shots of activity as well as to imply that the ensuing shot is the result of the watcher's imaginative thought. The position of the watcher at the window implies a relationship between beholder and beheld, the resolution of which is worked out gradually in a line of activity. The resolution between static and dynamic positions is the narrative energy of the film. Eventually, Griffith re-

84   85

Figs. 84–87. *The Girl and Her Trust* (1912)—Windows (condensed)

turns to the look projected from "outside" the interior, reversing the look
through the window. But by this time the abstraction of the look is being used
to unify different shots related to the same location.

As in *The Voice of the Violin*, characters appear outside the window looking in, but now the relationship of this look to the interior space is considerably more complex. In *A Country Cupid* (1911) a menacing lunatic looks in
the window of a schoolhouse and sees that the schoolmarm is alone. One of
the most obviously remarkable things about the use of the window in this
sequence (shots 37–41) is the inefficiency of the set-up to express anything like
a realistic point of view. The audience is presented with the same "omniscient"
view of Edith, the schoolmarm, that has been the view of the schoolroom all
along, and the graphic contact between observer and observed still lacks the
adjustment of angle that would confirm the reality of looking and observing.
One reason why Griffith may not have been looking for this adjustment, even
so late in his Biograph period, is that by 1911 the window had become a
proven cinematic link. Looks could be directed through the window at succeeding shots and related to preceding material. Windows became indicators
of the combination of immediate and imaginative relationships between spaces
in the world of the film, whether the confirming angle marked that relationship as "real" or not.

The use of windows in *The Girl and Her Trust* (1912) is especially interesting in this regard. Beginning with an interior that is nearly an homage to *The
Great Train Robbery* (Edison, 1903) (or perhaps just a comment on how difficult it still was to manage interiors nearly ten years after Porter's film), Griffith
gives a window view of a train pulling into a station, and then proceeds to
create a spatial composite of the interior and exterior shots of the station and
station house that demonstrates how far he had come from the initial desire to

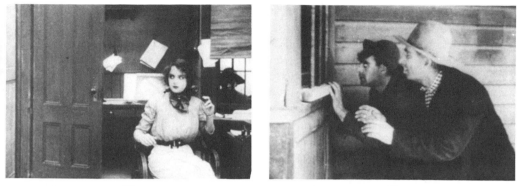

86   87

use the window to provide an extra dimension of realism to the interior of the stage.

By *The Girl and Her Trust* Griffith had totally reversed the utility of the window. Instead of amplifying the interior spaces with an extra measure of realism, the window creates a relationship between the interior spaces and exterior spaces of one location that combines the views of that location into a unified stage of dramatic activity. The window controls the ebb and flow of dramatic information that advances the narrative, but the look directed through the window also controls the viewer's ability to understand as a whole space the group of shots in which the dramatic event is presented. The fragmentation of the scene creates its anxiety. The looks ensure the spatial unity that intensifies that feeling.

The later Biograph films are typically divided into two movements, which can generally be characterized by the spatial opposition closed:open and the narrative opposition siege:chase. The interior (closed) space of *The Girl and Her Trust* is initially besieged by window. The telegraph office in this film consists of two interior spaces, and both of these spaces are accessible at first only to the intruder's gaze (figs. 84, 87). The windows in each interior room provide a view of the money being placed in the strongbox (shot 24, the set-up of shot 2 repeated) (fig. 85), and of the girl alone in the office (shot 49, the set-up of shot 1 repeated) (fig. 86). As the looks come from both the left (shot 23) and the right (shot 41), they create the same sort of composite stare that caught the young woman in *The God Within*. Taken together, these looks set the sight lines of tension across the interiors that make up the telegraph office and this occurs before any narrative action in the siege takes place. Most important, shots 23 and 40 (exteriors) cannot be related to any realistic point of view of the related interiors. The girl eventually sees the lurkers at her window in the background of shot 49, but an understanding of their position in the exterior space of the train station depends wholly on the resolution of the interior and exterior positions of the crooks, a matter of some importance for an understanding of the dynamic of the siege—that is, when and where the villains will break into the station house. The windows in this case provide a number of fronts on which the interiors are assaulted. They are also the bridge to the exterior space of the train station, for no shot of the exterior space fully reveals anything further about the dimensions of the train yard.

In the lover's exchange in *Love in the Hills,* a suitor and his country lass, related in a conversational passage of intercutting, both wind up looking left in their respective shots. This graphic indication suggests that they do not face each other over the cut, information that directly conflicts with the plot information that they are facing each other, screaming. It is true that looks do not seem to be Griffith's major structural concern in the creation of this sequence of verbal arguing. The eye is often drawn to the connectors and away from the center of the frame as Griffith displays an 11-shot battle of wits. This drama might have been attempted in one or two shots in which the guy would grab the lass and she would struggle and break away from him. But Griffith first separates the lovers (shots 4–7), then joins them in shot 8, and then separates them again on a dramatic reverse at the young woman's exit left and entry left with her back to the camera. The tension of the argument is conveyed with shortened shots and abrupt movements that precipitate cuts in no more than twenty frames (roughly a second). Interestingly, the tonal structure of the argument is allowed to confound the coherence of the sight-lines.

Griffith may have valued the effect of the reverse far more than he cared about the link between shots formed by the matched glances in *Love in the Hills* (1911 was also the year of *The Lonedale Operator,* another film that has a high incidence of reversing directions and producing seemingly unmatched actions over cuts). But so strong is the theme of looking in Griffith's films that an effect is almost always created whether willed or no. In *The Unchanging Sea* (1910), when looks do not meet "across the miles," the distance between the lost husband and the faithful wife seems to widen with the suggestion that he has forgotten and cannot or will not remember her. In *Fisher Folks* (1911) each entrance of the jilted sweetheart is preceded by the clear indication that she has seen her honey with another girlfriend, and her pursuit after them from shot to shot is reinforced by the pathetic second suitor who tags along at her heels, desperately wishing she would look back and recognize him.

Griffith becomes so comfortable with action projected along a look that he could make this structure the basis of the flow of activity through the world of the film. *The Female of the Species* (1912) has already been discussed in this context, but the look is used to advantage in a number of the desert films of 1912. In *Man's Lust for Gold* (1912), for instance, the look is combined with a very old idea about directional probability, backtracking, to plot a false trail across the spaces in the sequence of shots from 47 to 58. A claim jumper appears in an already familiar space (shot 47, repeating the set-up of shot 25) to dig for gold. This shot is followed by shot 48 (46), in which the real owners of the gold mine are shown to be on the claim jumper's track. In shot 48 (25), the claim jumper first travels to the left boundary of the frame, then backs out of the shot to the right, plotting a false trail across the frame, which he hopes the pursuers will take. He then backs into a new space (shot 50). This man is now separated from 49 (25) by a cut, but remains linked to the space by his look toward his pursuers. By 1912 the sense of the reality of that look could be maintained in this thoroughly arbitrary, landmarkless desert space because a doubly reinforced sense of direction relates it to the familiar space of 49 (25). Although the convention embodies a wild abstraction, the *sense* of realism, of the fact that the man is looking at his pursuers, is very strong, as is the feeling that he is hidden from them three times over: by the bush "behind" which he crouches in the foremost area of the shot; by the cut; and by the falsely plotted trail out of the frame. All three veils are interposed between the watcher-lurker and his pursuers, while the visibility of each of the parties and their relationship to one another in the world of the film are not compromised. So nice is Griffith's apprehension of this relationship that he does not worry about using shot 50, where the lurker crouches, as a resolution to this sequence: the pursuers travel through its background once more in the correct direction to continue the pursuit, although they miss the object of their search, the man "hidden" in the foreground.

True to Griffith's method, no device disappears, though it may be trans-formed by a new use. In *A Welcome Intruder* (1913) the look again passes over a cut, supposedly creating eye-contact. The connection is ostensibly straightforward, except for the interposition of a foreign element in the se-quence by which the eye-contact is suddenly and boldly transformed. In shot 17 a father stands on his front porch to say good-bye to his child for the day (fig. 88). His exit right from 17 is connected to shot 18 with an entry left and an exit right (fig. 89). Shot 18 ends with the entrance of the ne'er-do-well who will kidnap the child. He stays in 18 at the cut (fig. 90). The father's walk continues left to right into a new space (shot 19), where he turns to stare left and wave (fig. 91). The feeling that he is waving to the child, whom he really sees, is undoubted, yet when he turns to leave, walking to the background, the next shot given to the viewer is a repeat of 18, where the villain stands and also casts a stare left (fig. 92). Only as this villain begins to turn right in 20 (18) does the realistic object of the father's greeting appear. Shot 21 is pared down to child size, and shifted to the right, but is essentially the familiar space of the porch (17) and shows the child's returning wave (fig. 93). The sequence ends with a repeat of 18 where the villain continues his movement right and enters the bar (fig. 94).

One cannot resist the thought of Griffith actively playing with the realism of eye-contact in this sequence. At least he knew enough about the power of

Figs. 88–94. *A Welcome Intruder* (1913)—
Exposition (sequential)

88

sight-lines to withhold the object of attention long enough to interpose a "foreign" object (the villain) between the father and the child. This structure introduces the villain without obstructing or even disturbing the line of sight between the father and the child. The juxtaposition of these three shots becomes much more than a daddy waving to his child, a sweet moment though that is. A rash of implications breaks out in this combination of three shots that is unconfined by the realism of the look that cements them into a unit. While there is no doubt that eye-contact between father and child is accomplished, there is also an echo of the really "blind," but imaginative, stare of the mother in *A Drunkard's Reformation.* Although the father seems to look "past" him, the villain is introduced in a "central" position between father and child. There is a sense that the villain, too, has seen the father and the child in a significant way and a sense of presentiment, of consequence is injected into a simple, everyday action. When the villain abducts the child, it seems fated.

The second action sequence of *Swords and Hearts* (1911), the siege of the house, begins with a look. Jennie, the heroine, stares forward (shot 40). Soldiers ride (shot 41). The next shot is an interior (shot 42), the reintroduction of the familiar space of the parlor, shortly to be besieged. Jennie's shot is repeated, this time with her movement left, out of the shot, linked to Ben, the faithful servant, leaving the parlor to the right. The siege sequence follows this passage. Jennie next rides into a new shot, and Ben steps left into that same space in one of those coincidences of proximity that the viewer can only feel to be logical because both of these characters have been following absolutely continuous lines of activity in respective chains of shots that "logically" lead to such a conjunction of positions. At this point in the sequence (shot 62), Hugh, the hero, exits his sweetheart's mansion and looks left. Although he is only looking for his horse, that lightning sense of linkage between all the principals of this film is communicated in the conjunction of direction and sight-line.

89

90

91

92

93

94

During the course of Griffith's Biograph period, the look becomes more surely realistic in its directionality, but acquires overtones of contemplation, of rumination. A moment of privacy is maintained at the same time that the dimensions of the world of the film are being defined for the viewer. It is this dualism that finally marks Griffith's use of looking and observing. Having begun to use the look in an ambiguous way in his earliest films, perhaps of necessity, he never lost the habit or the inclination to retain the element of abstraction as part of the act of observation in his films. This allows him to develop a theme of the relationship between visual and emotional "sightedness" and create such tension around figures that are centrally placed in the frame but unseen by the characters whose attention they crave. In films such as *The Mills of the Gods* (1909), *The Awakening* (1909), *The Light That Came* (1909), and, most poignantly, *Through Darkened Vales* (1911), this tension between visibility and invisibility is the substance of the film. The utter, nerve-shattering revelation of her husband's infidelity is communicated to the young wife in *The Mothering Heart* in the exchange of looks between her husband and the vamp in a nightclub. Finally, although it is somewhat outside the scope of this discussion, the mooning sentry in *The Birth of a Nation* (1915) presents a delicious variation on the theme of looking that goes all the way back to some of Griffith's earliest Biograph films. This amorous soldier is related to all the Biograph characters whose resonant glances reflect the emotional depth of a particular dramatic moment. But by 1915, though the sentry practically steps on Elsie's skirts, his look is never spatially ridiculous. As he admires Elsie, but does not gain her notice, he recalls all the Biograph characters who were centrally placed in the frame, invisible to the objects of their attention, but visible to the audience. In this role the sentry's look is really meant for the audience's notice—a third-party exchange of appreciation for the heroine. It is Griffith's final comment on the spatial realism of the connection of sight-line to concrete object of attention.

On the most basic level, the look combined with activity over the cut reinforces the audience's orientation in the world of the film. When the look is an indicator of relationship between shots that emphasize position, a sense of place occurs that is real only in the context of the film. The look that smooths the actual discontinuity between the spaces of the film asserts that one shot is no further from another than one person can see, even if, according to the mise-en-scène, that look could not possibly be physically connected with the object of interest. But this was precisely Griffith's accomplishment: he defined "sight-lines" to mean that positions in the film are clear—that is, visible *to the audience*.

Time, Pace, Duration, Speed

As he strove to encompass larger dramatic subjects in his Biograph period, Griffith became occupied with the problem of time. He discovered very early that a cut might expressively interfere with the duration of an activity. This is to say that while Dollie's barrel floating down the river and over the rapids has a dramatic dimension, the real-time duration of this process drags against its inherent kinetic effect. In order to heighten the effect, Griffith sought to express, not only incidents, but whole histories made of incidents in the short space of a 14-minute film. The expressive restructuring of a dramatic event on the screen cuts into and alters its real-time duration, so he needed a means to signal the passage of time to his audiences.

Many signals would be introduced to indicate the passage of time in his Biograph films. Children would grow up and parents age. Furniture would be moved to depict a new era in a familiar space, such as occurs between shots 10 and 11 in *Faithful* (1910). Clocks had become an important element of mise-en-scène in many films by 1907, not always used very precisely. "In *Lost in the Alps* (Edison, 1907), the mother worries about her tardy children, . . . the clock shows 6:05 (she pointedly looks at it, calling our attention to the time). *Later,* one cannot ignore the clock's indication of the *same time* when we return to the set. . . . *Father's Lesson* (Hepworth, 1908) similarly presents a clock that seems painted onto the set but has moveable hands to indicate a different time whenever we return to that set (three times.)" [5] In *The Fatal Hour* (1908) Griffith presents the heroine tied up in a room with a large clock. The movement of the hands of the clock indicates how close she is to being blown up by the infernal machine the villains have set to destroy her. In *The Country Doctor* (1909) a clock appears in the hands of the distraught mother to indicate that the situation is becoming temporally acute.

The passage of time would be fade-signaled in *Fools of Fate* (1909), where the introductory passage of "meeting the stranger" is separated from the rest of the film by a fade. The device is not used with absolute precision: one understands only that some time has passed, without specifically knowing how long it takes for the crisis between husband and wife to develop over their new-found friend. But the use of the fade in *Fools of Fate* demonstrates Griffith's interest in developing a wide range of signals to clarify the passage of time in his films.

To convey the passage of time as a dramatic process, however, involved more than an assertion of mise-en-scène, a statement by title, or an effect such as a fade. What Griffith eventually settled for, within the constraints of the one- and two-reelers preferred by the Biograph executives, was the moment-by-moment development of a plot described in sequences of activity, interwoven by means of referential bridges between those sequences. While the temporal statement lost its specificity in these bridges, the audience's orientation in the world of the film was retained, and the temporal stage was set for the next moment-to-moment development of a series of incidents.

Shot Order

Shot order and the rhythm in which shots appeared before the audience played a part in the development of a sense of time in Griffith's films. When the barbarian Ingomar is sent off on a false trail by his enemies, the spatial mistake (he takes the "wrong" exit from the shot) can be interpreted as a loss of time as well as a step in the wrong direction. While the villains are escaping with the heroine (shot 15), Ingomar must take the time to retrace space 14 (shot 16) before he is on the "right" path to her rescue once again.

Griffith first learned that the repetition of shots in order, barring for the moment any intervention by editing the action through those spaces, imposes the rhythm of routine on a sequence of shots. The unity of an exterior with an interior can make a temporal statement, particularly when linked with the chain of shots extending a line of activity through the world of the film. The child's walk in *What Drink Did* (1909) offers an excellent example of such a structure. From shot 21 (the house exterior) to shot 26 (the saloon, introduced in shot 6), a little girl searches for her father. Thereafter, the link between the locales of the film, house and barroom, is formed by passage through these exterior shots. Linking significant exteriors with interiors and repeating the pattern in the child's walk gives a clear and simple picture of the dramatic opposition of the film, animated by a line of physical activity that literally keeps the film moving. *What Drink Did* is a cycle. It begins and ends with an expression of family unity. The degradation of the father and the resulting accidental death of his child becomes a historical process worked out by enclosing a repetitive activity (a child's walk) in a frame of family portraits. Banishing the outright allegorical stage play that brings the father to his senses in *A Drunkard's Reformation* (1909), Griffith confines the activity of *What Drink Did* to the banal and grinding routine of a child returning to a bar to call her father home. What Griffith approaches in *What Drink Did* is an effective structural mechanism in which "normal, daily" activity takes on a dramatic burden. A child walking is neutral activity in itself, but the film, climaxing in a brutal tragedy and encapsulated by two highly significant evocations of family unity, makes a leap toward greater significance.

The more often any chain of shots is asserted in the same relationship, the easier it is to "read" that chain, because the audience becomes accustomed to the relationships between the shots. *The Country Doctor* (1909) contains a core of repeated images in the walk that stands in contrast to the opening panoramic shots. An interior/exterior unit defining the locale of the doctor's house is linked to an exterior/interior unit that defines the locale of the other family in the film. Although both interiors have entrances in the left background, if the walk from the doctor's house to the house of the other sick child is considered a composite line of activity, the picture is a passage composed of two opposing directions. This opposition actually represents the general movement of the film, inasmuch as these directions are foreshadowed at the beginning of the film in the movement of the pan to the right through the valley to the doctor's house and echoed in the leftward panning retreat from the doctor's house and back to the valley at the film's end. This directional opposition is reinforced every time the doctor must go from one "end" of his journey between sick beds to the other. Passage through the exterior/interior units of the film is both rhythmical and easy to "read" because the flow of activity in the shot order, once established, is not altered. The fact that the "traveling spaces" are of a fairly uniform duration only underscores the equation that the audience is asked to make between the space to be traversed and the span of time between the two houses. As time literally runs out for the sick child in the doctor's house, the orderly passage of people across the two exterior spaces becomes maddeningly long.

At the outset of the story, the doctor's beloved child falls ill. This is immediately countered by the portrayal of the household of the second little girl of the film. The dramatic opposition of the film is posed to the audience in the juxtaposition of these two shots: should the doctor have to choose, which child will he save? Shots 4 and 5, the sick rooms, will be the poles of the doctor's walk. Their similarity is reinforced by the identity of the mise-en-scène, at least insofar as the positions of the children (foreground) and the crucial doorways (left background) through which the doctor must pass are concerned. It is the doctor who is forced to take the wider view of the film and to go from his own child to his duty at the bedside of another, for illness is not particular. The composition of the interiors makes other universal statements about the dramatic situation: the motherly need to nurture and protect is stated as a quality shared by the women in the film, and this statement emphasizes the isolation of the father/doctor's tragically split position.

The exterior images of *The Country Doctor*—the running spaces between the houses—create a tempo, an awareness of time as a factor in the drama. Each time the doctor or the housemaid who recalls him to his own child exits one of the houses, each must traverse a known series of spaces. Every time they return to the doctor's house, the two exteriors must be covered, and the exterior of the doctor's house is elided only once in the film.

For the viewer, the structure of *The Country Doctor* produces a compression of space between comparative portraits, and an expansion of space in the frantic, but stable, walking from one portrait to the other. It is in the comparison between these two statements that the pace of the film is created. The cutting pattern requires the audience to work, while the actors, except for the doctor and the housemaid, are for all practical purposes relatively motionless in a compositional and directional pattern. It is the audience that is directed to the doorways by the looks of the anxious mothers, the panicked flight of the housemaid, and the doctor's determined walk from one child to the other. It is the audience, not the character, that experiences the pastoral majesty of the enclosing pan that lifts the story to the level of a universal statement. It is, above all, the audience that understands that these events are only particulars in the all-embracing generality of the world of the film.

In *The Lonely Villa,* Griffith discovered that how long an event lasts on the screen is purely a result of the relationship between shots, rather than a function of the activity in those shots themselves. Shot order can make statements about duration. Since the viewer eventually knows how many rooms and how many doors constitute the locale of the siege, Griffith has given a gauge of the fact that time is of the essence. The shots of the father are very important to the overall sense of time in the film, but their number is directly related to the rhythm of assault and the regrouping of the burglars in the house. If the viewer knew the sequence of shots that led from the villa to the hotel, there would be a very exact sense of "when" the father was nearing the house. The viewer could judge "how close" by the number of shots successfully retraced. As it is, the tryptich must indicate when the father *must* come home. The shots of the father convey only that he is still on the way. Griffith had discovered that the duration of an event is a product of structure. Passage of time ultimately depends on the *way* the audience is involved in an evolving sequence of shots.

Griffith's later Biograph films give the impression of great speed. There is a notable increase in the number of shots (from the 13 shots of *The Adventures of Dollie* to the 111 shots of *Death's Marathon*). Griffith was able to improve the rate of cutting in later films by creating "readable" and probable continuity. The faster the audience can sense the structure in a suite of images, the more cuts can be made and the more fluid the films seem to be, especially if the viewer's eye is guided through the film along the paths of least resistance by the flow of activity from shot to shot. Griffith's continuity is based on reliable suites of images connected along the lines of least resistance, and this alone speeds up the activity in his films. But Griffith also devised means by which the realistic duration of an action could be curtailed with no sacrifice of realistic effect.

In *The Ingrate* (1908), although the course of the chase is mapped out from left background to right foreground, Griffith tries to make continuity in the chase order by having one person's exit from his shot "continue" a related line of activity instead of repeating a space. In other words, the pursuer does not repeat the chain of images laid out by the pursued. The viewer has no way of knowing whether the man trying to recover his kidnapped wife is on the "right" track. But the kidnapper and the husband each alternately travel from left to right across their respective images, and this gives a feeling of surface continuity to the discontinuous body of the chase. The potential spatial confusion is not as important as Griffith's intuition that the surface of continuity could unify deliberately discontinuous lines of activity. There is actually less raw activity in *The Ingrate* than in a film such as *The Call of the Wild,* made earlier that year—the relatively slow canoe race of *The Ingrate* cannot match the speed and volume of the horses chasing around in the earlier film. But in *The Ingrate* Griffith finds a way to circumvent the laborious recapitulation of each image by pursuer and pursued.

The sense of "goings on" in *The Ingrate* is increased because the audience's attention is productively split between interest in the shot at hand and a sense that an allied line of activity is exerting a certain thrust somewhere "else" in the film. This pressure could be immediately exerted by a character against an entrance/exit cut, or the action may remain to be completed in another shot. *The Ingrate* suggests that these cuts on action could even be "displaced"— that is, that continuity could be built by having character *B* continue the *line* of activity initiated by character *A,* although the viewer knows that the *spaces* each travels through are not connected. Although the spatial displacement of such a structure is potentially disorienting, Griffith proved that surface continuity could actually increase the efficiency of the narrative and the scope of the film. New information about both *A* and *B* could simultaneously be conveyed along one reliable line of activity.

Griffith had found a means to express more information in less space, a discovery that broadened the narrative time of his films. In *Fools of Fate* (1909) he was faced with the problem of dramatizing a series of expository events that precede the actual drama of the film. Since he must compress these events into a small amount of reel-time, Griffith utilizes displaced cuts on action to achieve a temporal ellipsis while preserving the sense of place and the flow of activity in the sequence.

The first eight shots of *Fools of Fate* are devoted to depicting the relationship between a man on a hunting trip and the man who saves his life. This sequence ends in a new woodland space, from which the first man exits left, leaving the stranger alone. The next sequence begins with the hunter's wife exiting a familiar space, the domestic exterior seen at the film's beginning (shot 9 repeats the set-up of shot 1). She leaves through the right foreground, as did her husband when he first left the house to go hunting. She meets the stranger in town and they exit the town image together through the right foreground, entering a tighter shot of a bridge, dramatically enhanced by the same kind of panoramic view that served as a backdrop for the first alienated wife in Griffith's films (in *The Planter's Wife,* made in 1908). The wife in *Fools of Fate* falls for the stranger.

Both the husband and the wife in *Fools of Fate* take expository walks from their home into the world of the film to meet and become involved with the same stranger. At the conclusion of the expository walks, Griffith shows the economy possible by employing spatial displacement. The wife's exit from the panorama through the right foreground is joined to the husband's entrance into the interior of a house that is revealed to be his own when the wife re-enters set-up 1 (at shot 13, the house exterior), and then enters the house interior (set-up 12 repeated at shot 14). Her entrance into the interior winds up the expository sequence of *Fools of Fate*.

The beauty of this sequence is that the husband enters the house in a way that reintroduces him into the world of the film smoothly and introduces a new space (the house interior, which will recur in the film) on the tail of another action: the wife's exit from a panorama to which the husband's activity is related only by the continuity of action. Griffith slips the husband, lost to the film for three shots, back into the film smoothly at just the right affective moment—the point at which he is betrayed—and the wife is used to reassert the basic logic of the locale from which both ventured out so unhappily. The economy of the structure makes room for elaboration—a more fully developed narrative picture.

Perhaps the most frivolous and delightful use of this method of expanding drama and retaining clarity by alternating the carriers of the film's activity occurs in *Love among the Roses* (1910). This film is trivial in everything except its facility and grace of movement, and these qualities serve very well to animate a film story that involves exchanges of identities, fortunes, and affections between two pairs of lovers walking through a particular garden on a particular day. Ease and grace are at the heart of this film about fiancé-swapping, and the means of accomplishing a happy resolution is the invisible cutting amongst the characters: from the beginning of the film all entrances are continuations of a previous exit and a lover is picked up or exchanged in transit. Only Mary Pickford stands still in the repeated set-up of shot 8, a stable point around which the merry-go-round revolves until the correct pairs of lovers emerge from the garden.

The smooth, matched cutting in *Love among the Roses* is the result of Griffith's long-practiced sense of directional continuity. In the few instances where he mars a line of activity, he is reinforcing the lovely velocity of some lover's earnest flight from the frame. In *Love among the Roses* Griffith shows an elegant knack for the kind of romantic comedy that consists of smooth paths to the heart of the beloved laid on straight lines through the heart of the frame. An ironic twist is provided when the winning lover rather than the jilted one succumbs to jealousy. Could this character have stood above this lovers' maze of crossing paths and crossed affections, he would have seen what the audience sees, that all the visual paths of the film are leading to the right heart-lands.

Love among the Roses is a wonderful example of action-generated space. Increasingly in Griffith's work the number of spaces traversed (and therefore the number of shots and the number of cuts between them) has less to do with the display of the plot and more and more to do with the dynamic tension building and resolving within the structure of the world of the film. The kinds of connections that unify *Love among the Roses* also occur in *The Marked Time-Table* (1910) at the transitions between sequences of shots. For instance, at the juncture of shots 39 and 40, the link is made by having one person complete another's activity over the cut. As it happens, the larger percentage of crosses from one shot to another in this film are not matched, although there are entrances and exits in all but six shots and the film has only eight basic set-ups, used fifty-four times.

The unifying scheme of *The Marked Time-Table* is a hybrid of surface continuity and the kind of "doubling" of actions that normally occurs in the chase. For instance, the sequence of shots 23–30 is constructed by having character *B* simply echo the actions of character *A* in respective shots. This means that the mother walks into a room, for instance, to have the son echo the direction of this action in a different, but allied, space. To have her leave her room and follow that exit with the son's departure from his shot seems to be the basic structural logic of this film. And the boy's actions—his entrances and exits—unify the first sequence. Whoever else enters and leaves a space, he is at least accompanying them. Another director might have shown the entirety of one character's action and followed it with the entirety of the other's, but Griffith insists on asserting the relationship between characters by interweaving the courses of their actions.

Displaced cuts on action allow Griffith to suggest the pace of an event without having to be absolutely specific about the span of time. *The Broken Doll* (1910) offers a good example of this effect. An Indian child who is sympathetic to a group of white settlers discovers that her tribe is about to attack the white settlers. But Griffith is not interested in playing with the proximity of the Indians to the child to generate the dramatic tension of the story. He does not have the tribe traverse the same ground on the child's heels to emphasize the urgency of her mission to save her white benefactors. In *The Broken Doll*, as has been discussed, Griffith uses the proximity of the Indians to the settlers they plan to attack to build the impact of the sequence.

To add to this final effect, Griffith unites the two races to the town by making each group graphically complete the other's line of action in their respective spaces. The whirling motion of the Indian dance in shot 19 begins in the same direction that the child takes as she exits her space to run to warn her friends. From that point, the race proceeds left and right through successive shots with alternating racers, Indians and child, bearing the responsibility of carrying the line of activity forward in the respective shots.

This cross-referencing development of a story is absolutely characteristic of Griffith's work. It insists on involving the audience in the creation of the narrative event. The audience's interest in each aspect of the race in *The Broken Doll* centers around such questions as "Who will reach the town first?" "Will the child save her white friends?" But the audience is given no opportunity to predict the outcome of the race to the town, as the child and the war party are traveling through different series of images. The sense of directional probability is very strong, but the sequence suggests speed and urgency rather than a specific span of time. The pressing question that arises in *The Broken Doll* is *when* either the Indian tribe or the Indian child will reach the white settlement. The audience's involvement is born of an anxiety induced by a sense of momentum coupled with an ignorance of the actual distance to be covered. When the first familiar image of the town appears, neither Indian child nor Indian group enters: the familiar entry into this shot does not match the Indian line of advance and indeed the Indians do not enter this shot. The anxiety is transferred to the other familiar image of the town, which contains the more likely connection to a leftward entry, suggested by the directional flow of the tribe. Again neither group enters. The audience has been teased by two misleading shots to prepare for a third, new image, into which the Indians do burst. To take full advantage of the directional impact of this conjunction of shots, Griffith even has the Indians leap suddenly into the frame in the midst of a quiet, affectionate moment—a boy and girl saying goodnight. This climax is rooted in the moment the child is separated from the tribe in shots 9 and 10. The left-to-right connection is meant to hit a goal with an impact, and it does. This thrust of activity carries the child from left to right through one more new space until she finally arrives at the squatter's cottage to warn her friends "in time" of the danger. The resolution of the film begins at this point.

By *The Modern Prodigal* (1910) Griffith was so sure that he could control the dynamics of the film's structure, that he freely breaks into the temporal continuity of its activity. The structure of the prodigal's escape from the evils of the city is used to set the stage for a secondary exposition in the film, the introduction of the sheriff and his son. Foreshadowing the second plot in the midst of an opening action sequence was not a new idea in 1910. Griffith freely broke into sequences as early as 1908 to develop affective relationships within the film. It is the sophistication and the expressiveness of the structure in *The Modern Prodigal* that makes it impressive.

A young man leaves home and his mother to find his fortune in the world. Griffith takes the first five shots of *The Modern Prodigal* to identify the wayward youth with the prodigal of the title and to link him to the biblical Prodigal Son, telling the story primarily in "symbolism," as the film's subtitle states. The opening image is pure portraiture, a picture of mother and son. The next image (shots 2 and 3, separated by a title) sharply recalls the panoramic formality of the enclosing shots of *The Greaser's Gauntlet* (1908). A road leads down to the city, floating visionlike in the far background of the shot. The hero descends into this city in shot 2 and returns from it in shot 3 in prison stripes, an escaped convict. This chase, which is the film's first physical activity, is delayed by all these "symbolic" references. There is the poignant return in shame to an empty home image and the patently biblical image of the ensuing shot, in which the young man eats "the food of pigs." The first five shots of *The Modern Prodigal* are geographically related over wildly discontinuous space and form an expository block on the basis of this surface of activity in a sequence that is also the allegorical prelude to the ensuing chase.

Two very active shots follow this prelude. The prodigal jumps over a fence into a field and crouches in some bushes—movement that indicates that he is being pursued. To find the pursuers, the film returns to the panorama (the set-up of 2 repeated at shot 7) to pick up the prison guards who have risen from the city to chase the prodigal. But at shot 8 Griffith breaks into this incipient chase to introduce a triad of shots (8 through 10) that concerns a new set of characters. In shot 8 a sheriff and his child are introduced. They exit the shot left and enter shot 9 in the left foreground, traveling toward an exit right. They enter shot 10 left and walk toward the right foreground, where the wife and mother sits on a porch. This sequence of shots ends with a family configuration, particularly emphasizing the relationship of the mother to the child, which can be compared to the opening situation of the prodigal, and the allegorical tone and the spatial unity of the first seven shots of the film reflect upon this introduction of the second family, in which the young son is also headed for trouble. Just as the geography of the first set of shots leads to the transition to this new set of characters, so the allegorical overtones linger just long enough in this second sequence to suggest that the audience will be seeing versions of the same story, each of which concerns a boy and his mother, in two sets of characters.

Although he had commonly cut discontinuous images together and freely interposed "foreign" images into developing sequences, Griffith had rarely intercut whole sequences of shots as boldly as he does in this film. The potential excitement of the chase, dependent on intercutting comparative images to elicit judgments about immediate proximity, is simply suspended in the interests of the affective content of the story. The sequence of shots from 8 to 10 is clearly meant to occur in real time and space. But Griffith deliberately places it in a structural opposition to the story of the prodigal, suspended as it is at a moment of tension, and this position causes the new sequence to oscillate between reality and metaphor. Griffith could afford these liberties in 1910 because he understood how to guide the audience's attention through the world of the film—with comparative portraiture; along well-defined lines of action; and between the moment-to-moment sequences of the film and the images that clarified the sense behind all the frantic activity.

He created the time in the reel for such construction with a new-found economy of form. The "white space" at entrances and exits was eliminated, and characters were already in place at the cut. The passage of action through the frame was curtailed without harming the integrity of the chase. The cross-referencing effect of intercutting was intensified as the number of shots increased and the quicker pace of the cutting challenged the audience's perception, as well as fulfilling its expectations.

In *The Modern Prodigal* Griffith returns to the guards to continue the chase. When they are seen again at shot 11, they have "already" reached set-up 6, where we left the prodigal. The prodigal has not yet left the frame, and Griffith uses this moment of real proximity to resume the chase. When the prison guards enter shot 11, the prodigal runs from it. They notice his movement and begin to follow him out of the shot, but do not complete an exit. When Griffith cuts to shot 12, the prodigal is already center frame, long shot. Only then do the guards start over the fence in shot 13 (11) to exit the frame. By shot 14, the prodigal has managed to get two spaces away from the guards, and again he appears at the center of the frame, in place at the cut, looking right. Cutting back to shot 15 (12), the guards are picked up already in the frame. When they exit, Griffith cuts to shot 16, with the prodigal in a new position: the camera pans with his entry into a stream to show him hide under a box floating there. Shot 17 (14) begins with the pursuers already in place, occupying the center of the shot, where the prodigal formerly stood. Shot 18 (16) shows the guards completing the chase order by arriving at the stream, but they are unable to recognize the prodigal hiding there "in plain sight." The camera pans left with the exit of the guards to close shot 18, signaling the completion of the chase sequence.

The Fugitive (1910) echoes many of these intuitions. In previous films, the proximity of pursuers to pursued was understood as each new piece of space was successively traded off for an old one in a series of shots. *The Modern Prodigal* proved that this practice gave the audience more information than it actually needed. In *The Fugitive* Griffith began to depend more heavily on the audience's awareness of the order and nature of a series of shots, making a scene memorable by the repetition of memorably detailed mise-en-scène.

In *The Fugitive* Union troops are pursued by Confederate soldiers. In shots 7 and 8 each group rises up over a ridge in turn, each exiting to the right. There follows a thematic opposition of shots (9 and 10) that alludes to the concern of respective mothers for the safety of their children. The actual engagement of both groups in the chase begins in shot 11: the Union troopers enter left—a matched action. The Confederates enter shot 12, a new space in the chain, and "see" the Union troops. In shot 13, the Union boys exit and the Confederates enter the frame, right foreground and right background respectively. In shot 14 the Union line of march is matched with a leftward entry into a new space. Shot 15 repeats 13 (11), with the Confederates storming around but not leaving the shot. Shot 16 repeats 14 to find the Union still occupying the same space. Finally, they exit. The Union mother's son, John, splits from his group to enter a new space, shot 17. Only then do the Confederate troops finally storm through shot 18 (16–14), and Johnny Reb follows Johnny Yank.

This curious, halting shot order obviously has some other goal than simple pursuit. It gives Griffith a chance to make an expressive statement about the situation of the two opposing armies and finally to single two personalities out of a general line of march. In this shot order Griffith also found a way to relate and emphasize only the essential information of the chase: where a person enters and where he leaves the frame; how he is oriented toward his pursuers in the order of the shots. The audience gets a coherent, moment-to-moment account of the chase, which begins with two groups whose only relationship is progress in the same general direction from two different spaces.

In *The Fugitive* Griffith identifies intercutting as an inherently cinematic activity, exclusive of action within the frame. Further, he arrived for the first time at a dramatic formula in which the audience in fact supplied much of the real activity of the film. The audience's participation in the film is created by exploiting the feeling that the same path of action must have been run through a shot if the entrance and exit marks are maintained. Intercutting suggests that the duplication of the trace is indeed being accomplished, even if it is never actually seen. Moreover, the intercutting suggests that action is continuing in more than one location in the world of the film.

So much did Griffith find this to be the case that he finally abbreviated the duration of action through the shot. This shortened shots and increased the pace of the intercutting. As long as the established trace is the basis of continuity, character B can be assumed to have completed a run through the entire frame, even if his recapitulation of the path of action is picked up in media res (as is the case in *The Modern Prodigal*). Because the audience is involved in creating the dimensions of such structure, there is an actual increase in the amount of space available in the one-reeler. This "space" created by the economy of expression in action sequences is then used to build characters, suggest emotions, and create the mental realm of the film (room is made for the comparative portraits of the mothers in *The Fugitive,* for instance).

The problems of time and pace did not lie in staging. If Griffith had had to confront action and the development of incident in real time, no matter how ingenious he was in staging, he would simply have fallen foul of the 14-minute length of the standard Biograph reel. The aesthetic of continuous activity was well established by the time Griffith began to make films, but he aimed to maintain the feeling of continuous action while simultaneously producing the dramatic effect of duration. For his own purposes, he preferred to stay within the bounded shot—frontal views not broken into a variety of angles. But Griffith did not need to be constrained by the real time/real space implications of that perspective.

By 1909 only economy was wanting, and the means to economize appeared in the link between the cut and the burst of activity through it. Displaced cuts on action revealed that once the trace of activity was established in the shot, any of the component parts—entrance, transit, or exit—could imply the completion of passage through the frame. Intercutting that clarified at least one of these components would produce a coherent composite image of the line of action. The old time-consuming format is exemplified in films such as *The Call of the Wild* (1908), in which the pursuer doggedly copies the line of activity traced through the frame by the pursued to "prove" that there is really a chase in progress, and panning with action takes up even more valuable screen time. Griffith found that the audience did not need to be convinced by the duplication of the entire line of activity, any more than it needed the confirmation of feet to prove the humanity of a body shown in close-up. In the production of continuity, as in all other aspects of film construction, Griffith found that he only needed to suggest strongly enough to make the audience complete the thought.

By the train chases of *The Lonedale Operator* (1911) and *The Girl and Her Trust* (1912), panning and tracking with chase activity is not aimless trailing motion. Nor do these camera movements cause shots to occupy more screen time than they are worth. The illusion of speed is the subject of shots in which the camera tracks with trains. Having discovered the benefits of creating a sense of orientation, and having learned the mechanics of orientation in the context of the door-bounded interior, Griffith could vary the audience's position in respect to the activity of a sequence and speed up or slow down its *sense* of the flow of the film without disorienting viewers or disturbing their sense of the reality of the world of the film. He had removed the sense that the moving camera was "in any way a specialty" by wedding its motion to the newly increased speed of his own structures.

This is especially true of *The Lonedale Operator* (more properly a race to the rescue than a chase), in which very few of the actions seem to "match" properly over cuts. Yet the dramatic reversal of the audience's position with respect to the engine of the train—now in the cab behind the engineers; now before the train as it rushes to the rescue toward the forecorner of respective frames—certainly leads Griffith to the radical separation of pursued from pursuer in sequences such as the train chase of *The Girl and Her Trust* (described on pp. 47–52 above). The total control of the audience's experience of the chase or race to the rescue and the ability to convey a sense of speed gradually broke the conventional pattern of following that had prevailed since the very early chases. The ability to convince the audience of the authenticity and logic of a chase in which neither party entered the other's frame until the very end of the sequence, as is the case in *The Girl and Her Trust,* depended on an ability to observe, learn, and adapt new ideas in a long, slow process of creating action structures.

Griffith himself reported that "as long ago as 1910, I was carrying on a series of experiments in film tempo: making one picture at normal pace, the next with underpacing, and the reactions of many audiences were carefully recorded."[6] Such experiments could take place in Griffith's Biograph period because of the volume of production and the control Griffith exercised over every phase of production. But the resulting body of work also indicates that a definite aesthetic inclination directed these experiments—one that structurally transcended the simple requirements of melodrama even as it clung to its outward appearances. As a whole, his Biograph period presents a body of films in which even routine projects contributed to the explication and clarification of Griffith's formal interests: structural unity through repetition; a dramatic impact that issues from the form of the film in which graphic tensions and resolutions involve the viewer in a process of speculation, anticipation, and expectation grounded in the changing dimensions of the world of the film.

It is not so much a sense of time as a sense of beat or emphasis that can be felt in the flow of a Griffith film. Often the effects are only felt by the audience in the way that Claire MacDowell, one of Griffith's actresses, explained a technique Griffith used to rehearse the troupe: "He had music played on the set. We didn't hear the music . . . we felt the rhythm. If one had asked what music we heard, we'd be unable to say it." [7]

Griffith was well aware of the need for tempo in drama. He said:

> In the opening passages of a photoplay, the tempo is usually maintained in multiples of three counts—six, nine, twelve. This is the cadence of the waltz, tranquil, soothing, almost hypnotic to the senses. When the action quickens, the director discards the waltz tempo and paces his scene in multiples of two, four, six, eight—the staccato beat of the two-step. [8]

Griffith found the sense of pace in the order of shots and the rhythm of cutting. The passage of time as an article of information (two minutes, two weeks, two years, twenty years) is sometimes simply signified by a title in the Biograph films. As plots become larger, it becomes more difficult to deal with exact time spans. But the relationship of two minutes of dramatic time to two minutes of screen time was a fertile area of inquiry. When Griffith contents himself with pace, the feeling that events have become accelerated or decelerated in the world of the film, he is able to attack the problems of time, duration, and speed with a range of solutions.

A Basic Frame   4
of Reference

Mack Sennett once remarked that Griffith was "the greatest in building suspense . . . [he] would take a pencil and concentrate the attention of the audience on little things, objects . . . suspense." [1] This observation surely refers to those sequences in which Griffith has audiences on the edges of their seats, when attention concentrated on the antics of children and animals gradually widens to encompass a sequence of action that involves a whole community—as is the case in *Fate* and *The Battle at Elderbush Gulch*. But it is impossible to escape the impact of constant reinforcement and identification in any Griffith film. Associations and concentrated moments arise from the recurrence of a familiar image in an evolving system of relationships between shots. Instead of spinning a film out like a ball of yarn, Griffith folds it back in on itself, creating layers of associations that collect mainly in repeated images, which are often highly condensed portraits. Two effects ensue. The first is that it is impossible to consider a Biograph film as a linear project proceeding simply from beginning to end. The model of a Griffith Biograph film is rather a web of constantly developing relationships, implications that are constantly clarified by reference to recurrent, and therefore increasingly familiar, images. Each shot in the chain is graphically interdependent and refers back to the world of the film for its narrative significance. Secondly, construction thrusts the plot toward resolution, which is usually defined as the point at which all the visual relationships coincide in a pattern of information held by the audience and the character simultaneously. The audience's ability to "read" a line of action is frustrated and facilitated by construction, so that the narrative effect arises from the balances and tensions between the shots.

The narrative effect of a Griffith film is thus based in the graphic processes of the film. The narrative results from the audience's understanding of how the physical activities of the film combine with the affective elements of structure in the discontinuous spaces of the film.

There is a risk of over-emphasizing *After Many Years* in a discussion of Griffith's Biograph films, but it embodies one of Griffith's most radical narrative intuitions: the juxtaposition of shots 8 and 9—the stranded Enoch and the waiting Annie Lee. This combination asks *where* the film event is occurring. In answering the multiple questions of location posed by the combination of these two images, we also begin to understand now narrative takes place in a Griffith film. "Where," of course, is first on a lonely beach and then on a familiar porch at home. But combined with the husband's looking into the locket, the wife's image is also in his mind, his memory, his thoughts. Ultimately, "where" is nowhere but in the order of the shots that gives rise to this speculation in the first place. But the combination of immediate impressions results in an unexpected blend of physical and mental realities.

Griffith obviously noticed this effect. Linda Arvidson, his wife, reports that he had to defend the film when he was making it. "It was the first movie without a chase. That was something for those days, a movie without a chase was not a movie. . . . How could there be suspense? How action? [*After Many Years*] proved to write more history than any picture ever filmed and it brought an entirely new technique to the making of films." [2] While Linda Arvidson concentrates on the "close-up" qualities of the cut to Annie Lee, Griffith also noticed the structural possibilities of the device. Speaking of his films generally in 1921 he noted that he adopted the "flashback" "to build suspense, which till then had been a missing quantity in picture dramas. Instead of showing a continuous view of a girl floating down stream in a barrel, I cut into the film by flashing back to incidents that contributed to the scene and explained it." [3]

The practice of "flashing" or "cutting" back becomes increasingly radical. Later in his Biograph period, Griffith would think nothing of repeating an image from a familiar locale in a newly unfolding sequence of activity. This "intervention" of a shot foreign to the action of the sequence must be understood as referential—the attempt to create a mental effect. Far from disturbing the integrity of an evolving locale, the reference shot will instead make it throb with implication and nuance. The intrusion of a reference shot into a new locale does not challenge the realism of the new sequence, because the reference shot is usually a familiar image. Griffith's use of familiar images not only contributes to the rhythm of instability and resolution in the evolution of the chain of shots, but creates a rhythm of conservation and progression in the evolution of the narrative. Every new motion or suite of images is rooted in an old one and referred back to an antecedent sequence or line of activity in the world of the film.

Portraits and Iconic Formulations

The foundation of the reference shot is Griffith's sense of portraiture. Distilled compositions were important to the narrative arts of the nineteenth century. "Stereographs, song slides, and popular chromolithographs placed great store in the important (and 'picturesque') moment. . . . Melodrama was equally partial to heightening its effects by 'freezing the frame'—literally stopping the action for a momentary tableau of special effect. . . . In the same vein the period's authors would sometimes interrupt, and sometimes conclude, their chapters with posed compositions." [4] Eisenstein discusses this phenomenon at length in relating Griffith to Dickens. [5]

The pictorial fashion seems to foretell the advent of the cinema. The nineteenth-century theater developed the habit of "realizing" well-known paintings at climactic moments. [6] The "tableau vivant" certainly carried over into the silent cinema. Karl Brown mentions that "the grouping of the scene of Lee's surrender [in *The Birth of a Nation*] was an exact replica of an engraving Griffith was holding in his hand." [7] The mise-en-scène of *Intolerance* was directly influenced by "familiar academic painting of Old Testament scenes." [8] But the use of portraiture in Griffith's Biograph films differs from these painterly precedents in some important ways.

Icon is a word laden with baggage from other disciplines, but it is still a useful term to indicate the sense of pictorial distillation in Griffith's referential images. Peter Wollen defines cinematic icons in terms given by Charles Peirce, the American mathematician and philosopher: "An icon . . . is a sign which represents its object mainly by its similarity to it; the relationship between signifier and signified is not arbitrary but one of resemblance or likeness. Thus, for instance, a portrait of a man resembles him." [9]

In the Biograph films there is concentrated effort to conventionalize certain compositions with a selection of pertinent details. These images are not symbolic, because they are specific to the world of the film. But Griffith's iconography *is* a generalization that is meant to be immediately recognizable and invite identification. These effects result from the conventions of composition (which may refer to extra-film culture); and to the recurrence of these compositions within the film (which refers the icons to other shots in the film.) In line with Griffith's own stricture against "specialties," the portraits do not halt the action to achieve their effect. The same image is repeated a number of times to perform an act of summary within the flow of the film, and in fact the flow of the narrative depends on the summarizing qualities of these images. Shot to shot, icons acquire a patina of memory as they accrue the weight of the film's history. Resemblance eventually forms a cross-film system of references in Griffith's oeuvre.

Earlier filmmakers used a version of this kind of composition to introduce characters. In Biograph's *The Widow and the Only Man* (1904), first the fellow and then the widow are introduced in mid-shot limbo, a practice that continued at Biograph in such films as *The Chicken Thief* (1904) and *The Fire Bug* (1905). Sometimes this kind of shot served as a coda, a final dramatic comment. Sometimes a bit of business was added to wrap up the film's action. The comic codas of Griffith's *Balked at the Altar* and *The Curtain Pole* (both

1908) are basically an opportunity for the performer to take the stage to do some final bit of business that comments on the action. In *The Curtain Pole*, for instance, the chagrined Mack Sennett eats the pole that has caused him so much trouble.

The most common formal characteristic of these introductory and coda shots is their special composition. Quite often they are the only mid-shots in films otherwise composed at long and medium distance, and they look surprisingly intimate compared to the rest of the shots in the film. But it was their ability to convey information in a condensed form, rather than their compositional impact, that struck Griffith.

Iconic construction was a refinement on these codas, and became a way of relaying the most condensed statement of unity and place in the film. Once again, Griffith was preceded by other filmmakers. Both Cecil Hepworth and James Williamson concluded films with intimate family portraits. These appear in films such as *Rescued by Rover* (Hepworth, 1905), *Black Beauty* (Hepworth, 1906), and *Two Little Waifs* (Williamson, 1907). In all cases these concluding images reflect the restoration of family unity and order imperiled by the events of the film. Griffith begins to use formal portraiture in exactly the same way, and since the result of a Griffith film is the viewer's acquaintance with a particular space and a process of relationship, the use of iconic compositions becomes particularly powerful in his films.

The final image in *The Adventures of Dollie* (1908) is a family portrait— mother and father gathered around the recovered child. This image in Griffith's first film summarizes the substance of the drama because it visually restores the family unit broken when Dollie was kidnapped by the evil gypsy. This sort of summary occurs seven times in Griffith's first sixty Biograph films, and the more closely this kind of image is identified with the resolution of the film, the more truly the family icon serves a structural function in framing the action of the film, suggesting a narrative process.

The family icon undoubtedly drew its inspiration from theater groupings appearing in the domestic drama that developed in nineteenth-century theatrical and pictorial art. Certainly, there is a thematic affinity between Griffith's family group and the images created by painters and scenarists of the nineteenth century to present the "humble life and character as imperiled by the law, sophistication and aggressive cupidity." [10] The fact that many of these portraits were serial—Cruikshank's *The Bottle* (1847) and *The Drunkard's Children* (1848)—or comparative—Solomon's *Waiting for the Verdict* (1857) and *Not Guilty* (1859)—indicates the structural continuity between Griffith's sense of narrative and the nineteenth-century pictorial arts. [11]

In Griffith's work these condensed regroupings are the formal expression of order restored after an assault on the family by fortune or fate. Offering the effect of harmony by similarity or irony by contrast, Griffith's iconography is overtonal in effect and its polar repetition always forms a historical relationship between the first and last moments of the film. In this way, the audience is placed and kept literally and figuratively in the world of the film.

In *Tavernkeeper's Daughter* (1908) the iconic poles of the drama appear, if faintly: in the course of the film a young virgin runs from the image of an unstable family (the mother is missing), prey to lust, to the image of a stable family unit where passion is dissipated and the rapist chasing the heroine is stayed by the holy sight of mother, father, and child.

This description surely represents an overstatement of the significance of *The Tavernkeeper's Daughter,* but it also suggests the effect of iconic enclosure. The formality of running from family to family has an inherent power to generate meaning, at least by implication. In *The Tavernkeeper's Daughter* the structure does not bear much of the weight of these implications. The enclosing family images draw most of their power from whatever the viewer or critic can supply. The importance of *The Tavernkeeper's Daughter* lies mostly in the fact that it gives the first hint of an organizational trend in Griffith's work. This use of the icon persists in *The Drunkard's Reformation* (1909). In *What Drink Did* (1909) the iconic frame derives its poignancy from the comparison between the family portraits that begin and end the film: the child who dies as a result of the father's drunken excesses is not there at the reconciliation when the family group is reassembled at the end of the film. The child's absence is noticeable, and the family's feelings about the loss are one of the subjects of this final shot.

In *The Greaser's Gauntlet* (1908) Griffith began to construct an iconic cycle based on the structural possibilities as well as the compositional qualities of the image. While the story it encloses in panoramic shots is still crudely constructed, the existence of the frame is in itself of interest. The panoramic frame has an allegorical tone: a woman sits in a natural vista. The very panoramic quality of this shot abstracts it from the lateral and diagonal world of the film's activity. The abstraction of this panoramic frame in *The Greaser's Gauntlet* makes it a distillation of familial stability, even though it is not certain that the comforting female of the frame is actually the Greaser's mother. The framing images identify her womanhood with the ideal the Greaser seeks to serve in saving the heroine, and the film resonates with tension between this generalized, highly placed womanhood and the details of the action surrounding the real-life woman.

Thematic orientation is not the only role played by the polar icons Griffith employs in this film. *The Greaser's Gauntlet* draws energy from the tension between the formal stability of the mother/woman sitting in the panorama and the more intimate dramatic activity the frame encloses. This tension is generated between the general verticality of remove in the mother/woman icon and the general horizontality of the spaces of the drama.

The production of typicality in Griffith's films is therefore the sum of many compositional situations. While some of the power of Griffith's iconography draws from cultural references, some of its impact is derived precisely from the film medium, given the state of the art between 1908 and 1913. When the Indian portrait appears in *The Mended Lute* (1909), it is already par excellence, exhibiting from the first the features it will retain whenever an Indian village and the qualities of Indianness must be evoked in the Biograph films. And some of these qualities are derived from the deep image with which Griffith worked: a line of tepees extends far back into the image on a diagonal from foreground to background. In the foremost picture plane, a largely ceremonial figure stands either right or left, giving the composition a foreground termination point. (This "ground" is often the tall James Kirkwood, and so strong was his identification with this graphic duty that he performs it even when he is not in an Indian costume, as in the period drama *The Duke's Plan*, 1909.)

The scene of farming that opens *A Corner in Wheat* (1909) seems timeless because of the combination of the figure of the circle (the composition of activity in the shot) with the actual repetition of the image at the end of the film (events come full circle), and the warped echo of that familiar circular figure in the body of the film in the composition of the image of the Wheat Pit, where grain and human futures are bought and sold by the Wheat King. What has been distilled in *A Corner in Wheat* is not the most typical farm—that is not the nature of Griffith's iconography. Griffith's typicality results from the audience's film-long acquaintance with a few simple facts that give it the impression that it "knows." Part of the complexity of the effect of a Griffith film arises from the interaction between shots that can be considered formal icons and the iconic process that arises from the associations that are enforced between shots by the way shots are related in the chain. Resolving icons become the result of the chain of shots more than of their conventional composition. They become recognizable in terms of the film more than in terms of whatever cultural baggage the audience carries with it into the theater.

This effect transforms the mid-shot codas. In *The Awakening* (1909), for instance, the wife nearly falls from a ladder onto her newly amorous husband. This comic business at the end of the film recalls the mid-shot codas, but issues logically from the previous chain of shots, and is therefore a spatial resolution as well as a portrait that states the thematic unity of the film.

By *The Modern Prodigal* (1910) the structure of the film interacts with the effect of iconic enclosure. The wayward prodigal travels from mother-icon to mother-icon, but the journey is interwoven with the other activity of the film, so that while the polar enclosure is the shape of the boy's personal drama, it is only one strand of the film's narrative. Griffith no longer had to rely on iconic enclosure to organize narrative. In *The Modern Prodigal* the comparative icons of mothers and sons create a thematic resonance in the enlarged scope of the plot.

The Female of the Species (1912) ends with a family portrait, though the family is not related by blood and is exclusively female. This icon is the expression of the resolution of the pattern of cutting—the repulsion and attraction that has generated the dramatic energy of the film. At first glance, it seems far removed from a film such as *What Drink Did*. What the last shot of *The Female of the Species* actually represents, however, is the total integration of the idea of the icon of *What Drink Did* into the body of the film. Examination of the beginning and ending of *The Female of the Species* reveals that it really does begin and end with family portraits, but they depend on the context of the process of the film and cannot stand with the polar self-sufficiency of the family portraits of *What Drink Did*.

In *The Mothering Heart* (1913) Griffith expands on the idea of burying the icons in the flow of the film to produce an overlapping sense of location with a psychological resonance. One sense of orientation in the film is produced from the directional flow of activity from shot to shot. But there is another orientational flow that results from the summarizing portraiture of the film. Lillian Gish portrays a gentle-hearted woman crushed by her husband's philandering. The iconic logic of *The Mothering Heart* is distilled in three images. In the opening moment of the film, the young woman is introduced on a garden path. In shot 18, she is seen in the laundry room of her house. Finally, the distraught woman breaks down, destroying a rose garden after the death of her child. The initial shot is sentimental portraiture of Griffith's favorite kind—it is a star-quality picture of Lillian Gish as well as a sundrenched image of petal-strewn maidenly innocence. Compositionally, the other two shots of the triad might not be considered iconic at all. The laundry room depicts a typical wifely chore, but it is too detailed, its composition "messier" than a formal portrait should be. The signature of the rose garden is too baroque. But taken together, these three images echo and reinforce one another. The fade in on the introductory image is recalled in the vignette mask of the rose garden image. The emotion of the rose garden is all the more violent and chilling for the resemblance it bears the composition and mise-en-scène of the initial moment of the film and for the comparison offered by the homely portrait of the laundry room. In the context of the film, these three shots summarize and distill the emotional essence of the film. In one sense, the film is extended from point to point of portraiture and resonates between two psychological poles: the wife whole and productive and the woman fragmented and mad with grief.

To discuss *The Mothering Heart* in this way may be stretching the argument a bit. But the provocation for this kind of analysis lies in Griffith's structural habits. He built invariable locales in his film, some as simple as exteriors that are always linked to certain interiors by the same line of activity, however many times the locale is repeated in the film. These invariable locales have their roots in the impulse to use formal compositions to create resonance in the film—a sense of comparison and contrast based on the recurrence of a familiar image or familiar set of images in the midst of the narrative process.

Repetition itself thus acquires an iconic flavor—it becomes a formally generalizing factor in Griffith's work. One presumes much from pictorial distillations, and these presumptions begin to reflect on other repeated shots. Repetition gives less formally composed, but constantly recurring, shots an iconic function. Two factors are largely responsible for this effect. The first is that Griffith is not particularly representational. He tends to produce all of his compositions—iconic or not—from a small number of easily identifiable features. What details exist blast out at the audience with the promise of significance. This is not so much a function of the camera position as of judicious selection, and that quality is evident in acting as well as in mise-en-scène.

Secondly, a simple set of objects makes a repeated impression on the viewer. It is interesting to speculate about whether this effect would be so strong if Griffith had not relied on cuts to organize his films to the extent that he did, or if he had not worked under the aesthetic assumption that a single shot bounded by a cut was somehow more "objective" than the moving camera. Whatever the impact a freer camera attitude would have had on Griffith's Biograph work, as it exists, the repeated shots have a somewhat stroboscopic effect of flashing before the viewer a simple set of facts that begins to function as a unit because the details are persistently associated by composition and position in the chain of shots. Any variation in the image is immediately noticeable (visible), and the tension between the growing familiarity of the repeated image and the endlessly contrasting effect of its recurrence in the chain represents a substantial contribution to the ebb and flow of narrative information in Griffith's films. The famous gate scene in *Birth of a Nation* (1915) is not just a triumph of Henry Walthall's acting skill, although that was surely formidable. The scene of the returning soldier pausing at the gate of his family home acquires an undertone of irony from the fact that he is traveling through a familiar space that has a history of sweet memories, now made bitter by war. And hovering at that gate with Henry Walthall are all the Biograph families whose fortunes were portrayed in similarly contrasting sets of domestic portraits.

Expository Groups

The interaction of iconic distillation—produced through composition and/or repetition—with the action sequences of the film generates the narratives of Griffith's Biograph films. It is an extremely efficient process—so much so that room was made in the reel for longer stories of deeper psychological complexity. Over the course of Griffith's Biograph period, he developed distinct story-telling structures that lend a sense of history, motive, and consequence to the chase and siege sequences that almost inevitably resolve the films. As he developed more film time, Griffith acquired the luxury of expository sequences. Information implied in the condensed iconic framing images could be explicated in a sequence of shots. Repetition ensured that the power of iconic effects—memory, thought, feeling, psychological depth— was retained.

Frank Woods used the painterly "Millet-like" qualities of the opening shot of *A Corner in Wheat* to excuse the fact that the sowing was completely inefficient and "unrealistic." [12] But his observation questions more than the realism of the framing images of *A Corner of Wheat*. Implicit in Woods' criticism is the recognition of Griffith's ability to make atmosphere pertinent to the rest of the film in such a way that the world of the film becomes self-referential, depending for its realism as much on its internal coherence and unity of tone as on what the viewer knows to be true from his experience of the world in which he lives.

In *The Ingrate* (1908) expository space is developed through a pan that takes husband and wife from their cabin to the lake in front of it and back again. Aside from the fact that this provides the audience with a very beautiful aesthetic experience, it locates the couple's relationship in a specific place and gives it a "natural" rhythm that stands in contrast to the violent events of the film. This is also true of the heroine's introduction in *Fisher Folks* (1911). She is present in the first image of the film on a cliff above a beach before she descends to the spaces in which she is involved in a literal chase that sends lover after lover until the "right" people are paired up. One of the most complex relationships of a pastoral introduction to the rest of the film is created in *The Country Doctor* (1909), where the rolling panorama is actually unfolded by a panning movement of the camera. This expository moment of repose links *The Country Doctor* with Griffith's first film, *The Adventures of Dollie*. But the panoramic spread at the beginning of *The Country Doctor* has the added effect of generality, of a quite literal distance, of which the drama of the film is a particular instance. The family icon succeeds the panorama in *The Country Doctor*. The pan succeeds the image of the doctor's family shattered by the death of the doctor's child. The restatement of the pan and the panorama at the end of the film restores a familiar structural image, as well as withdrawing into generality rather than a restoration of family intimacy that is meant to extend to all families. The opposition of the continuous space of the pan to the interior structure of activity invests the drama with a sense of self-referentiality that creates identities and parallels between the two families in the film and makes an almost allegorical case of the private drama of a doctor's choice between his family and his duty.

A comparison between the first and last moment of the film is very important to Griffith's explication of narrative. In *The Zulu's Heart* (1908) the child of the Zulu chief has died. The first shot is a scene of ceremonial mourning. Rather than introducing the action of the film immediately, Griffith devotes this first shot to the statement of a theme, parental feeling, that will be the subject of the film. The solemn tone of the first shot contrasts directly with the ensuing, increasingly violent and frantic, activity that takes place once the Zulu father is drawn into his tribe's attack on a white settler's wagon. The intense introductory moment allows Griffith to state the substance of the narrative as well as establishing a staging area for the film's subsequent activity. In the course of the struggle between the white settlers and the Zulus, the Zulu father, having lost his own child, sympathizes with the distress of a captive white mother when his tribe makes off with her child. The Zulu father saves the white child from execution. At the end of the film he is left alone again in a solitary space that echoes the mournful tone of the film's opening. The importance of *The Zulu's Heart* is that Griffith applied these discernable, analyzable compositional strategies to construct the drama. Although the effect is still accomplished in broad sweeps, Griffith is able to use the structure to endow the story with a set of feelings as well as a set of actions.

In many expositions, Griffith works on the audience's ability to project the film's resolution by comparing the first and last images. *After Many Years* begins with a walk up a garden path. On the verge of the plot's resolution, when the lost Enoch is already on his way home, the portrait of the family is restored to the film with the "wrong" father and husband in it. Griffith is able to make particularly good use of the tension between the projected visualization of stability restored (the reunited family) and what is occurring (the faithful suitor, the best man, is ascending into the father's place in the repeated family image.) This may be a simple transformation, but it is surely an effective one. The appearance of this configuration of the family portrait throws the rapidly approaching resolution nastily off course by assembling a pseudo-family instead of the authentic one promised by Enoch's return. Griffith was very fond of creating these effects in a bucolic setting (as in the films mentioned above). In *After Many Years* he takes advantage of the implications of peace, natural order, and cyclical rhythm associated with pastoral imagery to create a last moment of tension before the resolution. The simple sensuality of the flower-bordered image stands in marked contrast to the desert island upon which Enoch has been stranded. By repeating this atmospheric, expository image near the moment of resolution, Griffith is able to recall the original order of the world to the audience. This leads to the image of Enoch's front yard, where the "false" family is assembled before Enoch's eyes before the truth is revealed and the "proper" family configuration restores order to the world of the film (figs. 95–96). The repetition of a charged image for its collective power prepares for the resolution of the film.

Eventually, Griffith stated the premise of a film by comparing and contrasting the opening images. No method of exposition seems to suit Griffith as well

95   96

Figs. 95–96. *After Many Years* (1908)—Portraiture (sequential)

as this direct opposition of initial shots. In *The Call* (1909) a man's stable home is juxtaposed with the bizarre and ominous circus world of the woman he chooses to marry. Perhaps the combination of images in *The Call* suggests a progression rather than parallelism, but in *His Last Burglary* (1910) two family icons are directly compared to state the substance of the film. The two domestic images are differentiated only by the kinds of dishes on the shelves in the background. Otherwise, they exactly mirror each other. No matter what industrial necessity may have produced this similarity, the contrasting of empty and full cradles in respective images immediately sets up a direct iconic contrast that contains the narrative opposition of the film. The action of *His Last Burglary* will work to move the child from one cradle to another and back again, until the baby is restored to its "proper" place in the world of the film. The thematic development of *His Last Burglary* is aided by this juxtaposition of family portraits from which lines of converging activity are extended into the world of the film.

The Awakening is another film to start with contrasting situations in separate shots. While it is true that the boy of shot 1 also appears in shot 2, the viewer is also presented with an immediate comparison: the man in his club, a carefree bachelor; the woman in her parents' home, waiting to be wooed. In the first two shots the dramatic problem of the film is clearly presented. A similar exposition is made in *A Midnight Cupid* (1910). Griffith begins this film with contrasting images of two young men. These are spatially unrelated, shots arising from nowhere, and although titles mediate the discontinuity between these introductory images, identifying the two fellows, it is the juxtaposition itself that characterizes them by objectifying a set of oppositions: poor/rich; mobile/static; open space/closed space. This sequence in *A Midnight Cupid* demonstrates the use of intercutting to provide an effect by contrasting shots that are not inherently iconic. Locale and position are used to characterize and define these men and set up a situation in which they will actually exchange identities.

The intuition behind these expository practices is that a direct relationship will be relayed by the juxtaposition of two images and that the contrast between two clearly stated "portraits" will be a creative, rather than illustrative, experience. Such an exposition creates more time in the reel, because it suggests a great deal of incident but takes up very little real time. In *The Awakening,* for instance, Griffith continues to parallel the young people in separate shots until their marriage, so that he is actually able to convey a courtship with a satisfactory sense of duration.

The simple adversary opposition of images persists as an expository practice. In *The Slave* (1909) the opposition takes place in two separate moments of one long scene: a woman rejects one suitor; she accepts another and the events of the film proceed from her choice. In *The Mills of the Gods* (1909) successive shots picture the two women who will vie for the man in the film. In *One Is Business, the Other Crime* (1912) a poor couple in shot 1 is contrasted with a rich couple in shot 2.

In *The Mended Lute* (1909) the juxtaposition of the opposing groups has a more formal relationship to the chain of shots developing into the film—the opposition is not merely the film's motivating antecedent. The first shot, an icon of "Indian-ness," depicts the rejection of a suitor. An image of the accepted lover follows. These two opening shots are joined by a connecting look: the rejected suitor seems to look past the cut and "see" the heroine join the other man. This method of exposition is effective because it expresses a narrative relationship in spatial terms. The audience is forced to understand the drama in terms of the spatial tension between these complementary shots. In the course of the film, the opposing characters stand in a relationship of constructed continuity (the chase) as well as in a narrative opposition (accepted and rejected suitor), until the conflict is resolved and the rejected suitor is reconciled to the heroine's choice of a mate.

In *The Fugitive* (1910) Griffith developed a variation on the adversarial opposition of shots that once again asserted the importance of the film's structure. In *The Fugitive* he does not immediately introduce Johnny Yank and Johnny Reb in opposing introductory images. The eventual inclusion of comparative icons of motherhood in the introduction implies the brotherhood of these two men, as well as the universality of motherly affection that is the subject of the film. The five opening shots of the film, however, are devoted to building locale, a cluster of shots that defines the space around the Rebel home. This gives Griffith an opportunity to stage a scene of celebration and group activity at the film's beginning, but it also reveals the alignment of spaces in a locale that will be the stage of crucial activity in the rest of the film. Only after the task of establishing the film's familiar images has been accomplished does Griffith introduce the complementary icon of the Union mother and son (shot 6).

Icons and the social relationships they express were not the only introductory formulations that Griffith used in his Biograph period. Given the fact that the Biograph films were so short, Griffith often condensed the history of the characters into the first two or three shots to provide some dramatic motivation for the events of the film. Often these expository efforts were not as structurally useful as icons or iconic\shots. They tended to be left behind in the chain of shots, and the opportunity for resonance through repetition was lost. But these prologues are interesting insofar as they indicate Griffith's struggle to express a greater time span within a small amount of reel space. A mark of the difficulty Griffith had expanding the temporal scope of his films is the use of titles between repeated shots as an expository strategy. In *Was Justice Served?* (1909) the tense courtroom drama is preceded by long expository shots broken by titles that give a sense of the passage of time leading up to the case of mistaken identity that returns a hapless convict to the bar of justice. *A Convict's Sacrifice,* also made in 1909, begins similarly with a lengthy, reel-consuming passage. To indicate a passage of time that will make the plot of the film seem reasonable and give it a plausible duration, ten shots (the longest of which is a minute and a half) are paired by titles to tell the story of a convict's release, attempt to find a job, rearrest, and escape from jail. By *A Fair Exchange* (1909) Griffith manages to condense the whole history of a miser into three fairly lengthy shots, which at least indicate that there is some reason for his miserliness. In *In Old California* (1910) the use of paired icons allows Griffith to summarize a twenty-year span of narrative time into two shots that depict the respective lives of a woman and her rejected suitor until the moment "to date" at which the suitor reenters the woman's life and the action of the film proper begins.

Partial efforts at characterization may be seen in the development of deliberately metaphorical relationships between shots. For instance, when the Snapper Kid first appears in *The Musketeers of Pig Alley* (1912), he is preceded by a puff of cigarette smoke, a tag implying the quality of his character. The first sequence of shots (1–12) in *The Mothering Heart* is devoted to characterizing the motherly young woman by intercutting her image with the antics of two puppies who get stuck while playing with a tin can and need to be helped out. Griffith spends the first six shots of the film characterizing this woman as a sympathetic and tender soul before actually starting the film's action with the entry of the suitor into an already-familiar image. In *A Romance of the Western Hills* (1910) this association between characters and characterizing objects is even more elaborate. When the "White [man's] book" (the Bible) is flung out of the image of the Indian camp, it lands at the feet of the white scoundrel who will seduce the Indian maiden. While making a spatial statement of proximity, the flinging of the Bible out of the Indian icon also produces a pretext for the introduction of the antagonist and indicates his character. In the first two shots of *A Romance of the Western Hills* Griffith provides a condensed summary of the thematic concerns that the action of the film will explicate. He makes this statement in such a way that the spatial relationships upon which the continuity of the film depends do not lose anything to the summary, and are in fact clarified by the way in which the introductory shots appear in the chain. The Bible thrown out of shot 1 to the right enters shot 2 from the left and falls at the feet of the villain. The fortuitous appearance of this man is belied by the right-to-left trajectory of the book—two spaces are joined so naturally that the villain seems to belong to the sequence, and coincidence is turned toward probability.

A mature example of the process of introduction can be found in *The Birth of a Nation*. Griffith introduces Elsie Stoneman three times to the audience and each introduction performs a different structural function in the chain of shots. Elsie first appears in a familiar image: she comes out of a house onto a porch in the background of a shot that is still concerned with the activities of her brothers in the foreground. In the next shot, Griffith gives the viewer a metaphoric characterization of Elsie, showing only her feet, at which kittens play. Finally, there is a shot that is specifically devoted to letting the audience see Elsie's face, a star-quality, close shot of Lillian Gish.

All of these shots retard the movement of the plot proper. Three shots may even seem excessive unless one conceives of the type of filmmaking in which it is taken for granted that the viewer wants to know several things about Elsie at this introductory moment before the film resumes its action—a resumption that Griffith effects very nicely with Elsie's run from background to foreground toward her brothers, uniting the planes of the familiar image. These three shots relay three kinds of information about Elsie to the audience. The character is oriented in the context of a familiar image; characterized upon introduction; and given a romantic aura. These introductory shots are so interesting because of the balance Griffith maintains between their strictly self-sufficient characterizing function and the contribution each must make to the unity of the sequence of shots.

The very need for an expository chain of shots represents Griffith's triumph over the aesthetic of physical activity in early films. The idea of cranking up the activity in the film slowly after relaying some basic spatial and narrative relationships to the audience is already an improvement over the use of the first shots as simply the starting point of activity, or the basic introduction of people who will be performing the activity. The expository block has to accomplish these tasks in the Biograph films, of course, but Griffith also used the expository chain to create a point of stability from which the action of the film could be related. The expository block serves as a prologue to which the activities of the film are referred. The result may be a rhythmical complement or a dialectical statement in images that become familiar and stable as they are developed in the chain of shots. Above all, the expository block could be an organizational composite from which the rest of the film would develop spatially. This is why the expository chains in Griffith's Biograph period so often seem to have a feeling of timelessness or to exist in a momentary hush of activity. They create a field of polarity with the final shots or sequence of shots in the film, between which the activity of the entire film shoots like an electric arc.

Expository stability becomes a point of reference to which the film will return to resolve itself, and the expository block stands as the orientation point that gives a concrete objective as the goal of the film's resolution. In *After Many Years* the walk down the garden path is a recollection of the film's beginning. The resolution should restore this family image to the "right" configuration—that is, Enoch should return; the suitor should not take his place in this image. A contrast between stability and conflict is often created in the one-shot context of a walk—as has been seen in *After Many Years* and *The Ingrate,* to cite only two early examples. As early as 1908 Griffith was also developing expository sequences based on taking a walk. *Where the Breakers Roar* has a lengthy introduction for a film made in 1908: two shots through which young folk walk from an arbored garden to the beach, where they picnic. This is one of the earliest expository sequences that made use of a directional connection. It is totally unnecessary to the story except as a tonal unit that contrasts with the running activity on the beach where the girl is chased by a maniac. This chase echoes the shape of the walk, but changes its pace to a run.

By *The Cord of Life* (1909) the walk is being used to define a particular locale. The villain walks through two introductory and directionally related exteriors before he arrives at the apartment of the family he will attack. The story is developed in the context of these introductory spaces and the relationship between them becomes an important indicator of how soon the father will return to save his child, whom the villain has hung out of the window of the apartment by a rope. Since the dimensions of this locale are revealed to the viewer in the casual expository walk, Griffith is relieved of the burden of creating images that indicate the coming climax. He simply needs to reinforce relationships between images that have been familiar to the audience since the beginning of the film. When the father returns through these familiar images, the child's rescue is indicated.

The Restoration (1909) is a tragic version of *Love among the Roses,* and like the later film, *The Restoration* is almost entirely built of characters walking through suites of increasingly familiar images. Although the film initially seems to be a romantic comedy, it soon becomes clear that jealousy is the factor that will fatally color the exchange of partners along these garden paths. The young lovers are introduced in the midst of a jealous tiff; the mature couple's marriage is threatened by the husband's unreasonable suspicions. The combination of continuous movement with the recombination of couples within the repeated shots results in a crisis of identity that depends on the audience learning the locale well enough to understand that the people derive some sort of identification from their positions in the shots—positions that may be fatally misinterpreted by the people within the world of the film.

The tension arising from a comparison of positions could also be the dynamic of the entire film. In *As It Is in Life* (1910) Griffith creates a secondary exposition in a cluster of images that states the history of the film. At the end of the first sequence, a father and his fiancée visit two spots that become associated with their courtship. These shots and the passage of the couple from one to the other convey a sense of time in the courtship and prepare the audience for the complementary restatement of these images that is the exposition of the second sequence of the film. At the end of the first sequence, the father rejects the idea of remarriage in order to devote his life to raising his child. In the second sequence, the child, now a grown woman, is faced with a similar decision: should she marry or devote her life to her aging father? To begin this sequence, the father and daughter walk together to *that* vista, *that* panorama. Suddenly memory is infused into the film. The same setting, the same configuration recurs, but peopled differently. When the child in her turn must confront the choice between husband and father, she is courted in the same spaces the father appeared in, and the film acquires a deeper sense of history. The viewer is instantly reminded of the father's decision and is faced with the disparity between the parent's attitude and the child's; between the father's expectations and the actual facts. The father's bitter disappointment with the daughter's marriage is given a reasonable context of events in *As It Is in Life*, in contrast to all the Biograph films in which the father whimsically or selfishly rejects the daughter's choice of boyfriend.

In *A Country Cupid* (1911) the first three shots of the film introduce a three-sided configuration of characters: pupils, country lover, schoolmarm. A directional impetus makes this juxtaposition the structural as well as the historical beginning of the film. All three principals start off on paths to the right, which converge in shot 4. The interesting aspect of this exposition is that it begins the film with a process of convergence that normally signals resolution. In addition, the lines of activity are interwoven by the introduction of a lunatic, who is the only character to plot an absolutely "geographical" course through the shots on his way to the schoolhouse, where he stops at shot 19 (the set-up of shot 4 repeated) to look across the cut "at" the schoolmarm. The juxtaposition of shots for opposition and contrast has been joined to the expository walk in *A Country Cupid*. The sense of spatial relationship conveyed by the walk gradually reveals the dimensions of the world of the film, but only the geographical path of the lunatic suggests the relationship between the characters that will be the dramatic subject of the film.

Ease and naturalness of exposition mark 1911 as a particularly fine Biograph year. Condensation in exposition gives Griffith more space in the reel to develop activity. Secondary expositions are placed in the middle of a film as it becomes possible to indicate a new time sequence or construct a new locale. Structural coherence depends on the relationship of a series of physical activities to a central sympathetic hub—a shot or group of shots that is constantly referred to a developing line of activity. The appearance of sympathetic reference shots creates a continuity of interest rather than space, often determining the rhythm of presentation of the dramatic event by providing a stable familiar space to which the audience is constantly returned to reassess the balance of the spatial and dramatic tensions of the film. In *Swords and Hearts* (1911) the three images juxtaposed as exposition are recalled three times to serve as points of reference at transitional moments in the film. Three times the hero's house, his fiancée's mansion, and the cabin of the "poor white girl" Jennie, are recalled (shots 1–4; 11–13; 89–91) (figs. 97–106). The physical activity of the film is encompassed in the two forms of the chase and the siege, and the repeated clusters of images appear at the beginning and end of the action structures of the film, always providing a point of reference to identify the basic character oppositions that generate the narrative tension.

Swords and Hearts is bracketed by the introduction of normal families and the restoration of familiar "normalcy" at the end of the film. The final sequence of the film returns Hugh, the Confederate hero, to all the familiar images of his life, and the restatement of the familiar images operates to show the state of the film at the climax of its activity. In the end, Hugh's world is destroyed: his family mansion is ruined by marauders; Irene, his fiancée, has preserved herself and found a Union husband; only Jennie's loyalty is unchanged when Griffith reintroduces this group of images just before the end of the film. Hugh must recognize what the audience already knows: that Jennie is the heroine of the film. This recognition takes place in a newly planted field. The significance of such a pastoral image cannot be mistaken, but its effect also issues from the fact that it is a newly constructed icon of stability and order arising from the historical processes of the film (fig. 107).

The prologue suggesting the history behind the main events of *The Massacre* (1912) is so sophisticated that it can no longer be considered an addendum to the film, but must be seen in terms of the total film, although its spaces do not recur in the film. *The Massacre* begins with three simple sequences of *ab* intercutting. The alternation of the first pair of shots depicts the choice of one suitor while the rejected suitor looks on (shots 1–8). In the alternation of the second pair of shots (9–12), the rejected suitor relays the death of the husband to the woman who rejected him. In the third alternation (13–17), the woman dies and her child is adopted by the rejected suitor.

These three sequences very succinctly state the dramatic situation of the film: the grown ward is seen by her guardian as surrogate for the dead sweetheart—a process of identification relayed by the *ab* intercutting of the exposi-

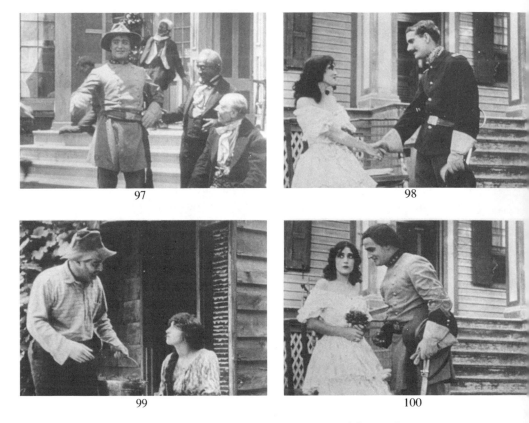

Figs. 97–107. *Swords and Hearts* (1911)—Iconic Groups (sequential groups)

tion. Also, the problem of duration in *The Massacre* is overcome by the dramatic immediacy of the three concrete events that make up the history of the film. The first event, the choice of a husband, is developed solely through intercutting. The rejected suitor never enters the shot in which he sees his intended fiancée pick another man. These first two shots are related solely by a directional gaze and remain an unresolved watcher-lurker situation. The second and third expository segments operate on a dynamic split between interior and exterior spaces, private and social events. In the third segment, the exterior where the maid retreats to weep after the woman's death is used to provide momentary relief from the intense concentration on the mother's death and the transfer of the child to the guardianship of the faithful suitor. Finally, Griffith overcame the difficulty of creating a context from which the drama of the film would logically develop by giving this history to the audience as a constructed experience rather than a simple assertion.

The examples given above should clearly indicate that Griffith rarely per-

101

102

103

formed a bit of exposition without taking the entire structure of the film into account. Each time the narrative object has been gained, a spatial project has been furthered or is being fulfilled. The deftness of Griffith's approach is felt in the ease with which the viewer grasps his opening ideas and follows Griffith into the film. It is difficult to think of any director until the Hollywood film-makers of the late thirties and early forties who could so surely and quickly set the film before the audience.

Resonance within the Chain of Shots

In *The Purgation* (1910) a young man is given a chance to make a new life for himself, and in the second sequence of the film he takes a position in a financial office. Shot 16 repeats the set-up of shot 1, the den of thieves that the young man has left. In shot 17 the hero is shown at work in his new office.

104

105

106

107

Shot 18 repeats the hotel room he and his robber friends assaulted in the first sequence of the film—a room containing the young woman with whom he has fallen in love and whose father is helping the hero begin anew. The combination of these images is the turning point toward a new sequence in the film, and it is absolutely characteristic that it points forward and backward in the history of the film. This kind of construction conveys and summarizes the basic elements of the plot to the audience. But it is of structural interest that this sequence of shots summarizes the "base" set-ups of the film: shots 1 and 2 are recalled at this transition and they point to the possibilities of the next section of the film. These familiar images bracket a new space (shot 17), the interior of the office that will be the staging image for the activity of the second sequence of the film. Far from being disoriented by the juxtaposition of three shots that have no ostensible spatial relationship, the audience is reassured by the repetition of the set-ups of shots 1 and 2.

Griffith uses this interplay between summarizing and propelling the narrative as a matter of course in such films as *A Summer Idyll* (1910). The fundamental opposition of this film is between a country life and a city life, a theme that receives a lengthy expository treatment in two images of city interiors, followed by an extended walk into the country that is headed by an icon of grandfather and granddaughter. The fact that the conflict will center on this opposition is not plain until, at shot 14, Griffith reintroduces the city into the shot order. Just as the hero is becoming interested in the country lass, the city woman pops into the film by way of a shot of her city parlor. This is followed by a repetition of the grandfather-and-child family icon. This juxtaposition of shots intends to reidentify the antagonists in this bucolic tussle for the young man's affections—a struggle the city woman wages without ever leaving her house to confront her rival. She simply sends letters to the country. The final half of the film is made up of three segments that are all referred back to the stable city icon, until the young man is gradually transferred out of the country locales and attracted back to the city where he "belongs." The repeated image of the city woman reinforces the symmetry in the sequence of shots and stands in opposition to the country icon as a very concrete visualization of the hero's options.

In *Comata, the Sioux* (1909), to allow her the luxury of a second choice, the film returns the wayward Indian maid to the shot of her first erring decision to marry a faithless white man. This film demonstrates the range of expression that can be achieved by repeating the same plot material in the context of familiar images. In *Comata, the Sioux* the heroine returns to the (almost literal) "crossroads" of her life to recognize the man who really loves her. In *The Mills of the Gods* (1909), when the disappointed young woman is left in a familiar image with the faithful suitor, she only reluctantly recognizes him and grudgingly bestows herself on him because she has lost the man she really loves. In *A Change of Heart* (1909) the suitor who is present at an actual crossroads, where the heroine literally took the wrong turn in life, is summarily and contemptuously dismissed. The basic situation and the structure are the same in all three films. The formal stability of construction serves as the base line over which the melody of the plot is played in either a major or a minor key.

Another means of building an infra-film history throughout the film is to refer all activity back to one stabilizing image, often a family icon. This shot is either the one from which the spatial relationships of the film will grow, or the one static image in the midst of activity. The chief quality of this sort of reference shot is its constancy—it serves as a point of stability in the midst of constructed activity.

Such is the case in *The Honor of His Family* (1909). The repetition of the image of the waiting father always refers to his son, who takes the family honor into the field of battle. This is a thematic matter, but the combination of the static, familiar image of the father with the frenzied activity of the battle is also a constructed effect. The father's position at the parlor window suggests a

Fig. 108. *The Honor of His Family* (1909)—
Portrait

look that is directly in contact with the actual events of the fight—although he clearly does not see the battle and spends much of his time facing the audience, toasting his son's valor (fig. 108). Most of all, the frequency with which the film refers back to this image (nine times in twenty-five shots) makes the father's image both a point of spatial reference and the location of the affective activity in the film. In the chain of shots, his is the central, stabilizing image, and it is not out of the question to say that Griffith uses this image to control the film, because with it he is able to suggest that the father's perceptions control the line of activity in the world of the film just as strongly as does the war in which the soldier is fighting. When the son runs from the battle, he eventually connects with the direction of the father's sight-line, and his actions are significant in response to the father's expectations about the son's behavior in the battle. Not all juxtapositions between waiting and activity suggest quite so powerful a sense of consequence, but in each instance where the stable image is joined to a line of activity, the same quality of communal life arises in the film, and Griffith is able to suggest the complicity (at least ideological or sympathetic) of all those concerned with the activity of the film.

These stabilizing images are an important source of the film's rhythm, punctuating sequences of activity. They are a collection point for all the thematic issues the film is raising. In *In Old Kentucky* (1909) the iconic image of the family unit, the portrait that opens the film, is rather long and represents the first sequence of the film. This icon is shattered by the Civil War: the brothers leave home and serve on opposite sides in the conflict. In the second sequence of *In Old Kentucky,* in the midst of the chase, it is to this icon of the home that the brothers literally return. Now enemies, pursuer and pursued, they return to the image that is a familiar and condensed statement of the unity that has been tragically sundered by the war. Of all the ways in which Griffith might have chosen to envision a conflict between brother and brother, this return to their actual home, the initial picture of harmony and repose, is a triumph of simplicity and efficiency. The idea is so simple and obvious that in the context of the film it works with a certain brutality—which Griffith does not scruple to exploit by expanding the home locale to include a new room, where the mother retreats to hide her Confederate son in her bed. The forceful entry of the Union son into this "innermost" room is almost too literally "meaningful." But the action in the context of the film is also a concrete visualization of the effects of the war on the family. The sense of violation issues from the structure.

Stabilizing images begin to appear more often in the context of intercutting. These shots are not the culmination of a series of images (appearing as though in summation), but actually function in the flow of activity through the chain of shots. *Love among the Roses* (1910) depends on the momentum built of the entrances and exits of the two sets of couples who swap and reswap partners in the course of their walks through a rose garden. In the midst of the activity, a shot is repeated: one young woman stands in the same set-up, neither exiting nor entering, providing the one stable point around which all the manic activity of the film swirls, a punctuating stillness in the midst of the easy flow of activity from shot to shot. This film is not a particularly deep one, but its rhythm is engaging, and Griffith ably exploits a structure that originally carried the more furious activity of the chase to make a charming comedy.

In *The Little Teacher* (1909) Griffith achieves an interplay of plot and subplot by interweaving the repeated image of the little teacher at the crossroads with images of the victory over a school bully. The latter process takes place over the greater number of shots, but in the repeated image a touching subplot is developed. The young teacher falls in love with a handsome surveyor, who helps her to control an unruly boy in her class, and she returns six times to the crossroads where she met this man, hoping that he will notice her and marry her. *The Mills of the Gods* is the most direct comparison to *The Little Teacher*. In the earlier film, the young woman simply stands near the man of her choice hoping that he will take notice of her, while the man remains stolidly oblivious of her and finally walks off with another woman. In *The Little Teacher* Griffith reserves one of the spaces of the film entirely for this dramatic yearning. The little teacher does not follow on the heels of her beloved as do so many suitors in Griffith's Biograph films. In shot 6 she stands waiting for the surveyor to claim her as his prize for having vanquished the school bully. This shot is spatially related to the rest of the film most strongly by the little teacher's look "toward" the shot in which the bully is subdued. Griffith uses this link by look to force this shot into a relationship with the physical activity of the film, until, with every repetition, it offers a more and more intense visualization of the heroine's expectations. At shot 19 (the set-up of shot 6 repeated), the problem of the bully has long since been resolved, but the film has just reached a dramatic pitch with the accumulated effect of the little teacher's occupation of the familiar image. She returns to the crossroads only to be cruelly surprised by the entry of her hero with his wife. This is, of course, another version of an image appearing in the wrong configuration, but this configuration refers specifically to the events in the world of the film, and its formality is entirely the result of the film's structure.

It is likely that the drama of *The Little Teacher* might have been visualized in any number of different ways, but difficult to imagine how it might have been constructed with the economy and power that Griffith achieves. The choice of repeating the image compounds the effect of the film in two ways. First, one is forced to consider the effect of the other shots on this image. Each juxtaposition colors the representation of the familiar image in which the heroine stands. Secondly, the changes in the repeated image itself form a basis of comparison, creating a sort of overtone of her expectations that stands in contrast with the information being relayed by the rest of the film.

Quite often, Griffith interjects a familiar image that is not necessarily spatially related to the chain in which it appears. These kinds of reference shots are more abstract than those that recapitulate and stabilize. They often have the effect of a lightning flash of significance and are images that have no other relationship to the matter at hand than to create such a mental effect. These images are rarely so firmly connected to the physical activity of the film as are the images of the lookers and the waiters who project the graphic thrust of their gazes across the cut to connect with loved ones "far away" in the discontinuous space of the film. Often, in the return to a specific shot, one finds a particularly self-contained content that is forced into a relationship with the organization of the world of the film through shot order alone. In *One Touch of Nature* (1908) the opening image of a mother distraught over the death of her child is interjected into a sequence in which a cruel gypsy woman is beating her child. The connection is obvious, but the juxtaposition of shots is a bold one, for it recalls the film's beginning to the viewer to force a comparison of two mothers and prepares for the fact that the policeman-father will rescue this selfsame child and bring her to his home to restore the icon of his family, incomplete since the first image, to its proper configuration—father, mother, and living child. The effect of this shot order is a statement of the film's theme and a foreshadowing of the film's resolution. This effect is only possible because Griffith is willing to inject "foreign" (and potentially disorienting) material into a developing sequence of activity.

Griffith's willingness to let the total effect of the film take place in the audience instead of on the screen often makes this return of the familiar image particularly effective. In the intense *Edgar Allen Poe* [*sic*] (1909) Griffith lends a sense of urgency to Poe's passage from office to office to sell his writing by cutting back to the shot (a closer view, but the same angle as the original view) of Poe's dying wife. The conjunction of shots produces a burst of significance. The full importance of Poe's anxious, frenzied attempt to sell his work is stated in the comparison with his wife's stillness. The combination of these two images generates real emotional power, as well as a parallel sense of time: Poe must make some money before it is too late. The eventual irony of Poe's wasted efforts is experienced by the audience, which knows the wife is dead before he discovers her.

The return to a familiar image for reference was not always so intensely dramatic. Griffith used the return to a specific shot to create some comic situations. In *The Little Darling* (1909) all the activity, from the visit to the toy store to the arrival at the train station, is referred back to the house to which the little darling is to go, where all await her arrival. Nothing changes in this house, but the cuts back to it increase the sense of comic anticipation by juxtaposing this image with information that the viewer has, but the darling's relatives do not: they have prepared for a tiny child; the darling is a charming young woman. The pay-off occurs when this disparity of information is resolved.

A similar effect is created in *They Would Elope* (1909). Each locale is complete unto itself: the young couple elopes; family and friends gather to toast their wedding. Intercut, these locales convey to the audience the comic irony of frantically trying to escape a family that is only too glad to see the marriage take place.

In the poker game of *The Last Deal* (1909) realistic and affective locales of the film are intermingled. The sequence is made up of two shots of a poker game in which there is no plot necessity to refer to the wife left at home. The viewer has already met the wife in the first sequence of the film and is well aware of her attitude toward her husband's gambling. Griffith maintains her presence in the film by interjecting her image into a sequence where it has only affective duty to do, the subject of which is not only who will win at cards, but how this will affect the wife, who is already worried about her husband's gambling habits. In addition, the space in which she appears becomes one of the crucial spaces of the next sequence. Her space, introduced in the context of the card game, is set up to be a familiar image, a point of reference that resounds back and forth in the history of the film.

This function emerges as early as *Through the Breakers* (1909), in which the idle mother "realizes" that something is amiss with her sick child in the midst of a party. At that point she actually receives word that she must rush home. The emotional telegraph precedes the actual revelation of the information of the film. Griffith specifies and clarifies this effect with intercutting. In *In Life's Cycle* (1910) Griffith introduces a shot of the girl's brother walking forward to look out the foreground in a sequence in which his sister is about to be seduced. The interposition of this shot of the brother at once deepens the sense of the girl's peril, although the connection is abstract and reflects only a vague intuition, a sudden chill the brother feels without knowing why. There is no indication that the brother actually knows what is going on—there is certainly no indication that his space has any "real" relationship to his sister's space. But he is nonetheless drawn into the dramatic moment on the basis of a sympathetic feeling. Griffith carries on this direct relay of emotional information throughout his Biograph period. In *Judith of Bethulia* (1913) the two lovers, Nathan and Naomi, are separated by the war. Naomi telegraphs her need to Nathan across the miles and draws him to her rescue, an effect achieved by the juxtaposition of shots of the lovers in the course of the film.

Often, the sympathetic or affective juxtaposition of shots introduces a new character and is retained throughout the film. In *A Welcome Intruder* (1913) a child is abducted and randomly placed in a wagon, which is then driven out of town. Intercut between shots of the father inquiring for his lost child at a police station is the introduction of the widow who will take the child to her heart. In shot 41 the father is walking into the station; shot 42 introduces the widow; shot 43 completes the father's entry into the station. At this point in the film, the viewer has no idea who this woman is. The title tells that she is the housekeeper of the men who have unwittingly carried the abducted child away from the father. Had Griffith waited until the men arrived at her house to introduce the shot of this woman, the sequence would have made perfectly good dramatic and logical sense. But he chose to sandwich her image into the sequence that winds up the father's desperate search for his child. This juxtaposition is a variation on the referential ideas Griffith had used to this point. The device is at hand when Griffith needs it to introduce a new character in an image that will itself become familiar in the film. In fact, this image is the goal of a line of activity being taken by the wagon, which has been intercut with the father's walk in search of his child.

The introduction of the widow prepares a "motivation" for the eventual relationship between this woman and the father. This relationship is primarily conveyed by the order of the shots. In the sequence of shots 59–61, the substance of shots 41–43 is repeated, but inside out. Now it is the father's image, the familiar home of shot 1 where the father was first introduced to the audience, that is sandwiched between shots of the widow in her home with the abducted child (figs. 109–11). The family portrait toward which the film is tending is half-assembled twice in *A Welcome Intruder*. It is only completed when the father returns to the widow's house at Christmas to offer her his hand and ask her to be the mother to his child (figs. 112–14). Finally, the three occupy the same shot (fig. 115).

In *The Rocky Road* (1909) a composite family portrait is made of three separate shots that appear at transitions between sequences of the film to suggest the span of time that renders the dramatic premise plausible. A child grows up and prepares to marry her father, whom she has never seen and therefore accepts as a suitor. The film begins with a strictly geographical intermingling of the paths of the young woman's mother and father—he abandons her in a drunken fit, and she follows him out of town. Sequence 2 intercuts two images of these people: the father sheds his life of drunken madness in a strongly composed image from which no one enters or exits; the mother begins a life of madness occasioned by his desertion. She and her child veer toward the left foreground in an image that echoes the diagonal that organizes the husband's stable image. A transitional sequence follows in which mother and child are found and taken in by a kindly farm family, although the mother is too crazy by that time to tell them that the child is hers or identify herself to them in any other way. The transitional sequence introduces the locale in which the next sequence will occur (shots 23 and 24, the farmhouse exterior and interior) and ends with a juxtaposition of the *father's* shot in his new state (prosperity), to the *mother* (madness), to the *child* (on her eighteenth birthday). This composite portrait not only summarizes the dramatic problem of the film (the separation of the family that may lead to the disaster of incest), but satisfactorily accounts for a passage of eighteen years.

In *The Rocky Road* Griffith had begun to mix methods of recapitulation used in other films. From *The Country Doctor* he took the repetition of iconic images (father, mother, child). From films such as *Comata, the Sioux* and *The Broken Locket* (both 1909) he took the recapitulation of the walk, a course of following that is not meant to achieve the end of catching. The form of the chase run through repeated images appears only briefly at the beginning of *The Rocky Road* to underscore the tragedy of the separation of the family.

This abortive chase order at the beginning of *The Rocky Road* interacts with the family icon broken into a suite of related images, repeated in substance in the course of the film (although father, mother, and child are repeated in order, the actual images change in the course of the film). This composite family portrait accomplishes several tasks. The first is the statement of the relationship itself, a sense that these people belong together, created by the fact that their images always appear in a cluster in the chain. The second task is a statement of the position of each family member in the world of the film as the story proceeds. The third is a composite image of the "natural" family configuration that stands in opposition to the unnatural image that is trying to assemble itself in the film.

Breaking up the family icon could be more useful than maintaining it as a simple image-portrait. In *The Rocky Road* each character could then do spatial work, as well as significant work in the film. Moreover, since it is the audience that holds the whole picture of the film, the splitting of the icon conveys orientation, relationships, a sense of history, a sense of foreboding, and a sense of memory that exists in the audience alone, for it is the audience that compares images in which madness, neglect, and simple ignorance deny the obvious connection between these three people and threaten to destroy them.

The combination of images itself conveys the sense of history, the theme of recognition and memory to the audience. The recapitulation of a suite of im-

Figs. 109–15. *A Welcome Intruder* (1913)—
Iconic Groups (sequential groups)

109

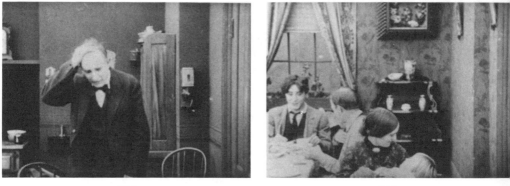

110   111

ages urges the audience to engage in this process of building an infra-film history just as it built the dimensions of the locale from activity. As with physical
activity, the strict order of the images assures that the audience will not lose its
way as the film begins to encompass greater spans of time and more complex
emotional effects.

Memory—A Matter of Reference

A tremendous amount of information is transmitted by the films once
Griffith begins to employ these methods of exposition that essentially rely on
increasing the number of ways shots can be related. This is true of sequences
in which modes of exposition (iconic; walking) have been combined, as in
The Modern Prodigal, where a point of reference serves to introduce new sequences; as in *Swords and Hearts,* in which a shot foreign to the spatial coherence of the sequence immediately at hand becomes the crucial space of the

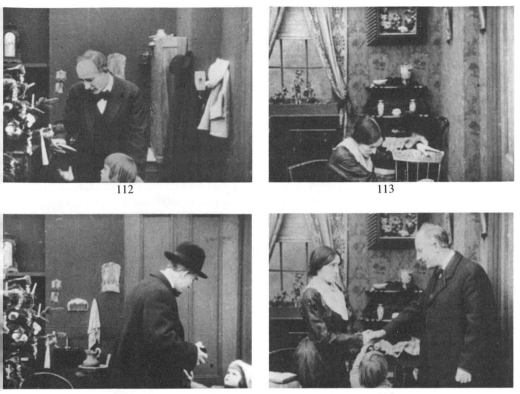

112

113

114

115

sequence that will be developed next; as in *The Last Deal,* in which the resolution of one part of the film is interwoven with the exposition of the next.

The heart of Griffith's approach to dramatic action is an ability to infuse memory, imagination, and desire into the processes of physical activity that display the plots of his films. Reference is the device used to create tensions between the immediacy of activity and the endurance of memory in the world of the film. These mental qualities are present in varying degrees in Griffith's Biograph films. Sometimes the sense of memory or imagination is shared between character and audience. Sometimes it is primarily the audience that makes the connection between two concrete instances in the film—an effect produced particularly by shot order. Sometimes, there is a strong sense that the viewer knows what the characters are thinking and feeling. In any case, the audience is led to believe that it knows more than the simple physical facts of the film.

The stage directors of the nineteenth century had established a method of depicting the thoughts of the characters in the drama. The "popular 'vision' sequence [was] a pictorial presentation of action proceeding within the mind of one of the characters on stage." [13] This appeared in early films as the "dream balloon." Although there are many examples, one of the best known examples of the "dream balloon" (and one of the most literal) is in E. S. Porter's *Life of an American Fireman*. "A firechief [is] asleep and dreaming in his office chair. [He sees] a vision, a dream . . . of a mother putting her child to bed. This scene dissolves to the ringing of an alarm at the neighborhood box." [14] Griffith abandoned the mediating "balloon" effect and ignored the possibilities of dissolving in favor of the direct juxtaposition of shots. Consequently, he achieved effects that were both more subtle and more ambiguous. These mental suggestions begin to be relayed as early as *Behind the Scenes* (1908), where Griffith implies a sort of sympathetic relationship between a mother performing on stage and her dying child by intercutting their two images. Forced to complete her stage act because "the show must go on," the mother cannot rush home when she hears that her child has taken a turn for the worse. Shot order is the only relationship between the mother and the child, and this creates the clear implication that the child is "in the mother's thoughts" during the performance. Placed as it is in the midst of this performance, the effect of the child's death is all the more striking. The spatial discontinuity between these two spaces suddenly coincides with the disparity between the viewer's knowledge and what the mother still hopes and believes to produce the dramatic impact of the sequence.

In *The Christmas Burglars* (1908) Griffith uses a rare dissolve to create this sympathetic relationship between characters very explicitly by joining two shots that are obviously unrelated spatially. A pawnshop owner who has played Santa to the family of a poor woman reads the letter her children have written to Santa. This shot (19, the set-up of 3 repeated) dissolves into the image in shot 20 (1) of the children dancing around the Christmas tree the pawnshop owner has given them, then dissolves back to him enjoying his anonymous good deed in shot 21 (3). The dissolve has the effect of identifying the man directly with his generous action, implying that he envisions the children's joy in a scene that conveys a sense of immediacy that is both mental and physical.

In *A Plain Song* (1910) the referential image intercut into the chain of shots resolves the film. It has both a more literal meaning and a more tantalizing position. The image Griffith repeats for affective emphasis in *A Plain Song* fits the temporal flow of the story, so there is a delicious ambiguity about when and where the shot occurs. Edith wishes to marry and escape her duty to her parents, one of whom is blind. She is standing in the railway station waiting to buy the tickets that will take her away with her fiancé when an old couple pass before her. Griffith underscores this entrance rather heavily with a title: "Remember thy father and thy mother," then cuts to an image of the young woman's parents, sleeping peacefully, unconscious of their abandonment. The actual shot of these people is the third and most concrete statement of the emotional coefficients of Edith's situation. Are they a mental image? Like the image of the wife in *After Many Years,* the image of Edith's parents in *A Plain Song* exists in at least two "places" in the film. The old people exist immediately, here, now in the chain of the shots for the viewer—temporally paralleling the young woman's position in the film. They also exist as a recollection—the memory of her own parents recalled to/by Edith by the passage of the old couple through the frame in the train station. This resounding recollection of the film's theme—filial devotion—begins the resolution. The end of this film finds Edith racing back to retrieve the note she has left for her parents. In 1909 this film would merely have ended with the daughter's return to her parents. But by 1910 Griffith is able to extract the last dramatic moments from the plot. Edith saves her parents from the knowledge that she would have abandoned them. More important, Griffith is able to dramatize the fact that awareness (rather than ignorance or unconsciousness) pertains to the resolution of the plot.

The relationship of the stranded father to the image of the faithful wife is usually a reciprocal one in Griffith's Biograph films. Annie Lee's look in *After Many Years* implies a reciprocal awareness, which creates a narrative dynamic of parallel waiting, rather than of a parallel action, as was more common in early films. Waiting is a visual theme that Griffith often creates by building patterns of reference in his films. In *Lines of White on a Sullen Sea* (1909) Emily and her suitor travel from her porch to the beach to the boardwalk, where he pledges eternal love to her. When her lover leaves to go to sea, the scope of the young woman's life is encompassed in this walk, and her return to the boardwalk indicates the resolution she awaits. But the audience discovers that the lover's return to this familiar image is impossible. When he faithlessly marries another woman, Griffith is able to contrast two views of the world of the film—Emily's and the audience's. All subsequent activity refers back to the circumscribed world of the walk, indicating the tragic problem of the young woman's illusions. Links created from this suite of images to the other locales of the film will not be made by Emily herself, and the associations the viewer makes between shots in the greater world of the film deepen Emily's immobility, abandonment, and tragic self-delusion. Her fantasy is maintained, rather than dispersed, in the second sequence of the film. The irony of *Lines of White on a Sullen Sea* is that the information that could free the betrayed woman—that the man she loves has married another—is withheld from her. She dies with the faithless suitor kneeling at her bedside, falsely professing his love to her.

In *The Unchanging Sea* (1910) Griffith combines previous structures. The viewer first sees a fisherman and his wife taking a walk through their fishing village—a walk that is an expanded version of that first blissful walk in *After Many Years*. Three shots express the dimensions of the village, and also, by extension, the life of the woman, who fears she has lost her man at sea, but spends the rest of her life hoping for his return. The comparison with *Lines of White on a Sullen Sea* is obvious: just as the ruined woman repeats the walk to the scene of what the audience knows is her betrayal, so the wife in *The Unchanging Sea* walks to the image in which she and her husband bade farewell. There she waits for his return. The rhythmical order of that walk organizes the experience of the wait. It is repeated three times in the course of the film, and all the other events of the film occur within its context: the child grows up, meets a man, marries; an old suitor courts the waiting wife. But all of these events occurring in this setting only remind the audience of the major fact of the film, the separation of the husband from the wife. And all the events of the film almost recede before the obsessive concentration of activity in these repeated images, the effect of which is to make the audience concentrate on the correct resolution of the film—the reunion of so faithful a woman with so haplessly lost a sailor.

Never had Griffith introduced so much stray material into the suite of familiar images and still maintained the concentration of character and audience on the "real" importance of these images. Both the husband and the wife are presented in dynamic situations that depict a process parallel to the immediacy of the separation the wife experiences. In one image the fisherman is shown in a village where he has found work following the accident at sea that has caused him to forget who he is. The wife's image, projecting the force of her look across the miles to her lost husband, is repeated eight times in the course of thirty shots, and it is the collected power of attraction in this image that builds the sense of history in one of the most touching portrayals of loss and recovery achieved in the Biograph films.

In all of these cases, one begins to get a sense of a family or a person with a definite life story—of events conveying more than an immediate meaning, and one cannot help but be dragged into the ruse that one is thinking and remembering along with the silent characters of the film, making associations as they make them.

The spatial and temporal ambiguity of such juxtapositions of shots is demonstrated in the introduction of the woman into the work day of one of her suitors in *Death's Marathon* (1913). The shot of her sitting in a sunlit arbor is at once memory, imagination, idealization—this latter implication created specifically by mise-en-scène. This shot is the viewer's introduction to the young woman and has a sense of immediacy that somewhat conflicts with the spatial and temporal unity of the day at the office that is the ostensible subject of the first sequence of the film. But by introducing the young woman in a sequence of related activity, Griffith makes sure that by the time she is actively involved in the film, the audience recognizes her and senses her importance, as well as recognizing an image that will become the familiar one in the next sequence of the film.

The power of imagination that Griffith taps for both character and audience creates the affective meaning of the film. The ability of the audience to take notice of the pertinent facts that expand Griffith's films from incidents to histories depends on the efficiency and clarity of Griffith's presentation. Usually, the combination of a strong composition with the repetition of shots ensures that proper notice is taken.

In *The Fugitive,* for instance, Griffith concludes with a moment that is so interior, so introverted, so private, that the viewer almost wishes to withdraw tactfully from it. The mother of the dead Confederate soldier, all alone in her cabin, pins a sprig of lilac to the soldier's uniform. At this moment many associations occur. The viewer understands all the events that have led up to this point and the moment itself occurs in a shot that has at least three distinct functions: it is, and has been throughout the film, the comparative icon to the shot of the mother of the Union soldier—a man who is now alive because the Confederate mother generously hid him; the shot has been the stage of the physical activity of the film, joined to allied exterior spaces to form a definite locale; and the shot is the staging area of the film's future, as the daughter and her rather bored fiancé leave the mother to mourn alone. The audience does not see the mother's future, but can make a good guess. Suddenly, the audience, always an omniscient observer in Griffith's films, possesses too much knowledge. The abandonment of so noble a woman is painful, and the viewer is almost embarrassed. The key to the force of this feeling is the combination of all these functions in one image culminating a chain of shots.

The secret of deliberation and repose in Griffith's work is the creation of the moment in which the viewer feels that he understands the thought of a stationary, silent character who stares into the space of an image that is all too familiar, but tragically transformed. It is this ruse that delivers the dramatic impact of Griffith's *The Painted Lady* (1912). A young woman had always met her lover on the same rustic bridge. A dramatic rush of imagination fills the gap left in this image when the young woman, mad with grief after having killed her lover, returns to imagine he still stands there with her. The consonance of audience and actor imaginations is not so much a matter of performance as of the impact of this return, of having to see an image once more that one knew in better, happier times.

One of Griffith's finest accomplishments was the structure that brought about this kind of accumulated effect. The two processes by which it was achieved were intercutting and repetition. Intercutting emphasizes the relationship between shots; repetition creates a sense of familiarity upon which the audience can rely. The effect of this process of construction is that the audience is led to fill the gaps Griffith could not fill in the one-reel format. Because the emphasis is on the cut, and the information in any one shot is at least partially created by its relationship with preceding and succeeding shots, Griffith could tone down the amount of information the actor had to convey by mime. Theatrical gesture was drastically scaled down in the course of Griffith's Biograph period. As further fragmentation became important to the development of sequences of action, the time in which actors and actresses could emote was even more radically curtailed. One need only compare the 1−minute shot of 1908 with the 1.5−second shot of 1913 to see that a change had taken place. But the subordination of acting to the rhythm of the film oddly enhanced the expressiveness of Griffith's troupe. As his Biograph period progressed, the types that populate the early films become more personalized. This is at least in part because of the process of intercutting shots that are repeated through their changes or in their resistance to change, which causes the audience to create personalities for the actors. At the same time, performances actually did of necessity become more controlled, more discreet.

Before Griffith's work, the main way to grab the audience's attention was to run with the plot. Griffith was very quick to realize that activity could be purely mental and did not have to rely on the physical token of the dream balloon or even the telephone and the telegraph to relay information across the miles of the film. A shot placed in the order of the chain can be read as an affective message regardless of what the audience knows about the real geographical distances of the world of the film. Moreover, Griffith did not confine his use of this affective potential to special instances. The affective image often became a reference point for the film's activity, and specific locales in the film are transcended by the pattern of the whole film, in which shot-to-shot relationships convey both mental and physical energy.

It was in the process of creating these reference points in his films that Griffith finally found the affective resonance he needed to vitalize his films and expand the range of narrative possible in a single reel of film. He was able to create films charged with the excitement of emotions as well as the rush of physical activity. In one sense, Griffith's "cuts back" were as much "cuts in"—that is, inclusions to give reference and emotional scope to activity immediately occurring. The transcendence of the requirements of physical activity to create spatial coherence helped to introduce a contemplative quality in Griffith's films. The possibility of "psychological" content in the Biograph films, the suggestion that each event is more than itself, is particularly the effect of placing reference shots in the chain. Each event extends the history of the film, emerging from a spatial context of interlocking geographical relationships to encompass an imaginative dimension.

Between 1908 and 1913 critics developed the following standards for screen realism: (1) psychology; (2) deliberate acting; (3) a credibly told story (with some doubts expressed as to the suitability of "serious" subjects for the screen); (4) dramatic consistency; (5) credible staging with realistic detail; (6) consistency of presentation, which included economy and a tempo suited to the subject; (7) structural soundness, with exact and fluid matching at doorways.[1]

These standards evolved slowly. A cursory examination of films made before 1908 reveals that the cut on action and the match between cuts on action were by no means structural norms. Recent evidence indicates that between 1902 and 1906 there were repeated instances of action overlapping at the cut—some of these involving cuts on the axis (as in Biograph's *The Widow and the Only Man*), others involving shot-to-shot continuity (as in *The Life of an American Fireman*.)[2] This overlap may not have been annoying or even noticeable to early audiences, who did not expect that the visual path would be smoothed for them through the film by actions "matched" over cuts.[3] Nonetheless, by 1909 Frank Woods, the "Spectator" of the *New York Dramatic Mirror,* was criticizing films for not exhibiting continuity cutting.[4]

Whether prints of Griffith's early Biograph work are edited correctly or not in the prints available for viewing today, the potential exists in the footage for an absolutely smooth passage of action from shot to shot. In the case of Griffith's first film, *The Adventures of Dollie,* this characteristic may reflect the Biograph expertise in producing chase films, such as *The Lost Child* (1904), as well as the experience of Griffith's cameramen, Billy Bitzer and Arthur Marvin, both of whom had directed films and worked with other directors before Griffith came to the Biograph Company. But the primacy of continuity cutting also reflected a structural response to the material Griffith worked with. The Biograph plots generally emphasize coincidence and achieve their emotional effects through dramatic irony. In an effort to visualize this material, Griffith sought to channel continuous activity through structures that would produce a picture of coinciding forces rather than forced coincidences.

Entrance and exit points in the frame suggest Griffith's early feeling for building continuity with action. In *The Fatal Hour* (1908), for instance, the ride to the rescue is displayed on a background-to-right-foreground diagonal that simply states that the rescuers are coming "toward" the heroine, who occupies a position in the right half of her image and is tied to a bed watching a clock ticking off the minutes of the fatal hour of the film's title. Although there was some early trouble negotiating interiors, as exemplified in the confusion of place in *The Bandit's Waterloo* (1908) and the conflicting directions of *For a Wife's Honor* (1908), Griffith generally tended toward matching activity over cuts. By *The Curtain Pole* (1908) a sense of rhythm enters into the film, with the arrangement of diagonals alternating directions across the faces of successive shots. At one point, the direction of the chase in this film is even reversed. In *The Criminal Hypnotist,* made a bit later in 1908, Griffith effects his first actual reverse of action over the cut, shifting the direction across the cut from toward to away from the camera.

Most of these films would not be considered the major projects of 1908, yet even this "routine" work shows a tendency toward formal unity within the flow of activity. Although early transitions between interiors and exteriors were roughly executed, exterior activity already showed a basic understanding of the principles of matching the line and direction of one person's activity in the shot to the line and direction of activity in the succeeding shot. When one character walked through a space and exited, "following" or "chasing" could be shown by having the pursuer duplicate that walk and that exit. "Catching" was signified by having the pursuer enter the image while the pursued still occupied the shot, a process of "chasing" that may be extended over two or three shots before actual contact is made.

The Call of the Wild and *The Red Girl* (both 1908) contain examples of such structures. The first film that seems to indicate an awareness of the fact that matched actions could function outside the chase is *'Tis an Ill Wind That Blows No Good* (1909). In this film, the continuity of a woman's walk bridges the spaces between two dramatic sequences of shots.

By 1909 Griffith was able to build a whole film from actions that were smoothly matched over cuts. The general tendency was to simplify a situation spatially while retaining activity as the basis of continuity. The shot-bounded lateral took the burden of interior activity, while the chase diagonal was a basic exterior line of action, although, as with the child's walk in *What Drink Did* and the doctor's path in *The Country Doctor,* the lateral was also used in exterior construction. *The Cardinal's Conspiracy* is the first film to display the practice of shooting architecture from a low angle, and buildings and rock formations assume a more imposing pictorial role in Biograph films from this point on. But for all its monumentalism, *The Cardinal's Conspiracy* also flows. It was one of the first films that accommodated a variety of levels in the frame upon which activity could be staged. Unlike its predecessors, *When*

Knights Were Bold (Biograph, 1908) and Griffith's own *Love Finds a Way* (1908), *The Cardinal's Conspiracy,* which takes the form of a walk, grace-fully reaches a dramatic goal by extending a line of activity from shot to shot until the dramatic resolution is reached in the form of a physical objective, a final shot in a chain of shots. The resolution of the father-daughter conflict over marriage partners in this film is a literary affair, but the outcome of *The Cardinal's Conspiracy* also refers a physical point of departure to a physical point of arrival on a walk through a garden.

"The recent viewing of films made in 1907 confirms a hypothesis that film-makers of that period, whatever the exceptions, systematically avoided com-plicating the structures of their films, perhaps so as not to mislead the audi-ence," [5] André Gaudréault writes. Once Griffith seized control of the power inherent in the discontinuous spaces of his films, he never seems to have wor-ried that the audience might not "follow" the line of his thought. Eventually, he could literally insert any number of shots into a sequence without disturb-ing the sense of the film's logic. The awareness that an audience can be en-couraged to seek the wholeness of graphic completion, the unity of a series of shots presented to it, is not explicitly acknowledged in Griffith's work, but it is the implicit basis of all construction in his Biograph period. The insertion of new shots in the order of the chain takes advantage of the freedom of dis-continuous spaces. It is the smooth flow of activity through these spaces that convinces the audience of the correctness of the order of the world viewed and leads to an acceptance of connections between shots that are much wilder to contemplate than to experience.

The audience's awareness of shot order is often most important in signaling the convergence of all the lines of activity in the film. This signal may be conveyed actually (all the characters appear in the same space) or affectively (a node of shots comparing the positions of all the characters in the world of the film). The convergence of lines of activity may be the resolution of an entire film (*The Lonely Villa*); or of a sequence of the film (*The Modern Prodigal*); or of a sequence that resolves the film (*The Primal Call*).

There may be an indication that the character has eluded this convergence, based on the fact that the pursuers complete only a limited number of the shots that the pursued has "traced out." This occurs in *The Modern Prodigal* (1910), where the pursuers are simply "lost" when the prodigal ducks under a box floating in the middle of a lake. Griffith exploits this idea of losing pur-suers in the order of shots more fully in *Swords and Hearts* (1911), where the pursuers are held in position for five shots until they finally lose track of their quarry, who has been advancing to new spaces. In *The Girl and Her Trust* (1912), although the space outside the train station is a composite of relation-ships to interior positions, the number of doors that separates the thieves from the heroine signifies the consequence of converging lines of activity. In the second sequence of the film, this convergence of activity is developed in complementary suites of images in which pursuer and pursued are "matched" graphically (size, direction) before they actually begin to enter each other's spaces.

In a Griffith film, the illusion of continuous activity is extended over discontinuous, but often-repeated, spaces. Matching the line of activity from shot to shot indicates that the discontinuous spaces are at least directionally related—one can say that one space lies to the right or left of another without knowing anything more about "where" the characters are in the world of the film. Given the condensed format of the Biograph reel and Griffith's appreciation for speed and motion, the control of activity by a cut was more efficient and effective than the explication of a real continuous geography full of material extraneous to the dramatic point of the film.

Pippa Passes (1909) illustrates a principle of continuity in Griffith's films. Griffith seems to have intuited that the audience would feel a character to be moving even when that activity is interrupted by a number of shots delineating the dimensions of, and displaying the action of characters in, another locale of the film. In the first sequence of *Pippa Passes*, for instance, Pippa exits the left foreground of shot 2 and only reenters the film in shot 6. At that point she makes a graceful entrance from the right that suggests that the continuity of her walk is carried over from shot 2. The continuity of Pippa's passage is based on the creation of such "geographical" linkage, and her walk becomes the thread of continuous action that unifies the entire world of the film, although she appears only intermittently in the course of the film. These appearances occur just often enough to assure the audience that her energy has not flagged or disappeared from the world of the film. The same kind of geographical link joins sequence 1 to sequence 2. After Pippa passes out of shot 6 (traveling to the right), two shots occur, a portrait of reconciliation appears back to back with another portrait of discord that Pippa's passing soothes. When Pippa reenters the film, there is another firm geographic link to her line of activity (flowing left to right). This intermittent assertion of directional continuity in *Pippa Passes* allows Griffith to generate a great deal of energy in the film by implication, an accomplishment of obvious importance to a man confined to reels approximately fourteen minutes long.

Pippa Passes is important because it represents Griffith's first major victory over "forbidden" material. Early critics, even the enlightened Frank Woods, felt that film, with its populist roots and its penchant for melodrama and action, might *naturally* be unsuited to serious artistic achievement. This question was usually posed in terms of whether adaptations of "serious" literary works might be filmed successfully.[6] Griffith approached the premier screening of his film of Robert Browning's poem "Pippa Passes" with trepidation, and emerged with an unqualified success.[7] It is no surprise to find that it is a dynamic pattern of passage, of walking, that provides the very satisfactory coherence of the film. The geography of this walk carries the sense of

Browning's poem, even though the lives Pippa affects seem to be the more obvious dramatic material. Characteristically, Griffith centers the effect of this film in construction and achieves an overall tone of fluid grace. One might compare Vitagraph's *Francesca da Rimini* (1907) or Griffith's own version of *Rigoletto, A Fool's Revenge* (1909), to *Pippa Passes* as examples of adaptations that have turned into tableaux and therefore become frozen in cultural pretensions.

Griffith is hardly unique in his use of a number of entrances and exits in the frame, but he is unique among early filmmakers in his insistence that these entrances and exits be definitive. It is true that occasionally action will slip through oddly joined shots, or the same set-up will be reached from a number of different directions. But generally this is not the case. The question "where" is a major dramatic issue in Griffith's films (how close is the villain? how near is the hero?) and one that finds expression specifically in terms of composition, shot order, and the direction of activity through the world of the film. The audience may not know an exact location in terms of city streets, but has a very clear sense of where in the film characters are located with respect to each other. The careful connections between shots constructs a web of relationships among shots that lets the audience know what to expect, not so much in terms of plot and narrative (although that is a corollary kind of information) as in terms of the order of the film itself. The question "where" can be answered with reference to the other shots in the film.

Increasingly, spatial relationships within the frame are affected by the realization that space between shots can be absolutely manipulated because it is absolutely abstract. Griffith's films may often have disappointingly light and banal plots. Although some social points are scored, Griffith is too often just as happy with the conclusions that the family unit is the solution to society's ills; that it is right to be angry with the rich, but not to strike out at them; and that women are the general hope of the universe. But, remarkably, Griffith generates feelings in his films that far outstrip the banality of the material—one is constantly surprised to find oneself deeply moved by one of these melodramatic little chestnuts. This effect has sometimes been attributed to the fact that Griffith was able to elicit performances of remarkable subtlety and delicacy from his actors and actresses, and that this acting was enhanced by his decision to use close-ups—to concentrate the camera's eye on the human face. While Griffith's repertory company was indeed remarkable, more emphasis must be placed on the fact that by the end of a Griffith film, the viewer has experienced a very complex set of abstract graphic relationships that feel normal, realistic, and even familiar. These feelings are elicited by the experience of the film as a total effect, rather than a series of performances, no matter how commanding.

Griffith had no timetable of development in his Biograph period. He may not have been absolutely aware of all the effects produced by the structures in his films. Yet, even if the structural consistency in his Biograph period is intuitive, the ever-evolving shape of the course of activity gives evidence of the fact that Griffith felt that the narrative effect was generated, rather than illustrated, in the cinema. Many alterations were made in basic structures. Some experiments were dropped, others only infrequently duplicated. But while it may have taken Griffith some time to realize exactly what he had discovered (and while he may have spent the rest of his life trying to put it into words) structures evolved during his Biograph period served as the foundation for all of Griffith's later work.

Dramatic activity in the cinema began with the simple charm of movement, to which early filmmakers such as Georges Méliès, Edwin S. Porter, and the directors preceding Griffith at the Biograph Studio added the magnitude of crowds and the speed and impetus of running bodies. The comic mayhem of people spilling in and out of the sets of such Méliès one-shot films as *The Inn Where No Man Rests* (1902) and *The Magic Lantern* (1902) quickly challenged the limits of the frame and burst out of the shot at the cut in the early chase films of Hepworth and the fabled Sheffield Photo Company, credited by some as "one of the first, if not the first, to popularize the chase film." [8] Continuous activity achieved speed. Griffith's contribution to the cinema was to take this speed and channel its energy into drama—the running was toned down and the impact of cutting and assembly was made to suggest human emotion, thought, and psychology. In fact, this latter effect was the creation of the audience, engaged as it was in understanding the relationships Griffith created between shots through which physical activity ran like an electric current.

The dramatic effect of Griffith's films is based on a deliberately constructed continuity, and to achieve this coherence, Griffith had to control several structural variables. He controlled visibility within the shot. He insured that what he thought was important—a face, a gesture, a detail—would be seen by the viewer. To this end, he employed a *bounded* shot, a unit of mise-en-scène in which only rare changes in camera angle occur, and in which the volume of the actor's figure (long shot to close up) is usually varied only by the actor's movement through the frame. In some cases, there is a direct cut into or out from the actor's figure. This basic unit is *repeated* many times in the course of the film. The consequences for visibility are obvious: the image becomes so familiar that any variation is immediately noticeable. In fact, these variations can be glaring changes, as with the absence of a beloved family member in a formally composed portrait scene that resolves the film. The basic unit is also *discontinuous* with other spaces in the film. Close examination reveals that Griffith's unit of construction is basically spatially discrete, exhibiting very little angular or linear overlap with its sequential neighbors. Discontinuity means that the relationship between shots is of necessity constructed and artificial, no matter how "natural" the transition between one shot and an "adjoining" one seems to be.

The decisions exercised in regard to visibility were not all aesthetic ones. The Biograph Company liked Griffith to work quickly and economically, and the pressure of production schedules alone may have militated against a variety of angles that would have mitigated the effects of repetition and discontinuity. In any case, repetition and discontinuity are two of the definitive characteristics of Griffith's Biograph work, and the decisions he made about narrative construction demonstrate that these definitions were at least functionally recognized.

Having controlled visibility within the frame, Griffith also needed to control the flow of physical, and eventually emotional and psychological, activity through the world of the film. Continuity cutting suggested that the audience could be convinced that two shots, two spaces, were adjoining bits if activity passed fluidly between them, providing an uninterrupted flow that directed the eye from one shot to the next. The Biograph films reveal three basic principles governing the flow of physical activity:

1. Action inscribed across the face of the shot creates continuity from shot to shot, regardless of actual elisions of space between shots. Actual discontinuity can be bridged by the audience's assumption that if action flows from one shot directly to another, those spaces are immediately adjoining. Place in the film can therefore be constructed instead of illustrated.

2. The space of a film depends on the structure of activity. The perceived coherence and character of the world of the film depend on the manner in which activity flows through it. It can be perceived as a physical space with definitive destinations and boundaries: a house whose door neighbors try to break down; an opposition of country and town, in which intercutting shows a father and a lover contending for the affections of a daughter. It can also be perceived as mental space, because without the confirming flow of physical activity, direct intercutting suggests a dramatic relationship. The mental realm of the film thus also becomes a spatially determined entity. Though we know they are not actually spatially contiguous, the telephone exchange seems to lie "between" the mother (on the right) and the child (on the left) in *The Medicine Bottle*. This effect results from the fact that a spatial composite results from discontinuous construction, whether physical action bridges the "gap" between the shots or not.

3. Continuous action may be implied when the line of physical activity is interrupted in intercutting. Actually, the basic intuition for intercutting occurs as early as 1903 in Edwin S. Porter's *The Great Train Robbery*. At the height of the physical activity, as the robbers are about to get away, Porter returns the audience to set-up 1, where the telegraph operator is freed. In the next shot, the viewer sees the townsfolk dancing *unawares, even as* the robbers are escaping with the goods.

These two concepts, "unawares" and "even as" are the cause of much of the narrative tension in Griffith's films, and cutting away from a particular line of activity to a waiting person or to a pursuer is a very common strategy for suggesting to the audience that the growing awareness of the characters within the world of the film is a dramatic issue. Sergei Eisenstein illustrates at great length the literary roots of this practice, using a passage from Charles Dickens' *Oliver Twist*. "We have before us a typical and, for Griffith, a model of parallel montage of two story lines, where one (the waiting gentlemen) emotionally heightens the tension and drama of the other (the capture of Oliver)," Eisenstein concludes.[9]

A resolution of this dramatic tension is often accomplished when the disparity of information between the audience and the character within the film is overcome. Griffith accomplishes this in film space and film time by a structural resolution of the tension between two spaces that have been held "apart" by intercutting—at first simply accomplished by switching from shot *a* to shot *b* over a contended doorway. When will they break through?

Griffith found that under certain conditions, the audience could *imagine* the action of the film. While one character is running, the other is not perceived to have stopped, but to keep coming on. Cutting itself increases the amount of activity in the Biograph films. The almost excessive intercutting of some of the late Biograph films plays directly on this balance between the actual physical movement within the frame and the activity generated by the relationships between shots. Intercutting taught Griffith that, as Porter's work suggests, dramatic excitement is generated if a sequence of activity is interrupted. The audience is required to "work" at assembling a composite picture from increasingly smaller bits, arriving at a faster rate. The flow of information is curtailed by the cut, and the audience can be made curious and anxious.

But intercutting also involves viewers in a sort of spatial speculation that forces them to imagine activity not seen, and this allowed Griffith to alter the classic form of the chase. In the classic structure a criminal (for instance) runs into a shot in the background (in early films this entrance is preceded by empty space in the frame). The entrance and exit points and the path of the progress through the frame determine the dynamics of the chase. If the pursuer copies them, for instance, he is "on the trail." Griffith found that he could begin the pursuit with the chasers already on the trail, eliminating first the empty frames and then the entrance itself at the head of the shot. He could cut between pursuers and pursued while both were in transit through respective shots in the chase order. As long as he cut back to the pursuers within the sequence of shots defined by the activity of the pursued, he could advance the latter two or three shots ahead of the pursuers and still make the audience believe that the pursuers are on the way.

The more Griffith cuts between segments in the chase sequence, the more activity the audience is forced to relate in the moment-by-moment progress of the chase. Cutting itself therefore constitutes cinematic activity. The audience projects activity through the course of the chase and in a sense can be led to "predict" the presence of persons already running along an established path in the chase sequence. More important, Griffith's films suggest that viewers will continue to envision activity in all parts of the film's structure until they are *told to stop*. The filmmaker can be in control of the audience's curiosity and imagination as well as of the actual events that take place in the world of the film.

Griffith makes this process look quite "natural" to the viewer because it is so formally logical. But one has only to consider *Physician of the Castle* or the otherwise histrionically effective *A Tale of Two Cities* to see how quickly such spatial "normalcy" evaporates from the world of the film when clear relationships between shots are not indicated. When these links are dispensed with, the world of the film breaks down and disintegrates into mise-en-scène, which, while compelling and even inventive in some cases, may ultimately not be as dramatically effective or as emotionally satisfying as Griffith's exciting treatment of basic plots.

An audience can follow a story from the mere serial order of shots. But Griffith never seems very satisfied with that. It is impossible that he doubted the capacity of his actors to convey the information of the film. It is equally impossible that a man who made almost five hundred films in five years lacked invention. More likely, the search for structure is related to the fact that Griffith discovered, at least in an intuitive and repeatable way, that locking a structure into the body of the film has narrative consequences. If one considers Griffith's work to be formally determined by its narrative material—as Eisenstein clearly does—then it must be admitted that he at least found the perfect visual coefficients for the melodramatic stories he favored.

Finally, the tension of a Griffith film is divided between the viewer's need to concentrate on the image itself and the need to construct the world of the film. If deliberation and repose mean anything at all in Griffith's work, it is as a description of these complementary processes of contemplation and construction that the viewer engages in while watching a film of Griffith's Biograph period.

Knowledge and experience have robbed us of the simplicity we need to feel the excitement audiences felt at the first images. But the leaves on the trees—those trees that Griffith found so beautiful—have never ceased to exercise their power over audiences and image-maker alike. Each filmmaker breaks through the layers of imagery to which audiences have become hardened. The manipulation of multiple places and multiple times remains the creative problem posed to each succeeding filmmaker. And each new artist tries to create a fresh arrangement of locations and tenses that will bring the audience to the level of feeling that the cinema alone is able to reach. Later directors, using a greater variety of angles and shot dimensions, working with hours rather than minutes of reel-time, would achieve more complex effects than Griffith achieved in his Biograph period. But Griffith's short Biograph films—with their controlled spaces, their creative use of discontinuity, their concentration on the relationship of the order of the shots to a physical line of activity that binds the shots together—first tapped the "spontaneous way of seeing" that makes the cinema world seem more *present* than everyday reality and transforms everyday reality into the world of the screen.

Notes

Introduction

1. Jean-Luc Godard, *Godard on Godard,* trans. Tom Milne (New York: Viking, 1972), p. 135.

2. Richard Schickel, *D. W. Griffith: An American Life* (New York: Simon and Schuster, 1984), p. 154.

3. D. W. Griffith, "Youth, the Spirit of Movies," *The Illustrated World* 36 (October 1921): 194–96, in *Focus on D. W. Griffith,* ed. Harry M. Geduld (Englewood Cliffs, N.J.: Prentice-Hall, 1971), p. 59.

4. Eileen Bowser, "Toward Narrative, 1907, The Mill Girl," in *Film before Griffith,* ed. John L. Fell (Berkeley and Los Angeles: University of California Press, 1983), p. 331.

5. Maurice Merleau-Ponty, *Sense and Non-Sense,* trans. Hubert L. Dreyfus and Patricia A. Dreyfus (Evanston, Ill.: Northwestern University Press, 1964), p. 49.

6. D. W. Griffith, "Five Dollar 'Movies' Prophesied," *The Editor,* April 24, 1915, pp. 407–10, in *Focus on D. W. Griffith,* ed. Geduld, p. 34.

7. Frank Woods, *New York Dramatic Mirror* 68, no. 24, August 7, 1912, in Myron Osborn Lounsbury, *The Origins of American Film Criticism, 1909–1939* (New York: Arno Press, 1973), p. 15.

8. Frank Woods, "Reviews of New Films," *New York Dramatic Mirror* 62, no. 1599, August 14, 1909, p. 15, in George Pratt, *Spellbound in Darkness* (Greenwich, Conn.: New York Graphic Society, 1973), p. 62.

9. Quoted by E. Bowser, "Toward Narrative, 1907: *The Mill Girl,*" in *Film before Griffith,* ed. Fell, p. 332.

10. Hugo Munsterberg, *The Film: A Psychological Study* (New York: Dover, 1970), p. 30.

11. Horace Kallen, "The Dramatic Picture vs. the Pictorial Drama," *Harvard Monthly* 50 (March 1910): p. 23, in Lounsbury, *Origins of American Film Criticism,* p. 37.

12. D. W. Griffith, "Tomorrow's Motion Picture," *The Picturegoer* (London), June 1928, p. 11, in *Focus on D. W. Griffith,* ed. Geduld, p. 68.

13. Lev Kuleshov, *Kuleshov on Film: Writings of Lev Kuleshov,* trans. with an introduction by Ronald Levaco (Berkeley and Los Angeles: University of California Press, 1974), p. 129.

14. Munsterberg, *The Film,* p. 28.

1. A Basic Shot

1. Lewis Jacobs, *The Movies as Medium* (New York: Farrar, Straus and Giroux, 1970), p. 13; Thomas W. Bohn and Richard L. Stromgren, *Lights and Shadows* (Port Washington, N.Y.: Alfred, 1975), p. 18; Robert Sklar, *Movie-Made America* (New York: Random House, Vintage Books, 1976), p. 24.

2. Edward Wagenkneckt, *The Movies in the Age of Innocence* (New York: Ballantine, 1971), p. 31.

3. Interview with Cristy Cabanne, Barnet Braverman Papers, unpublished MS, Museum of Modern Art Archives, New York.

4. Schickel, *D. W. Griffith: An American Life*, p. 579.

5. Ibid., p. 494.

6. A. Nicholas Vardac, *From Stage to Screen: Theatrical Method from Garrick to Griffith* (Cambridge, Mass.: Harvard University Press, 1949), p. 169.

7. John L. Fell, *Film and the Narrative Tradition*, (Berkeley and Los Angeles: University of California Press, 1986), p. 18.

8. Ibid., p. 14.

9. Ibid., pp. 19–20.

10. Ibid., p. 14.

11. Tom Gunning and Charles Musser, "Cinema c. 1905," lecture presentation, Collective for Living Cinema, New York, April 29, 1979.

12. Henry Tyrell, "Some Music Hall Moralities," *The Illustrated American* 20, no. 335, July 11, 1896, p. 76 in Pratt, *Spellbound in Darkness*, p. 17.

13. Richard Arlo Sanderson, *The Development of American Motion Pictures Content and Technique Prior to 1904* (New York: Arno Press, 1977), p. 89.

14. Fell, *Film and the Narrative Tradition*, p. 54.

15. Ibid., pp. 92–112.

16. David Levy, "Edison Sales Policy and the Continuous Action Film, 1904–1906," in John L. Fell, *Film before Griffith*, p. 215.

17. E. Bowser, "Toward Narrative, 1907: *The Mill Girl*," in *Film before Griffith*, ed. Fell, p. 335.

18. Martin Meisel, *Realizations: Narrative, Pictorial and Theatrical Arts in 19th Century England* (Princeton, N.J.: Princeton University Press, 1983), p. 39.

19. Vardac, *From Stage to Screen*, p. 169.

20. André Gaudréault, "Temporality and Narrativity in Early Cinema, 1895–1908," in *Film before Griffith*, ed. Fell, p. 322.

21. Ibid., p. 322.

22. Bowser, "Toward Narrative, 1907," in *Film before Griffith*, ed. Fell, p. 330.

23. Frank Woods, "Reviews of Licensed Films," *New York Dramatic Mirror* 63, no. 1638, May 15, 1910, in Stanley Kauffmann, *History of American Film Criticism* (New York: Liveright, 1972), p. 39.

24. Robert M. Henderson, *D. W. Griffith: The Years at Biograph* (New York: Farrar, Straus and Giroux, 1970), p. 20.

25. Ibid., pp. 19–20.

26. Interview with Sam Landers, Barnet Braverman Papers, unpublished MS, Museum of Modern Art Archives, New York.

27. D. W. Griffith, "Movie Actresses and Movie Acting," in *Focus on D. W. Griffith*, ed. Geduld, p. 55.

28. Schickel, *D. W. Griffith: An American Life*, p. 117.

29. Henderson, *D. W. Griffith: The Years at Biograph*, p. 54.

30. G. W. Bitzer, *Billy Bitzer: His Story*, with introduction by Beaumont Newhall (New York: Farrar, Straus and Giroux, 1973), pp. 204–7.

31. Kemp Niver, *D. W. Griffith: His Biograph Films in Perspective*, ed. Bebe Bergstrom (Los Angeles: John D. Roche, 1974), p. 2.

32. Schickel, *D. W. Griffith: An American Life*, p. 123.

33. Bitzer, *Billy Bitzer: His Story*, p. 70.

34. D. W. Griffith, "The New Stage Supplants the Old," in *Focus on D. W. Griffith*, ed. Geduld, p. 39.

35. Sergei Eisenstein, *Film Form* (New York: Harcourt, Brace and World, 1949), p. 234.

36. Kuleshov, *Kuleshov on Film*, p. 128.

37. Niver, *D. W. Griffith: His Biograph Films in Perspective*, p. 7.

38. Interview with Sam Landers, Barnet Braverman papers.

39. Vardac, *From Stage to Screen*, p. 47.

40. Fell, *Film and the Narrative Tradition*, p. 21.

41. Interview with Sam Landers, Barnet Braverman papers.

42. Ibid.

43. Bitzer, *Billy Bitzer: His Story*, p. 96.

44. Interview with George Beranger, Barnet Braverman papers.

45. Ezra Goodman, "Flashback to Griffith" (magazine and volume unidentified), March 28, 1948, Museum of Modern Art Archive, New York.

46. Interview with Cristy Cabanne, Barnet Braverman papers.

47. Henry Stephen Gordon, "The Story of David Wark Griffith," *Photoplay*, June–November 1916, in *Focus on D. W. Griffith*, ed. Geduld, p. 37.

48. D. W. Griffith, "What I Demand of Movie Stars," *Moving Picture Classic* 3 (February 1917): 40–41, 68, in *Focus on D. W. Griffith*, ed. Geduld, p. 52.

49. Mrs. D. W. Griffith (Linda Arvidson), *When Movies Were Young* (New York: Dover, 1969), p. 66.

50. D. W. Griffith, "Pace in the Movies," *Liberty Magazine*, 1926 (number unspecified), Museum of Modern Art Archive, New York.

2. A Basic Line of Action

1. Sanderson, *Development of American Motion Pictures Content and Technique Prior to 1904*, p. 89.

2. "Introduction to the Film Section," *Complete Illustrated Catalogue of Moving Picture Machines, Stereopticons, Films,* Kleine Optical Company, Chicago, Illinois, November 1905, pp. 206–7, in Pratt, *Spellbound in Darkness*, pp. 39–41.

3. Schickel, *D. W. Griffith: An American Life*, p. 108.

4. David Levy, "Edison Sales Policy," in *Film before Griffith*, ed. Fell, p. 207.

5. Eileen Bowser, program notes on *A Tale of Two Cities, The Yaqui Cur*, and *Fate*, March 28, 1978, Museum of Modern Art, New York.

6. Gordon, "Story of David Wark Griffith," *Focus on D. W. Griffith*, ed. Geduld, p. 36.

3. Basic Structures

1. Eisenstein, *Film Form,* p. 223.
2. Ibid., p. 234.
3. D. W. Griffith, "Insert Titles: Their Use," from "Don't Blame the Movies!" *Motion Picture Magazine* 31 (July 1926): 33, 82, in *Focus on D. W. Griffith,* ed. Geduld, p. 65.
4. John Huntley, interviews for British television shown in conjunction with "Early British Studios," nine programs prepared by David Francis, National Film Archive, England, presented by the Museum of Modern Art, New York, October 4–8, 1985.
5. Gaudréault, "Temporality and Narrativity in Early Cinema," in *Film before Griffith,* ed. Fell, p. 326.
6. D. W. Griffith, "Pace in the Movies," *Liberty Magazine,* 1926 (number unspecified), Museum of Modern Art Archives, New York.
7. Interview with Claire MacDowell, Barnet Braverman papers.
8. Griffith, "Pace in the Movies."

4. A Basic Frame of Reference

1. Interview with Mack Sennett, Barnet Braverman papers.
2. Mrs. D. W. Griffith, *When Movies Were Young,* p. 66.
3. D. W. Griffith, "Innovations and Expectations," in *Focus on D. W. Griffith,* ed. Geduld, p. 56–57.
4. Fell, *Film and the Narrative Tradition,* p. 59.
5. Eisenstein, *Film Form,* p. 218–23.
6. Meisel, *Realizations,* p. 358, for one instance among many illustrated.
7. Karl Brown, *Adventures with D. W. Griffith* (New York: Farrar, Straus and Giroux, 1973), p. 75.
8. Schickel, *D. W. Griffith: An American Life,* p. 313.
9. Peter Wollen, *Signs and Meaning in the Cinema* (Bloomington: Indiana University Press, 1972), p. 122.
10. Meisel, *Realizations,* p. 148.
11. Ibid., illus., pp. 126–29, 134–37, 295, 298.
12. Frank Woods, "Spectator's Comments," *New York Dramatic Mirror* 63, no. 1641, June 4, 1910, p. 16, on "Deliberation and Repose," in Kauffmann, *History of American Film Criticism,* p. 40.
13. Vardac, *From Stage to Screen,* p. 17.
14. Ibid., p. 181.

5. The Organizational Moment

1. Kauffmann, *History of American Film Criticism,* pp. 20–40 passim.
2. Gaudréault, "Temporality and Narrativity in Early Cinema," in *Film before Griffith,* ed. Fell, p. 319–20.
3. Gunning and Musser, "Cinema c. 1905."
4. Frank Woods, "Reviews of New Films," *New York Dramatic Mirror* 62, no. 1599, August 14, 1909, excerpted in Pratt, *Spellbound in Darkness,* p. 62.

5. Gaudréault, "Temporality and Narrativity in Early Cinema," in *Film before Griffith,* ed. Fell, p. 328.

6. Frank Woods, "Ghosts," *New York Dramatic Mirror,* September 11, 1909, in Kauffmann, *History of American Film Criticism,* p. 35.

7. Mrs. D. W. Griffith, *When the Movies Were Young,* p. 130.

8. Rachael Low and Roger Manvell, *The History of the British Film,* vol. 1, *1896–1906* (London: Allen and Unwin, 1948), p. 25.

9. Eisenstein, *Film Form,* p. 223.

Selected Bibliography

Published Material

Arnheim, Rudolf. *Film as Art*. Berkeley and Los Angeles: University of California Press, 1969.

Balshofer, Fred, and Arthur C. Miller. *One Reel A Week*. Berkeley and Los Angeles: University of California Press, 1968.

Barthes, Roland. *S/Z: An Essay*. Trans. Richard Miller. New York: Hill and Wang, 1974.

Bazin, André. *What Is Cinema?* Vol. 1. Trans. Hugh Gray. Berkeley and Los Angeles: University of California Press, 1967.

Bitzer, G. W. *Billy Bitzer: His Story*. New York: Farrar, Straus and Giroux, 1973.

Booth, Michael. *English Melodrama*. London: H. Jenkins, 1965.

Bowser, Eileen. Program Notes for *A Tale of Two Cities, Fate,* and *The Yaqui Cur*. New York: Museum of Modern Art, 1978.

Bowser, Eileen, ed. *Biograph Bulletins*. New York: Farrar, Straus and Giroux, Octagon Books, 1978.

Brown, Karl. *Adventures with D. W. Griffith*. New York: Farrar, Straus and Giroux, 1973.

Eisenstein, Sergei. *Film Form*. Trans. and ed. Jay Leyda, New York: Harcourt, Brace and World, 1949.

Faure, Elie. *The Art of Cineplastics*. Trans. Walter Peach. Boston: Four Seas, 1923.

Fell, John L. *Film and the Narrative Tradition*. Berkeley and Los Angeles: University of California Press, 1986.

Fell, John L., ed. *Film before Griffith*. Berkeley and Los Angeles: University of California Press, 1983.

Gallen, Ira H. "Birth of the Movies Took Place in the East." *Backstage*, November 12, 1976.

Geduld, Harry M., ed. *Focus on D. W. Griffith*. Englewood Cliffs, N.J.: Prentice-Hall, 1971.

Godard, Jean-Luc. *Godard on Godard*. Trans. and ed. Tom Milne. New York: Viking, 1972.

Goodman, Ezra. "Flashback to Griffith." Museum of Modern Art Archives, New York, March 28, 1948.

Graham, Cooper C., and Steven Higgins, Elaine Mancini, and João Luiz Viera. *D. W. Griffith and the Biograph Company*. Metuchen, N.J., and London: Scarecrow Press, 1985.

Griffith, D. W. "Pace in the Movies." *Liberty Magazine,* 1926. Museum of Modern Art Archives, New York.

Griffith, Mrs. D. W. (Linda Arvidson). *When the Movies Were Young.* New York: Dover, 1969.

Hamilton, James Shelly. "Putting a New Move in the Movies." *Everybody's Magazine.* Undated. Museum of Modern Art Archives, New York.

Henderson, Robert M. *D. W. Griffith: The Years at Biograph.* New York: Farrar, Straus and Giroux, 1970.

Hendricks, Gordon. *The Edison Motion Picture Myth.* Berkeley and Los Angeles: University of California Press, 1961.

————. *Beginnings at Biograph.* 1964. Reprint. New York: Arno Press, 1972.

Jones, Bernard, ed. *Cassell's Cyclopedia of Photography.* 1911. Reprint. New York: Arno Press, 1973.

Kauffmann, Stanley. *The History of American Film Criticism.* New York: Liveright, 1972.

Kuleshov, Lev. *Kuleshov on Film: Writings of Lev Kuleshov.* Trans. with an introduction by Ronald Levaco. Berkeley and Los Angeles: University of California Press, 1974.

Lescaboura, Austin C. *Behind the Motion Picture Screen.* New York: Munn and Co., 1919.

Lounsbury, Myron Osborn. *The Origins of American Film Criticism, 1909–1939.* New York: Arno Press, 1973.

Low, Rachael, and Roger Manvell. *The History of the British Film.* Vol. 1, *1896– 1906.* London: Allen and Unwin, 1948.

Meisel, Martin. *Realizations: Narrative, Pictorial and Theatrical Arts in 19th Century England.* Princeton, N.J.: Princeton University Press, 1983.

Mercer, John, comp. *Glossary of Film Terms.* University Film Association Monograph no. 2. Philadelphia: Temple University, 1978.

Merleau-Ponty, Maurice. *Sense and Non-Sense.* Trans. Herbert Dreyfus and Patricia A. Dreyfus, Evanston: Ill.: Northwestern University Press, 1964.

Metz, Christian. *Film Language: Semiotics of the Cinema.* Trans. Michael Taylor. New York: Oxford University Press, 1972.

Munsterberg, Hugo. *The Film: A Psychological Study.* New York: Dover, 1970.

Niver, Kemp. *D. W. Griffith: His Biograph Films in Perspective.* Edited by Bebe Bergstrom. Los Angeles: John D. Roche, 1974.

O'Dell, Paul. *Griffith and the Rise of Hollywood.* With the assistance of Anthony Slide. New York: A. S. Barnes, 1971.

Pratt, George C. *Spellbound in Darkness.* Greenwich, Conn.: New York Graphic Society, 1973.

Ramsaye, Terry. *A Million and One Nights: A History of the Motion Pictures through 1925.* New York: Simon and Schuster, 1926.

Robinson, David. *A History of World Cinema.* New York: Stein and Day, 1973.

Sanderson, Richard Arlo. *The Development of American Motion Pictures: Content and Technique Prior to 1904.* New York: Arno Press, 1961.

Schickel, Richard. *D. W. Griffith: An American Life.* New York: Simon and Schuster, 1984.

Sklar, Robert. *Movie-Made America: A Cultural History of American Movies*. New York: Random House, Vintage Books, 1976.

Slide, Anthony. *The Griffith Actresses*. So. Brunswick, N.J.: A. S. Barnes, 1973.

Stern, Seymour. "Griffith: The Birth of a Nation, Part I." *Film Culture* (Spring–Summer, 1965).

Vardac, A. Nicholas. *From Stage to Screen: Theatrical Method from Garrick to Griffith*. Cambridge, Mass.: Harvard University Press, 1949.

Wagenknecht, Edward. *The Movies in the Age of Innocence*. New York: Ballantine, 1962.

Unpublished Material

Barnet Braverman papers. Museum of Modern Art Archives, New York.

Letter to Lionel Barrymore, July 15, 1943.

Letter to Dorothy Bernard, October 1, 1944.

Letter from Dorothy Bernard, October 10, 1944.

Interviews:

Lionel Barrymore

Dorothy Bernard

Joseph Aller

Joseph August

William Beaudine

Christy Cabanne

Donald Crisp

Allan Dwan

James Flood

Dorothy Gish

R. H. Hammer

Dell Henderson

Rex Ingram

James Kirkwood

Sam Landers

Henry "Pathé" Lehrman

Garrett Lloyd

Claire McDowell

Mae Marsh

Albert Ray

Mack Sennett

Stanner E. V. Taylor

James Smith

James Waldron

Gunning, Tom, and Charles Musser. "Cinema c. 1905." Lecture presentation, Collective for Living Cinema, New York, February 23, 1980.

Hinds Radio Series. "D. W. Griffith's Hollywood." Script 9, *The Lonedale Operator.* February 1, 1932. Museum of Modern Art Archive, New York.

Hinds Radio Series. "D. W. Griffith's Hollywood." Script 14, "Mae Marsh's Acting." February 26, 1933. Museum of Modern Art Archive, New York.

Hinds Radio Series. "D. W. Griffith's Hollywood." Script 21, "Biograph Days." March 19, 1933. Museum of Modern Art Archive, New York.

Huntley, John. Interviews for British television shown in conjunction with "Early British Studios," nine programs prepared by David Francis, National Film Archive, England, presented by the Museum of Modern Art, New York, October 4–8, 1985.

Release Order of Films Discussed

This list is partial. For a complete list of the Griffith Biograph Productions with production and release dates, see Robert M. Henderson, *D. W. Griffith: The Years at Biograph* (New York: Farrar, Straus and Giroux, 1970), Appendix. For listing in release order with cast information, see Cooper C. Graham, et al., *D. W. Griffith and the Biograph Company* (Metuchen, N.J., and London: Scarecrow Press, 1985).

Griffith Biograph Films

1908

The Adventures of Dollie
The Redman and the Child
The Tavernkeeper's Daughter
The Bandit's Waterloo
A Calamitous Elopement
The Greaser's Gauntlet
For Love of Gold
The Fatal Hour
For a Wife's Honor
Balked at the Altar
The Red Girl
Betrayed by a Hand Print
Behind the Scenes
The Heart of Oyama
Where the Breakers Roar
The Zulu's Heart
The Vaquero's Vow
The Devil
The Barbarian, Ingomar
The Planter's Wife
The Call of the Wild
After Many Years
Taming of the Shrew
The Ingrate
The Pirate's Gold
The Guerilla
The Curtain Pole
Money Mad
The Feud and the Turkey
One Touch of Nature
An Awful Moment
The Christmas Burglars
The Criminal Hypnotist
The Honor of Thieves
A Rural Elopement
The Sacrifice
The Hindoo Dagger

The Salvation Army Lass
Love Finds A Way
The Girls and Daddy

1909

Those Boys
The Cord of Life
Trying to Get Arrested
Those Awful Hats
Edgar Allen Poe [sic]
The Golden Louis
His Ward's Love
The Prussian Spy
The Medicine Bottle
The Deception
Lady Helen's Escapade
A Fool's Revenge
I Did It, Mama
The Voice of the Violin
Jones and His New Neighbors
A Drunkard's Reformation
Confidence
'Tis an Ill Wind That Blows No Good
A Baby's Shoe
The Cricket on the Hearth
What Drink Did
The Violin Maker of Cremona
The Lonely Villa
Was Justice Served?
The Country Doctor
Jealousy and the Man
The Cardinal's Conspiracy
A Convict's Sacrifice
Sweet and Twenty
The Slave
They Would Elope
The Mended Lute
With Her Card
The Mills of the Gods
The Sealed Room
1776, or The Hessian Renegades
The Little Darling
In Old Kentucky
Comata, the Sioux
The Broken Locket
A Fair Exchange
The Awakening

Pippa Passes
Fools of Fate
The Little Teacher
A Change of Heart
His Lost Love
Lines of White on the Sullen Sea
The Gibson Goddess
In the Watches of the Night
The Expiation
What's Your Hurry?
The Restoration
The Light That Came
In the Window Recess
Through the Breakers
A Corner in Wheat
The Redman's View
The Rocky Road
Her Terrible Ordeal
The Call
The Honor of His Family
The Last Deal
The Duke's Plan

1910

His Last Burglary
In Old California
Faithful
Gold Is Not All
As It Is in Life
A Romance of the Western Hills
The Unchanging Sea
Love among the Roses
The Marked Time-Table
The Purgation
As the Bells Rang Out
The Usurer
In Life's Cycle
A Summer Idyll
The Modern Prodigal
The Broken Doll
The Banker's Daughters
Simple Charity
The Fugitive
A Plain Song
The Golden Supper
When a Man Loves

1911

Fisher Folks
The Lonedale Operator
The Primal Call
The Indian Brothers
A Country Cupid
Swords and Hearts
The Battle
Love in the Hills
Through Darkened Vales
The Transformation of Mike

1912

Iola's Promise
The Girl and Her Trust
Fate's Interception
The Female of the Species
One Is Business, the Other Crime
When Kings Were the Law
A Beast at Bay
Home Folks
Man's Lust for Gold
Man's Genesis
A Pueblo Legend
The Painted Lady
The Musketeers of Pig Alley
Brutality
The Massacre
The Burglar's Dilemma
The God Within
Fate

1913

A Welcome Intruder
The House of Darkness
The Yaqui Cur
Just Gold
Death's Marathon
The Mothering Heart
Her Mother's Oath
The Battle at Elderbush Gulch
In Prehistoric Days
Judith of Bethulia

Other Films

1898

Burglar on the Roof (Vitagraph)
Comic Faces (G. A. Smith)
Rip Van Winkle (Biograph)

1900

As Seen Through a Telescope (G. A. Smith)
The Big Swallow (Williamson)
Fire (Williamson)
How It Feels to Be Run Over (Hepworth)
A Quick Shave and Brush Up (G. A. Smith)
Story Told by Feet Only (G. A. Smith)
(Spiders on a Web) (G. A. Smith)

1901

The Execution of Czoglosz (Edison)
Grandpa's Looking Glass (Biograph, c. 1901)
The Pan American Exhibition (Edison)

1902

The Inn Where No Man Rests (Méliès)
The Magic Lantern (Méliès)
The Rival Cyclists (Williamson)
The Soldier's Return (Williamson)

1903

Firemen to the Rescue (Hepworth)
The Great Train Robbery (Edison)
The Life of an American Fireman (Edison)

1904

The Chicken Thief (Biograph)
The Escaped Lunatic (Biograph)
*How a French Nobleman Got a Wife through the New York Personal
    Columns* (Edison)
The Lost Child (Biograph)
The Moonshiners (Biograph)
Personal (Biograph)
The Scarecrow Pump (Edison)
The Widow and the Only Man (Biograph)

1905

The Firebug (Biograph)
Rescued by Rover (Hepworth)
Tom, Tom, the Piper's Son (Biograph)

Wanted, A Dog (Biograph)
The Watermelon Patch (Edison)

1906

Black Beauty (Hepworth)
The Policeman's Tour of the World (Pathé)
The Silver Wedding (Biograph)

1907

Boy, Bust and Bath (Vitagraph)
The Elopement (Biograph)
Francesca da Rimini (Vitagraph)
Lost in the Alps (Edison)
The Love Microbe (Biograph)
The Mill Girl (Biograph)
That Fatal Sneeze (Hepworth)
Truants (Biograph)
Two Little Waifs (Williamson)
Under the Apple Tree (Biograph)
Wife Wanted (Biograph)
Yale Laundry (Biograph)

1908

At the Crossroads of Life (Biograph)
Father's Lesson (Hepworth)
Nurse Wanted (Biograph)
Physician of the Castle (Pathé)
When Knights Were Bold (Biograph)

1909

Father Buys a Picture (Rosie)

1911

A Tale of Two Cities (Vitagraph)

Index of Film Titles

Index

Compositor: G & S Typesetters, Inc.
      Text: 10/12 Times Roman
   Display: Helvetica
   Printer: The Murray Printing Company
    Binder: The Murray Printing Company